S0-AJC-969

The Virgin of El Barrio

QUALITATIVE STUDIES IN RELIGION

GENERAL EDITORS: Penny Edgell Becker *and* Mary Jo Neitz

The Qualitative Studies in Religion series was founded to make a place for careful, sustained, engaged reflection on the link between the kinds of qualitative methods being used and the resulting shape, tone, and substance of our empirical work on religion. We seek to showcase a wide range of qualitative methodologies including ethnography; analysis of religious texts, discourses, rituals, and daily practices; in-depth interviews and life histories; and narrative analyses. We present empirical studies from diverse disciplines that address a particular problem or argument in the study of religion. We welcome a variety of approaches, including those drawing on multiple qualitative methods or combining qualitative and quantitative methods. We believe that excellent empirical studies can best further a critical discussion of the link between methods, epistemology, and social scientific theory, and thereby help to reconceptualize core problems and advance our understanding of religion and society.

Evangelical Christian Women: War Stories in the Gender Battles
Julie Ingersoll

*Every Time I Feel the Spirit: Religious Experience and Ritual
in an African American Church*
Timothy J. Nelson

*The Virgin of El Barrio: Marian Apparitions, Catholic Evangelizing,
and Mexican American Activism*
Kristy Nabhan-Warren

The Virgin of El Barrio

Marian Apparitions, Catholic Evangelizing,
and Mexican American Activism

Kristy Nabhan-Warren

CABRINI COLLEGE LIBRARY
610 KING OF PRUSSIA ROAD
RADNOR, PA 19087

NEW YORK UNIVERSITY PRESS

New York and London

✗ 56591058

NEW YORK UNIVERSITY PRESS
New York and London
www.nyupress.org

© 2005 by New York University
All rights reserved

Library of Congress Cataloging-in-Publication Data
Nabhan-Warren, Kristy.
The Virgin of el barrio : Marian apparitions, Catholic evangelizing,
and Mexican American activism / Kristy Nabhan-Warren.
p. cm. — (Qualitative studies in religion)
Includes bibliographical references and index.
ISBN 0–8147–5824–X (cloth : alk. paper) —
ISBN 0–8147–5825–8 (pbk. : alk. paper)
1. Guadalupe, Our Lady of—Cult—Arizona—Phoenix.
2. Mary's Ministries.   3. Ruiz, Estela, 1936–
4. Mexican American Catholics—Religious life—Arizona—Phoenix.
I. Title.   II. Series.
BT660.G8N33   2005
269'.2'092—dc22   2004021667

New York University Press books are printed on acid-free paper,
and their binding materials are chosen for strength and durability.

Manufactured in the United States of America
c 10 9 8 7 6 5 4 3 2 1
p 10 9 8 7 6 5 4 3 2 1

Contents

Acknowledgments

This study has consumed me for many years now, and I have received encouragement and support from family, friends, and colleagues along the way—each of whom has enhanced the project in his or her own special way. But first of all, I want to express my deepest gratitude to the Ruiz family, who have put up with my endless questions over the years, and whose members continue to impress me with their devotion to the Virgin Mary and to each other. I know that dedications usually come at the end of acknowledgments, but I want to dedicate this book, before I continue, to Estela and Reyes Ruiz, who welcomed me into their family and who reminded me, through their words and actions, of the importance of family and its interconnectedness to one's faith, whatever it may be. Moreover, the men and women of Mary's Ministries I have interviewed and befriended through the years have been generous in sharing their experiences as Mexican Americans and as Catholics. As a result, they have shown me what it means to be people of strong ethnic and religious identity, and have never ceased to inspire me.

In addition to having been blessed with such engaging interlocutors, I have been equally fortunate to have had professors who excelled both as researchers and as teachers. I have learned much from each of them, and working with them, individually and collectively, has helped shape me into the scholar and teacher I am today. At Arizona State University I worked closely with Tod Swanson, Moses Moore, Alberto Pulido, John Corrigan, and Linell Cady. Each in his or her own way offered me incisive critiques as well as abundant encouragement to pursue this project on Mexican American devotion to the Virgin Mary. Linell has worked with me since my Arizona State days, where she was a member of my Master's degree committee, and later, my dissertation committee. She has unstintingly shared her enthusiasm, warmth, and encouragement along the way.

If I had not studied at Arizona State for my Masters degree, and had not received the support I enjoyed there, this project simply would not have come into being.

While I was a doctoral student at Indiana University in Bloomington, I worked closely with Michael Jackson and Carol Greenhouse, both of whom taught me, by example, what it means to be a social-cultural anthropologist. Michael taught me how to be a good listener, how to ask good questions, and just as important, how to allow anthropology to inform theory, rather than the other way around. I thank him for these gifts. For her part, Carol has been a constant source of support since my time at Indiana, and has never failed to inspire me and to demonstrate her love of learning. Our meetings over coffee and lunch were important moments in my graduate school career; Carol's gestures of collegiality always came at the right time and her words of encouragement were taken to heart. Stephen J. Stein has shared his knowledge of American religious history and has helped me contextualize this project through the years. David Haberman pushed me to consider the "bigger picture" and to think through why someone who studies pilgrimage in India, for example, would be interested in reading this book.

More than any other graduate school professor, I want to thank my mentor, Bob Orsi. Bob is an exemplary scholar and teacher and manages to meld his scholarship and teaching quite beautifully in the way he tells a story. His many works are masterful storytelling; his interlocutors are kept front and center and the story is woven around them. I aspire to live up to his standard of engaged and searching scholarship. This project has benefited greatly from his critiques, comments, and questions over the years.

I have also been supported by colleagues both at Berea College in Kentucky and at Augustana College in Illinois, where I currently teach in the Department of Religion. Jill Bouma, Stephanie Browner, Steve Pulsford, Carol de Rosset, and Peggy Rivage-Seul of Berea College all actively encouraged me in this project and offered insightful comments that have helped shape the contours of this book. My colleagues in the Department of Religion at Augustana have also offered words of encouragement and support—Ritva Williams, Dan Lee, Gary Mann, Bob Haak, Elise Feyerherm, and Nirmala Salgado, thank you.

This project has also benefited from the comments, questions, and suggestions I have received over the years in various public talks and conferences where I have presented the findings collected in this book. I especially want to thank my friends and colleagues Tim Matovina and Kathleen Sprows Cummings of the CUSHWA Center at Notre Dame for their support, especially in the final stages of this project, and for granting me the opportunity to gain valuable feedback at the Spring 2003 American Catholic Studies Seminar. The seminar participants gave me helpful feedback, and Victoria Sanford offered an especially cogent critique as well as words of encouragement.

Writing this book has been a long and arduous journey, but also pleasurable, because of the support I have had over the years. Jennifer Hammer, my editor with NYU Press, has been simply amazing, an ideal editor who has offered both her insightful comments and her encouragement. She has always been available to answer the questions of this first-time author and has been a strong advocate for this project. My series editors, Mary Jo Neitz and Penny Edgell, have given me strong feedback and have, as a result, helped me sharpen my focus and improve my writing. The comments from the two outside reviewers were especially helpful, and I want to extend warm thanks to R. Stephen Warner for his incisive questions, concerns, and suggestions.

I would also like to thank Augustana College's Jeff Abernathy, Dean of the College, for his support of this project. Because of Jeff's advocacy, I was able to hire Martin Tulic, professional indexer, whom I would also like thank for his superb work.

I want also to thank my family for their support over the years. My parents, Randall and Linda Nabhan, have always emphasized the importance of family, and because of this I was better able to understand my friends in South Phoenix and their core values. As long as I can remember, my mom and dad have always shared their pride in advanced education and have encouraged me to pursue my interests and passions. My sister, Kelly Nabhan, has been another source of support and has helped to lift my spirits by always offering a listening ear when I really needed to talk through some ideas.

There are many, many friends and colleagues who have given their support through the years, but no one more so than my partner, my husband Stephen Warren. Steve has been my best friend and companion since we were undergraduates, and he understands me better than anyone. As a gifted U.S. historian in his own right, Steve's scholarly and teaching interests dovetail with my own, and our ongoing conversations on the interplay of ethnicity, religion, and history inform this book in many ways. Thank you, Steve, for always being there.

Finally, I want to acknowledge a person who is, quite honestly, the center of my life these days. My son, Cormac Nabhan-Warren, who is just shy of seven months old as I write this, is a constant joy, full of wonder. From the moment he was born he has helped me put life and work in perspective. Thank you, Steve and Cormac, for showing me that there is indeed life, and a rich one at that, outside of academia—and that I need to step out into it and enjoy it.

Fe (Faith), *Familia* (Family), and *Communidad* (Community)

Mexican American Devotion to the Virgin Mary

> I tell everyone, all you need to do is to trust Her and take hold of
> Her mantle and She will turn your life around.
>
> —Estela Ruiz, March 2002

When I sat down at my computer to write this introduction, I tried very hard to think of a way to make the religious and cultural world embodied in a South Phoenix backyard shrine that has become so familiar and fascinating to me just as intriguing to a wider audience. I wondered how I could best portray the family I had grown to care for and to admire and respect while maintaining academic critical standards. I also pondered how I could adequately show my gratitude to the numerous women and men who, over a period of ten years, shared their stories with me. If it were not for these interactions and experiences, this book would simply not exist. Because my academic and personal journey with Estela Ruiz, her family, and her extended circle of friends all began at the shrine to the Virgin of the Americas, I will start with one of my early encounters with Estela, the Marian visionary whose apparitions of this Virgin have become the focus of her and her family's life, as well as the lives of many South Phoenix Hispanos and Mexican Americans.[1] This book is my attempt to portray and to analyze their rich and compelling Catholic world.

It was December 4, 1993, and I was the lone academic, and a somewhat nervous non-Catholic to boot, a non-Hispana "other" (at least, I felt "other" in the beginning of my fieldwork) in a sea of devout Mexican

American Hispano pilgrims who had journeyed to the shrine to see *la Virgen* and to pay her respect. We all sat on plastic chairs or kneeled on carpet remnants in the half-acre backyard space. Ruiz family members and intimate friends sat in a semicircle next to the altar and family members took turns holding various young children. Devotional music proclaiming Mary's holiness played loudly from speakers, and candles were lit on the front altar to the Virgin of the Americas. The large oil painting of this Virgin was flanked by statues of Santo Niño de Atocha, Rosa Mystica, and Our Lady of Fatima. A poster of the Mexican Virgin of Guadalupe hung to the right of the Virgin of the Americas, and vases with pink roses stood on both ends of the wooden altar. To the far right of this front-and-center altar stood a life-sized statue of the Virgin of Guadalupe, surrounded by those ubiquitous grocery-store variety Guadalupe candles, petitions from believers, and flowers-both real and plastic-in styrofoam cups. All around the backyard space, men and women prayed the rosary, kneeling or sitting in anticipation of Estela Ruiz's arrival.

After the rosary was prayed by the approximately two hundred pilgrims, Estela stood up to read the message she claimed the Virgin of the Americas had given her that morning. A large woman ("I have big bones" is what she jokingly says) with a mass of snow-white, short curly hair, Estela was the center of attention. She read from a typed sheet of paper, in a clear and unwavering voice, and the attention of the large crowd crammed into the small back yard focused on her. The sounds of babies crying, and the whir of police narcotics and anti-gang helicopters flying overhead, were all that competed with Estela's steady voice. In this particular message, Mary showed herself to be a loving, gentle mother by thanking her "children" for gathering to listen to her; yet she also displayed a stern side, chastising them for following the "ways of the world" and being deceived by Satan's wiles. As Estela read the message, I looked around the crowd, observing and scribbling notes in my notepad. All eyes were on her—men and women rocked back and forth fingering rosary beads, mothers cradled their young children in their arms, and families sat huddled together drinking hot cocoa provided by the Ruiz family and served by volunteers from the barrio.

At the time I observed this backyard rosary and events, I was a young graduate student at Arizona State University and had been interviewing Estela weekly for my Master's thesis. I was intrigued by her status as a visionary and her life before her visions, which was, she readily acknowledged, quite different from other visionaries, most of whom were devout, churchgoing Catholics before their apparitions. A self-described former "career woman," a "feminist" and "lapsed Catholic" who "wasn't always there for my children," Estela says that before her apparitions she was very different from the woman she is today. According to Estela and members of her family, the Virgin's intervention in her life made her a "changed woman" who was "available" to her children, husband, and grandchildren as she had never been before.

Over the course of nine years, from 1989 to 1998, Estela became a highly sought after personality among the many women and men who journeyed to the shrine. At the biweekly rosary sessions in her backyard shrine, and most especially at the annual December retreats just described, she was practically mobbed by middle-aged and elderly women (and some men) who competed to gain her attention and to tell her their stories. I jotted in my notebook at the time that Estela was a "Catholic star." Indeed, she had a commanding presence, and from the first time I met her I was intrigued, and even intimidated. Little did I know at that time that I would be spending a good part of the next ten years of my life observing her and her family, taking part in their rituals, sharing meals with them, joking, laughing and crying with them, and thinking about them when I was not in South Phoenix. I knew that the stories of this woman and her family were fascinating, but I also realized that they reflected Mexican Americans' lives and realities in the Southwest and throughout the United States.

The Ruizes are in many ways a typical middle-class Mexican American family that works hard to maintain familial ties, the Spanish language, and Mexican American Catholicism, all the while negotiating "Mexican" and "American" identities and creating new ones in the process of carving out an ethnic identity that is anything but static. Estela, her family, and the many pilgrims who come to the shrine and who involve themselves in Mary's Ministries and ESPIRITU have stories to tell that can shed light on how we understand the construction and overlap of American Catholic, Mexican American, evangelical, class, and gendered identities, and how those understandings might be revised according to a changing cultural landscape. And by studying the lived religious world of these people, we can learn about the construction, contestation, and maintenance of Hispano-Mexican American religion, and religion in the contemporary United States more broadly. While this is a case study of a Mexican American woman, her family, and a community of faithful men and women, it is also a study of an American religious phenomenon, one that reflects prominent American religious themes of charismatic leadership, grassroots piety, entrepreneurial ingenuity, and imagination.

What lies at the heart of this study is how a manifestation of the Virgin Mary gives hope and meaning to people's lives, and how the Virgin's appearances and messages are the foundation for a creative Mexican American Catholicism that is being shaped by the Ruiz family and their ministries. The Catholicism nourished at the shrine is loyal to the institutional Catholic Church but is also a grassroots, independent phenomenon that encourages devotionalism, religious activism, and ethnic religious life. Marian devotees' narratives of conversion and change through their contact with the Virgin, and of how their faith is nurtured in the shrine-based community, are explored in depth in this study. Their stories show religion as a dynamic personal, familial, and social process. These women and men communicate with Mary, Jesus, and the saints at this barrio shrine and claim to have transformative experiences; many have personal encounters with the Virgin Mary and say they are "spiritually healed," "touched," and "kissed" by the Virgin.

A Family's Healing

The language of healing through Mary's touch was a prevalent theme throughout my fieldwork, and it explains and defines in many ways the easing of religious, ethnic, and racial "in-betweenness" that many post-1965 ethnics like Mexican Americans experience. According to Estela, her family, and the devotees of the Virgin, Our Lady of the Americas has "healed" their personal and familial crises—they have created a new *nomos*, to borrow the sociologist Peter Berger's terminology, centered on the Virgin's love and healing powers, to replace the anomie, or chaos, in their lives.[2] One conversation I had with Estela and Reyes Ruiz a few years ago can instruct us in how Mary is credited with healing the strife in Mexican American families.

Both in their mid-sixties, Reyes and Estela—"Stella," as Reyes referred to her—were holding hands near the colorful altar and now-indoor, air-conditioned shrine to the Virgin of the Americas. They were fretting lovingly over each other's health: Reyes over Stella's severely arthritic knees, which make it difficult for her to walk without help; and Estela over his bone cancer, which was diagnosed in the fall of 2001 and caused Reyes sig-

Estela and Reyes Ruiz, winter 2002, inside the backyard chapel. Photo by author.

nificant distress and pain until his death in the summer of 2003. As he spoke about his relationship with the Virgin, Reyes fingered the rosary that was always wrapped around his wrist, and when she spoke, Estela glanced fondly over at the portrait of the Virgin of the Americas that Reyes had painted in 1989.

On this warm March day, I asked them to describe what they continually and affectionately referred to as their "journey" with the Virgin Mary. Both focused on the healing that had occurred in their family and what they saw as the Virgin Mary's palliative spiritual powers. They talked more about how the Virgin grants them the strength to endure in their pain and struggles than about any "failure" of the Virgin to heal them physically. Reyes characterized his and Stella's pain as vehicles for better spiritual lives and ultimately for sanctification—what Robert Orsi has called the devotional ethos of sickness and pain in American Catholicism.[3] Both Stella and Reyes focused on their own and their children's renewed spiritual health—a result, they said, of the Virgin's loving embrace and guidance.

As she spoke of her "great love" for and experiences with the Virgin of the Americas, Estela described a sense that she and the Virgin were both mothers trying to keep their families and communities intact. Looking over to the portrait of the Virgin, she commented, "We have experienced such a tremendous healing in our family, and on a greater level I really think that the Blessed Mother is trying to build bridges between people, between the races. She brings people together, and I am trying to do that too, with my work in the school and when I am invited to fly around the country to give talks."[4] Reyes nodded in agreement with his wife and added that it is *la Virgen* who is the impetus and inspiration for everything that they and their family have done in the past ten years: the 1988-1989 family's "conversions" to God and to Mary; the 1989 building of the backyard shrine in honor of the Virgin; the 1993 founding and operation of the Catholic evangelizing group Mary's Ministries; the 1995 start-up of ESPIRITU Community Development Corporation; and the late 1990s international evangelizing that has become the newest focus of Mary's Ministries.

As they reminisced about the past and talked about their plans and hopes for the future, both Estela and Reyes spoke with enthusiasm about their "calling," which they believe has made an impact on the hundreds of pilgrims who have visited the shrine each year since the apparitions were made public in the spring of 1989. This Mexican American family's multiple organizations and endeavors are deeply rooted in and draw on commitments to *familia* (family), *fe* (faith), and *communidad* (community). Even as they are rooted in these lived "traditional" realities, however, they also work to create new manifestations of them. A close study of this family, its organizations, and the members of its community will show how some contemporary Mexican Americans are addressing their ethnic and racial in-betweenness and are reinterpreting what it means to be a family, to have faith, and to be part of a community.

While this is a case study of one family and their religious community, the Ruiz family is more typical of Hispano-Mexican American families than it is different; their struggles are reflected in the many stories I have been told by Mexican Americans in South Phoenix and by those who journeyed to the shrine from California, Texas, New Mexico, and Chicago. The ways in which this family and members of Mary's Ministries challenge stereotypes and assumptions of Hispanic American Catholics mirror the ways in which Mexican Americans challenge the stereotypes imposed on them each and every day. Like other third-, fourth-, and fifth-generation middle-class, ethnic Mexican American families, the Ruizes exhibit tensions over becoming middle-class, hearing their children and grandchildren speak English as their first language and watching them choose pizza over *carne asada*. They grapple with how to be true to their Mexican

Catholic identity in a pluralistic, non-Catholic, and non-Hispanic society, and they refuse to be "melted" into one American society.

One way the Ruizes and members of Mary's Ministries have maintained a sense of difference is in how and where they live. While they can afford to move out of the barrio into newer South Phoenix subdivisions, the Ruizes have all chosen to remain in the barrio because they feel a strong connection to each other and to *la familia*, much like other Hispanic families.[5] The importance that the family places on kinship is evident when we look to their housing patterns: Estela and Reyes's home is flanked by Fernando and Leticia's on one side, and Armando and Peggy's on the other. Little Rey and Norma and their son Reyes Moises live a few blocks away, as do Fernando and Leticia's oldest child, Xochitli, with her fiancé and two young daughters. Daughter Becky lives with her husband, De Angelo, and their two children, along with a daughter from Becky's first marriage, about a mile away from Estela and Reyes, and youngest daughter Rosie and her husband, Ronnie, live a mile and a half south of Estela and Reyes with their three daughters. This family and the organization it founded, Mary's Ministries, mirrors Mexican American Catholic, ethnic, and familial realities, and its devotion to Mary signals not only its strong connection to Mexican ethnic notions of family, faith, and community, but also a sense of difference from the rest of United States culture. Yet at the same time, this particular family and its Marian-based organizations signal a desire to be like other Americans—the Virgin's inclusive messages portray this yearning.

The Virgin of the Americas, the evangelization programs, and community development can be viewed in one sense as bridges that connect Mexican and American cultures—the Virgin is a *mestiza*, as are the members of the Ruiz family, the Hispano-Mexican American children involved in the Virgin's "cause" (to bring Americans back to God), and those who journey to the shrine to be in her presence. The Virgin of the Americas is bilingual (she speaks Spanish and English), and she claims to appear for "all of My children." Also significantly, she asks to be called by the same name given to the Mexican Virgin of Guadalupe, eleven years later, in 1999, by Pope John Paul II. Yet although the Virgin of the Americas is a *mestiza*, she is *not* the same as the Virgin of Guadalupe *mestiza*. The latter appeared in a completely different context: in sixteenth-century Mexico, to the newly "Christianized" Indian Juan Diego.

The Virgin of the Americas, by contrast, appeared in a late twentieth-century Mexican American barrio to a woman who was struggling with being a successful, middle-class Mexican American woman who transgressed cultural, gendered boundaries. In many ways, the Virgin who appeared to Estela adds to and complements the already existing strong Guadalupe devotions in the Southwest, and in other ways she is a challenge to the Mexican Virgin, for she makes demands of her "children" and has requested her own shrine and devotions. This double devotion to the Virgins in Estela's backyard shrine, and the complementarity and contestation that lie within the devotion, will be explored more in subsequent chapters, primarily in chapter 7.

The apparitions of this Virgin to Estela are a means for her and her family to deal with the struggles and challenges of what Orsi calls the "inbetweenness" of cultures and identities.[6] The Ruizes and the majority of those who make a pilgrimage to the shrine are neither black nor white, but "in between" the two. As Richard Rodriguez writes, "Brown bleeds through the straight line, unstaunchable—the line separating black from white, for example. Brown confuses. Brown forms at the border of contradiction; the ability of language to express two or several things at once, the ability of bodies to experience two or several things at once."[7] Those who pray to the Virgin at the shrine and those who have devoted themselves to Mary's Ministries are ethnically, culturally multifaceted; their Mexicanness "bleeds" into their "Americanness." In one sense the Virgin is a cultural bridge—to return to Estela's earlier observation. Neither Mexican nor American but both, like the Virgin of the Americas, the Ruiz family and the many others who are part of their organizations and who make pilgrimages to the shrine, are cultural, linguistic, ethnic, racial, and religious border-crossers. They occupy multiple worlds and are skilled at borrowing from all of them. Yet as with all metaphors, the idea of the bridge between cultures is incomplete, because it tells only part of the story. Sometimes the bridge breaks down and the connections are interrupted, even broken.

The idea of *mestizaje*, eloquently put forth by Virgilio Elizondo more than thirty years ago and written about extensively by academics ever since, puts a positive, mostly uncritical spin on in-betweenness. The *mestizaje* thesis posits that the in-betweenness of cultures that is accompanied by feelings of marginality to one or the other, or both, is overcome through syncretism—Mexican Americans do not have to choose one identity over the other because they *are* both. According to the thesis, *mestizos/as* are border-crossers who benefit from—and who should be empowered by—being part of two worldviews and lifeworlds.[8] But the problem is that multicultural reality is not seamless; it is contested, confusing, and difficult for people to maintain, and *mestizos/as* need a way to deal with their pan-identities. According to Elizondo, it is the Virgin of Guadalupe who has been, and continues to be, a locus for theological reflection and ultimate belonging for *mestizos/as*—especially for Mexican Americans. But the apparitions of the Virgin of the Americas, a bilingual, light-skinned Virgin, to a middle-class Mexican American woman complicate this assertion. This Virgin—and not Guadalupe—is appearing to a community of Mexican Americans who claim to have experienced "healing" and "true happiness" because of her messages and visits to Estela Ruiz. Most, if not all, of these women and men have felt ethnic and racial shame, anger, and frustration.

Mary's Ministries' recent turn to Latin American evangelization signifies Mexican Americans' search for ethnic authenticity and the desire to discover an American identity across borders. While I discuss this new focus and its significance in this book, my primary concern is the Ruizes' and their devotees' lives in South Phoenix and their individual and collective responses to Estela's apparitions of the Virgin. Thus, I primarily focus on Mary's Ministries evangelization in the United States. I do not claim to represent in this book all Mexican Americans, or a normative "Mexican American experience" that does not exist; of course, there are multiple realities and experiences rather than a universal lived experience. I do, however, know that this particular family represents lived Mexican American realities in the Southwest: growing up in-between cultures as both Mexican and American; living through and being part of the Chicano movement; experiencing racism; being part of a strong Catholic religious heritage; watching Protestant evangelicalism take hold in the Southwest; and making sacrifices to attain to middle-class America. What the narratives of these lived realities tell us about is the painful process of Americanization and *mestizaje*. In their quest to maintain both Mexican and American identities, and Catholic and evangelical identities, the Mexican Americans in this book, like many other immigrant and ethnic peoples, have faced and continue to experience the tensions and struggles that accompany the process of becoming American. In the largest sense, this family is representative of Mexican Americans' realities in the American Southwest; they are in many ways ordinary in their dreams, hopes, and failures, yet their experiences with the Virgin and what has transpired make them somewhat extraordinary.

Lived Catholicism: Popular and Official

Another way this Mexican American family and its religious organizations challenge assumptions about Mexican Americans specifically and Catholics more generally is that they are devoutly Catholic in addition to being the sponsors of a popular, backyard-shrine-based Catholic phenomenon. Estela's and Reyes' shrine is an alternative Catholic space and it embraces Mexican American culture in its material Christianity. Although this perception is finally starting to change, the American Catholic Church hierarchy has for many years assumed that Mexican Americans are not good churchgoing Catholics, that they are largely "unchurched," and that their piety is superstitious, weak, and not truly Catholic.[9] On the other hand, others have reified popular Catholicism and have assumed that Mexican Americans who practice popular Catholicism (and do not attend church regularly) are the "real" or true/indigenous Catholics.[10] This rather one-sided perspective of ethnic and religious identity assumes that when Mexican Americans start to attend mass more regularly they lose their ethnic identity and become overly Americanized.

For their part, scholars of Catholicism have assumed that Catholicism of the church ("official") and Catholicism of the people ("popular piety") are separate and largely different religious phenomena, and that Mexican American Catholics (like other immigrant Catholics such as Haitian, Filipino, Dominican, Cuban) fall into the latter category. Robert Orsi challenges this dichotomy of popular and official in the second edition of his seminal work *The Madonna of 115th Street*. He argues that the terms "popular" and "official" are largely unhelpful, that "the designation *popular religion* in relation to American religion was, among other things, a code for Catholic-like ritual and devotional practices, deemed inappropriate and even incomprehensible on the religious landscape of the United States."[11] For the most part, there has been a lack of appreciation for Catholicism that takes place outside of the church ("popular") by those who focus on the institutional church, and there has been an inability or unwillingness to recognize the overlap of what has been called popular and official Catholicism, as well as irreconcilable tensions that arise from this mixing of genres.

Mary's Ministries poses a direct challenge to the categorization of popular and official, and paves the way for new understandings of Catholicism. The Catholicism that they live, display at the shrine, and promote through their evangelization efforts shows the interplay of church Catholicism, backyard-shrine Catholicism, evangelicalism, gender politics, feminism and postfeminist backlash, and ethnic politics and dreams. In this book I examine this multifaceted lived Catholicism, and I contend that this is the direction Catholicism in the Americas is taking. The Ruizes' Catholicism, which is continually evolving, represents the next wave in American Catholicism—a religion that is lay-initiated and created, sculpted to fit the needs of people, even as it remains within the historical folds of the institutional church. What is so intriguing about this family and its organizations is that they are loyal to the institutional Catholic Church and are faithful churchgoers even as they pose a challenge to the American Catholic church through their alternate Catholic space—the Marian shrine and community charter school—and their evangelizing endeavors in the Southwest, Midwest, and Latin America.

Católicos y Evangélicos

While they are devout Catholics, *católicos*, all Mary's Ministries members are also evangelicals, *evangélicos*, who strongly believe that the Catholic church needs to become more engaged in the world and who incorporate practices similar to their Protestant evangelical counterparts and competitors in the Americas, primarily Pentecostals and Mormons. As evangelicals, they believe in advertising and promoting their faith and they desire a direct experience with the Holy Spirit. And, as is evident in Mary's Ministries faith courses, they strongly encourage a more charismatic style of worship, which includes faith healing and the experience of glossolalia—speaking in tongues. We can see that these men and women use evangelical language of being saved—testimonies at Mary's Ministries faith courses clearly distinguish between their lives of sin "before" and their newly constructed selves "after" they found Jesus and Mary. As saved individuals who have been "converted," these people emphasize spreading the word of God through evangelization. Inextricably tied to their focus on evangelizing is their awareness of the increasingly successful Protestantization—or, more specifically, the "Pentecostalization"—of Mexican American and Latin American Catholics.

Mary's Ministries does not ignore the Protestant evangelical challenges; instead, its members incorporate evangelicalism into their Catholicism, and in doing so they widen the parameters of Catholicism and Catholic experience. The organization tries to balance critiques of Protestants with the language of inclusion and acceptance of non-Catholics, with mixed results. Mary's Ministries' language combines a curious mixture of ecumenism and Catholic triumphalism. The organization operates outside the Catholic Church hierarchy while it simultaneously courts that hierarchy's support. The Ruiz family and members of Mary's Ministries and ESPIRITU are Catholic and they seek the Church's approval, but ultimately they constitute and run a separate Catholic organization. On this level, the family and its organization reflect changes on the late twentieth-century and early twenty-first-century American religious landscape, pointing to what Robert Wuthnow calls the "restructuring" of contemporary American religions—the phenomenon of laity taking charge of their spirituality and creating religious spaces, sanctuaries, outside of church walls.[12] The Ruizes are loyal to the Catholic Church, but they are also critical of it and say that their church is not doing enough for the Hispanic community. They have interpreted the Virgin's apparitions to Estela as a venue for addressing both their immediate community's needs and concerns and larger, more global issues.

Yet this demarcation of borders between Protestantism and Catholicism is accompanied by their use of the language of unity and ecumenism: "Mary appears for all of us," "She wants us all to go back to God," and "We are all Her children." This language and their actions link the Ruizes' and Mary's Ministries' endeavors with post–Vatican II Catholicism more generally, and with other Hispano-Mexican American Catholic groups in the Southwest more specifically. Mary's Ministries engages in and encourages pre–Vatican II Catholic exceptionalism, post–Vatican II ecumenism, and ethnic grassroots piety, sometimes simultaneously and at other times exclusively.

An Ethnographer's Pilgrimage and Method

When I called Estela in 1997 to tell her about my dissertation and I told her of my desire to write about her and her family's experiences and religious and community endeavors, she welcomed me and arranged it so that I would stay with her youngest son, Rey Junior ("Little Rey"), and his wife Norma. I was nervous as I flew out to Phoenix from Bloomington, Indiana, for I had worked almost exclusively with Estela from 1992 to 1994 and I wondered if her family and community would be as welcoming as she had been. I was not Catholic; the Evangelical Lutheran Church of America was my affiliation at the time. I am also not Hispanic, though I have a strong command of Spanish as a result three months in an intensive Spanish-language school in Cuernavaca, Mexico the preceding year, in preparation for my fieldwork. My worries were soon abated, for the most part, by the welcome I received from the Ruizes and from Mary's Ministries members, who enthusiastically embraced the project. I tried to be as open as possible about my intentions, and my religious background and marital status (I had been married for four years at that point) were public knowledge. I was honest about my intentions: I was there as a participant-observer, a Ph.D. candidate in Religious Studies at a large secular state institution, and a feminist anthropologist who wanted to see how this particular religious Mexican American family lived its Catholic faith and its ethnic, racial, and linguistic identities. Yet my openness did not mean that I did not have challenges in the field; I did, and the lines between emic "insider" and etic "outsider" broke down more and more the longer I stayed. The longer I stayed in South Phoenix, I found, the blurrier the boundaries became between myself, the Ruizes, and my other interlocutors.

As this project on one level represents how people make and maintain connections with each other and form a community, it is appropriate, even auspicious, that it came into being after a series of connections that ended up linking me to Estela Ruiz and her family. I was twenty-one years old and unmarried when I first began this study for my Master's degree, and I drove from Tempe to see Estela in South Phoenix each week. My initial entry into the community of South Phoenix came about through my interest in Mexican American gang culture, which was covered extensively in the city's newspapers. I had been particularly interested by one article about an activist priest, the late Father Doug Nohava, who worked with *cholos* and *cholas*, boy and girl Hispano gang members, in South Phoenix. I was intrigued by these young men and women, who wore large tattoos of the Virgin of Guadalupe on their backs, and I arranged to meet with Father Doug one afternoon, to talk with him about his work. It was he who introduced me to Arturo Weis, a forty-something "O.G." (Original Gangster), one of the founders of the South Side Posse gang. Arturo introduced me to several gang members, all of whom talked about the significance of their tattoos, the rosaries they wore that matched their gang's color, and why they genuflected in front of St. Catherine's Catholic Church. It was in South Phoenix that I was introduced, by a group of *cholos* and an O.G., to alternative spaces of Catholicism—and to the knowledge that Catholicism could be lived in the streets and in the form of tattoos and gang-colored rosaries. Over lunch one afternoon at Poncho's restaurant, Arturo mentioned that he wanted to introduce me to "a special woman I know" because he knew how interested I was in the Virgin of Guadalupe. So after lunch we drove over to Estela and Reyes's house. It was on this day in September 1992 that my intellectual, academic, and even spiritual journey began with this family, in this community.

Before I continue, I think it is important that I let the reader know a little more about my background, because we all have very specific reasons for studying what we do, and our life interests almost always overlap with the studies we pursue. My fascination with the intersections of race and ethnicity, religion, and culture began when I was quite young, living in northwestern Indiana—in Gary until I was five, and then in Portage until I went to college. For those readers unfamiliar with Gary and Portage, they are part of northwestern Indiana's "Region" or, as insiders call it, "*Da Region.*" This section of Indiana is rich in thriving ethnic groups and enclaves: Irish, Polish, German, Syrian, Lebanese, Greek, Mexican, Puerto Rican—the list is extensive. Northwestern Indiana challenges and effectively deconstructs the melting pot thesis.[13] My own ethnic heritage is Lebanese (paternal grandfather), Swedish (paternal grandmother), and Polish and Croatian (maternal grandparents); my Lutheran upbringing is because of my stalwart Swedish grandmother, who made her family practically the only non-Catholics in the Nabhan clan. My interest in Catholicism, like my fascination with race and ethnicity, also began when I was young; my mother's family was Catholic and my mother converted to Lutheranism when she married my father in 1967. Although at that point she officially became "Lutheran," I like to think that she was and still is Catholic in her heart—she follows the pope's travels and messages diligently, sends me clippings of traveling Mary statues in the Region, and lets me know when there is a television special on Catholic pilgrimage. My research interests have been a way for my mother to relive and recapture her own Catholic memories and imagination.

It was when I met Maricella in the seventh grade and became best friends with her that my interest in Mexican American culture was encouraged. I fondly recall afternoons of listening to the Mexican pop group Menudo with her in her shag-carpeted basement and making up dance moves, talking all the while about which group member we thought was the cutest. Marcie picked the one who would make it to stardom, Ricky Martin, of course. Marcie's mom was the kindest woman I knew and she made us amazing lunches of beans, rice, and *carne asada*—all typical and boring for Marcie, but savory and exotic cuisine for my palate, which was used to lots of typical "American" foods like Kraft macaroni and cheese and tuna casserole. I was amazed and perplexed that Marcie would prefer Doritos and hot dogs to her mother's delicacies; when I was there, I ate as much as I could. Marcie's father was always courteous to his daughter's friend who was at his house every day, but he was self-conscious about his English and his wife did the talking for the family—she was the pubic persona, in addition to Marcie and her younger sister.

I never attended church services with Marcie and her family but I did attend birthday parties and one memorable *quinceñera*, in which Marcie was part of the court. I was fifteen at the time and was in awe of the beautiful dresses, the way the men and women doted on the young woman who was celebrating not only her birthday, but her rite of passage into Mexican American womanhood. I felt shy and a little awkward there, as I did not know any Spanish at the time; I just smiled a lot and observed the happy, vibrant people who surrounded me in this brightly decorated East Chicago lodge. Marcie and I ended up not hanging out as much in high school; I recall being upset with her because I didn't understand why she lashed out at her parents, and I couldn't understand her continual arguing with her mother. For her part, she thought I was way too serious and that I worried too much. Growing up in a strict immigrant Mexican Catholic household, Marcie faced issues with which I was unfamiliar, and I did not see what I now understand to be conflicts in religious, racial, and ethnic identity. Marcie agonized over and rebelled against her in-betweenness in her teens.

So this book is, in large part, one leg of a long existential and intellectual journey I began at a young age, a search to understand my friend and her culture, and I thank her for introducing me, unknowingly, to what became my mission: to understand the crossings of religion, race, and ethnicity, specifically in relation to Mexican American culture. What began with a personal encounter with my girlfriend's lived experiences developed into a scholarly fascination and, in a circuitous fashion, ended up as an intensely personal commitment to portraying the Ruiz family and their socio-religious endeavors.

Becoming Part of the Familia: Ethnographic Method

My meetings with Father Doug, Arturo, Estela, and Armando were the first connections I made in what came to be an ethnographic project based on making and maintaining connections with a core group of pilgrims who visited this shrine. This project has from the beginning been an open-ended study, meaning that I did not enter into the research with a specific objective; I let the conversations I had be the guides for the direction the research eventually took.[14] It was the conversations themselves that made me realize that I could not separate Estela's identity as a Marian visionary from her relationships with her husband, children, friends, and neighbors, and that the concatenation of visionary and shrine was a social phenomenon. I realized early on that in order to evoke this phenomenon in the fullest way possible, I would have to integrate Estela's experiences with her family's, with those of the members of Mary's Ministries, and with those of the pilgrims who journeyed to the shrine. Because all these narratives were and are deeply entwined, taken together they give meaning to the shrine and to the Virgin and her messages.

In the fall of 1998, thanks to Estela's prompting, Rey Ruiz Jr. and his wife, Norma Ruiz, invited me to stay with them for what was the bulk of my dissertation fieldwork. They were my gracious hosts, and I lived with them and their teacup poodle, Basia, for three and a half months. During this time I had my own bedroom and bathroom—a real luxury in South Phoenix. Norma had even decorated the room with a new maroon bedspread and curtains in anticipation of my arrival, and she had purchased a new television for the living room, as the old one had quit working weeks earlier. I remember her telling me, "I know you will be so busy and that you will want some time to rest and watch the soaps!" I spent many hours talking, eating, and yes, watching television and renting movies with Rey and Norma those three months I was in South Phoenix, and I always stay with them on return visits.

As important members of Mary's Ministries, Norma and Rey answered many of my questions and helped put me in touch with other key contacts in the larger Phoenix Catholic community. It was Rey who explained in detail the connection between his mother's visions and those of Father Jack Spaulding, priest of St. Maria Goretti parish in Scottsdale from 1982 to 1996, and the group of nine young adult visionaries. He later went out of his way to introduce me to Father Jack after evening mass at St. Thomas the Apostle Church in Scottsdale, where Father Jack was the head priest from 1996 to 2002. Father Jack was immediately warm and receptive, in part due to my connection with Rey, and we scheduled an interview for the next week. Rey also introduced me to administrators of the Tempe-based evangelical organization City of the Lord and invited me to come along to several of his meetings with them, which helped me better understand Mary's Ministries' evangelical influences and connections.

For her part, Norma took me along to baby showers, birthday parties, and shopping excursions with other Ruiz family members—all of which helped this project immensely by giving me access to the family's social networks. Fieldwork truly is "deep hanging out," as Renato Rosaldo aptly calls it.[15] It was through these outings with Norma that I also began to appreciate the gendered nuances in the family and in Mary's Ministries. Going to Sunday mass at Saint Catherine parish with Rey, Norma, and other Ruiz family members allowed me the opportunity to meet members of the community and Mary's Ministries, as well as the then newly installed parish priest, Father Charles "Charlie" Goraieb. For his part, Father Charlie was a source of knowledge on the Catholic charismatic movement and *cursillos* in Arizona and it was he who helped me understand the connections between Mary's Ministries and the larger movement.

Armando and Fernando Ruiz also helped me to build connections by inviting me to key meetings related to their community planning for South Phoenix. I sat in on several meetings of the Arizona State Board of Charter Schools and of ART, the Phoenix architectural firm that designed the charter school and is continuing to work with the Ruiz family and ESPIRITU members on community development plans. Fernando invited me to tag along with him and Rosa María for an afternoon of surveying South Phoenix single-family housing units, which gave me important insights on their commitment to providing low-income residents with affordable housing. Breakfasts, lunches, and dinners with members of Mary's Ministries and Ruiz family members all provided me with invaluable insights into the social networking of Mary's Ministries members and their religious reform commitments. One memorable lunch appointment with Fernando at a Mexican food stand in South Phoenix provided me with a wealth of information for chapter 6; we talked for close to an hour and a half over steaming tacos and frijoles about Fernando's personal commitment to religious reform in his community and how the Virgin Mary had led him and his entire family to their urban reform efforts.

Other Ruizes were generous with their time, too. Estela, though extremely busy with all of her administrative duties at the school, scheduled a total of five interviews with me in the fall of 1998; they ranged from one to three hours and took place at her office and in her home. I spent many hours with Reyes Sr., talking over juice and pastries at his kitchen table as well as on our rides back and forth on the school golf cart (he used it to travel from his home to the school, where he did maintenance work). High school principal Becky Ruiz also made room in her full schedule to talk with me about her commitments, and Rosie invited me on several occasions to tag along with her and her two young daughters while they ran errands; we had some wonderful discussions during excursions to K-Mart, the doctor's office, and lunch at the Knock-Kneed Lobster. Peggy Ruiz was also generous with her time, and I drank many glasses of fruit punch and ate numerous treats while we talked at her and Armando's house. In addition, Leticia Ruiz, Fernando's wife, incredibly busy then in her capacity as a high school vice principal and mother of six, made room in her schedule to talk while she was preparing dinner.

Mary's Ministries members outside of the Ruiz family were generous with their time and tolerant of my endless questioning. Many joked with me about my incessant note-taking and the portable notepads I always had with me. "There's the professor," they would tease. These men and women sat with me, sometimes for hours, and told me about their experiences with the Virgin of the Americas, the Virgin of Guadalupe, and their relationship to the shrine. During these meetings, which usually took place over breakfast or lunch, I not only asked questions and listened, but was asked questions about my own participation at the shrine, my interest in the visions, and my relationship with the Virgin Mary. I tried to be as honest as possible in addressing these questions. Usually I discussed my attraction to the Virgin Mary as a powerful female symbol and voiced my admiration and fascination for Mary's Ministries and all its activities. Sometimes I was asked questions that made me uncomfortable, such as when I was asked if I had "felt" or been "touched" by Mary; in these instances I responded that I felt a sense of peace and contentment at the shrine but was unsure whether that meant that I had "felt" the Virgin's touch. My response, which was that I felt secure and happy ("muy contenta") at the shrine, was an honest assessment of how I felt, and was usually interpreted as my having experienced the Virgin Mary's touch. Whether or not *I* believed that I had been called by Mary was inconsequential, as it was clear to many others that I had been sent by Mary to study them and their organization.

Reflexivity

What I have learned from knowing and working with members of the Ruiz family and Mary's Ministries is that the kind of social participation an ethnographer experiences is determined by the kinds of interactions she has with her interlocutors; the extent and the kind of participation she is able to undertake is determined by both herself and her "subjects." My own ethnographic experience took various twists and turns; it changed depending on the conversation I was having, where that conversation was taking place, and who was telling me his/her story.

Women, for example, tended to be more descriptive and open about their experiences with the Virgin Mary and less guarded in their narratives. Location mattered less to them; they revealed personal information freely whether we were talking at the shrine or in a local restaurant. The men I interviewed tended to be more guarded in providing me with details, perhaps because of my gender and my relatively young age. I found it easier to ask personal questions of women than of men—my level of comfort tended to be greater with women, and as a result the conversations tended to be more revealing.

In my experience, the ethnographic endeavor affords the scholar a special kind of look into others' lives, a look that is simultaneously openly honest and voyeuristic. Ethnography can afford a depth and understanding of others' lives, but it can and does pose challenges to the ethnographer who is taking certain risks—epistemological, moral, and existential.[16] In my own experiences in South Phoenix, I found it necessary to put myself "out there" and to make myself vulnerable by disclosing personal details of my own life, and to be ready to answer the questions that would invariably arise.

One such occasion took place at the 1998 shrine retreat; I was sitting near the shrine early in the morning when several women around me looked up in the sky and exclaimed that they had just seen the sun "dance." I went around and talked with these women and asked them what exactly they saw in the sky; after describing their sightings a couple of them asked me if I had seen the sun dance. I responded that I had not, and I remember feeling like some sort of imposter. Although these women did not voice their distrust of me, *I* felt out of place, and any feelings of inclusiveness I had felt before this moment left me as I grappled with my identity vis-à-vis these pilgrims. I had wanted to lie and to say that yes, I *had* seen the sun dance, but instead I said "no," I had not. I felt that the truth was necessary, even though it might create distance between myself and these women.

As Ruth Behar writes, the risk in writing anthropology is that the anthropologist makes herself vulnerable, and it is this vulnerability, this ability to feel and to express the emotions we experienced in the field, that lies at the heart of the ethnographic pursuit.[17] I believe taking such "risks" is necessary during one's fieldwork—for who are we to demand that our "informants" hand over personal information about themselves, information that is sometimes quite painful for them to discuss, if we refuse to share something of ourselves?[18] I find it hard to believe that ethnography can be successful if the researcher does not engage in reflexivity and assess her own beliefs, desires, and hopes. For example, I was forthright with Norma and Rey about my position on birth control, and we engaged in a lunchtime debate over the issue. Although I was afraid at the time that they would be offended, I found that my disclosure gave our relationship a greater level of honesty. On the other hand, I was not able to muster the courage to disagree publicly with their stance on abortion—I was unwilling to take a risk in this instance because I feared moral indictment.

The task of translating conversations that took place in the field onto paper for public viewing poses ethical questions. How does the researcher, for example, incorporate detailed and personal information given to her by her "informants," interlocutors, who in many cases have become friends with whom the researcher has eaten and joked, laughed and cried, as I did with Rey, Norma, the Ruizes, and many of my friends in Mary's Ministries? And should some stories and details be omitted, even if the informant has given his/her consent? I have grappled with such issues as these for several years, and in addressing them I have found it helpful to imagine my informants and friends in South Phoenix as family members when I am writing about them. I have taken the advice of the anthropologist of religion Tod Swanson, who proposes that "writing like a relative" can bridge the gap between the writer/author and his/her informants.[19] Swanson goes on to write that this imagining and thinking about one's informants as family applies only to those researchers who have actually developed relationships in the field. He acknowledges that the danger of this position is that some writers can exaggerate their relatedness with their informants and can mask the differences of social positioning.[20] I find Swanson's advocacy of familial relations and metaphors to be helpful in my own work, as I have developed long-standing relationships with the Ruiz family and with other members of Mary's Ministries. Since Ruiz family members and my friends in Mary's Ministries refer to me as their "spiritual daughter," "sister," and "friend," the familial analogy Swanson describes is helpful. I am working within a language of intimacy that is already in circulation. When I sat down to begin writing this study and faced all of the issues involved in writing about people with whom I have worked and lived, thinking of them as family helped bridge the divide between field research and writing and the anxiety that accompanies the writing process.

As I have discovered, fieldwork can take unpredictable turns, and the researcher must be prepared to go with changes in tempo and time in ways that can challenge her personal boundaries. For example, when I was taking part in a week-long Mary's Ministries faith course, it was expected that I would evangelize along with a partner, or "spouse," assigned to me by the group, on the seventh day in selected South Phoenix neighborhoods. I had already decided that in order to really understand the community's evangelizing focus I would have to be more than an observer—I would have to participate. The boundaries I had set up in my mind that distinguished me from the rest of the twenty-five or so candidates were directly challenged when I too was asked to distribute rosaries, prayer cards, and literature about Mary's Ministries. "Don't worry, *hija*," Estela told me, laughing. "It's only for the day!" She must have seen the look of shock on my face as I was thinking to myself, "I already have a husband, and I certainly don't want another." What made it even more challenging was that Tony (my "spouse for a day") brought his young niece and nephew along with us as well, creating the perception that we were indeed a "family."

If I wanted to enjoy the benefits of participation, I decided right there, I would have to experience the sensation of being uncomfortable at times such as this. With this in mind, I joined Tony in telling residents of South Phoenix about the organization and its goals. I reconciled my angst about becoming overly involved with the organization and thereby clouding my academic vision with the knowledge that I was, in a way, practicing for the writing of this book: on a very basic level, I was letting others know about this group and the significance of its activity. Yet despite these assurances, which helped me bracket academic pursuits and personal relationships at the time, I was aware that on a deeper level, as Karen McCarthy Brown notes, the "lines long drawn in anthropology between participant-observer and informant" were being broken down and blurred, and that "the only truth is the one in between; and anthropology becomes something closer to a social art form, open to both aesthetic and moral judgement.

This situation is riskier, but it does bring intellectual labor and life into closer relation."[21]

Recent anthropological literature on reflexivity has concerned itself with this blurring of boundaries, defining anthropology more as an art form than as a science. Reflexivity, in relation to ethnography, is defined by Jay Ruby as "breaking the thrall of self-concern by its very drive toward self-knowledge that inevitably takes into account a surrounding world of events, people, and places."[22] As Ruby writes, reflexiveness is different from solipsism, self-absorption, and self-reference because it "pulls one toward the Other and away from isolated attentiveness toward oneself."[23] The goal of reflexivity is to break down, as much as possible, the boundaries that exist between the researcher and her informants, and this necessitates the ethnographer's inward, critical turn. Reflexivity experienced during the fieldwork enhances the writing process because the writer, by being open to the blurring of boundaries, develops a greater understanding not only of herself but also of the group she is studying.

While this blurring (like my involvement in the day of evangelization) carries risks, it also affords the researcher insights that are not gained through merely observing or through setting limits on participation. In reflexive anthropology, the researcher must be prepared to be flexible in her ideas of time and space and to be asked the very questions she asks her informants—who want to know more about her, too. Doing ethnography involves the exchange of ideas, and ethnographers must be forthcoming about themselves if they expect their informants to talk freely about themselves.

While this can be stressful, there is no way around it; ethnography necessarily involves mutuality. Connecting with one's informants is rewarding and ultimately makes that uncomfortable feeling worthwhile; learning to "go with the flow" is a necessary part of doing fieldwork. Some of my best conversations were unplanned, such as the time I stopped by Reyes's and Estela's place after a morning jog to see if Reyes could meet with me sometime that week for a taped interview. The best time for Reyes, it turned out, happened to be at that very moment, and there I was, sweaty, out of breath, and without my tape recorder and notebook. Nevertheless, I accepted Reyes's invitation to sit down at the kitchen table and talk. For close to two hours, over juice and doughnuts, he spoke with me about his Catholic faith and his Mexican American identity. He also asked me personal questions about myself and about my own faith, which I did my best to answer honestly. I never tried to pretend to be someone I was not, and I think that the Ruizes respected that. Sometimes my difference—primarily my not being

Catholic—made me and them uncomfortable, but as Estela said to me in the spring of 2002 before I departed for Berea, Kentucky, where I was teaching at the time, "the Blessed Mother just wants each of us to be the best Catholic, Lutheran, or whatever religion we may be. Just go out there and be the best you can be." This ecumenical language, which is one of the hallmarks of Mary's Ministries, managed to reassure me at the time.

Chapter Outline/Structure

In the seven chapters of this book, my primary lenses of inquiry are how Estela, her family, and her community find deep meaning in their Marian piety, meaning that translates into empowerment. However, finding empowerment does not mean that contradiction and constraint are left behind. Like Estela, many women find a deep sense of satisfaction in Mary's Ministries, but they must make compromises in order to fit within certain proscribed gender roles and codes. This family, *familia*, and their community, *communidad*, challenge the divisions between popular and official piety, divisions between Catholicism and evangelicalism, and the *mestizaje* thesis that sees ethnic identity and blending in mostly glowing terms.

In chapter 1 I delve into Estela Ruiz's life before and after the visions and analyze the effects the apparitions of the Virgin of the Americas have had on her. I pay special attention to her self-described shift from feminist to faithful Catholic woman, and I explore the ways in which her status as a visionary has enabled her to actually expand her base of power—in motherhood, education, and the spiritual realm—while giving the perception that she is a "traditional" woman. Chapter 2 provides an in-depth account and analysis of *fe y familia*, faith and family. In it, I explore the Ruiz family's overlapping experiences with the Virgin of the Americas and discuss their connection with another Catholic prayer group, Father Jack Spaulding and the nine young adult visionaries of Scottsdale's St. Maria Goretti Church. The significance of these meetings will be explored, as a Mexican American family from South Phoenix is united with a wealthy Anglo group from Scottsdale.

In chapter 3 I analyze and comment on the messages of the Virgin of the Americas to Estela, placing them within the historical landscape of contemporary Marian visions. The messages to Estela are distinct in that they express a toned-down apocalypticism and assert in a postmillennial way that women and men can avert destruction through their good works.

These are also the only apparitions that encourage social justice and are the basis for the Ruiz family's barrio-based community reforms.

The family-spawned Catholic evangelizing organization Mary's Ministries is the focus of chapter 4, in which I provide a thick description and analysis of this contemporary grassroots Catholic phenomenon, and chapter 5, where I further analyze and contextualize it with other Catholic movements. Mary's Ministries reflects an ethnic community's aspirations and is intriguing because it combines Catholic and evangelical beliefs and rhetoric and aims to reform the Catholic Church from the outside. ESPIRITU Community Development Corporation, under whose auspices Mary's Ministries functions, is the focus of chapter 6, in which I pay attention to the NFL-YET charter school and community development and the networks that have helped made the Ruizes' goals realizable. Finally, chapter 7 comes full circle and returns to the shrine space as a center of healing and hope for those who journey there. In it I draw on women's and men's narratives and analyze the meanings of pilgrimage. How these men and women relate to the Virgin of the Americas and to Guadalupe—through touch, sight, smell, and sound—gets to the heart of lived religion. And, through the pilgrims' stories, we are able to see the entwined realities of popular and official Catholicism.

Throughout this study I try very hard to maintain rigorous academic standards. This book is an academic account of a community; it is not a journalistic report. At the other extreme, it is not a hagiography. While this family and the members of its organization strive to be saints, they are not, and they would be the first to say so. So while I have a deep and lasting respect and admiration for the Ruiz family, and for the men and women I met and with whom I formed friendships, I try to portray them in a way that illuminates their place within contemporary Catholicism in the United States and, more generally, within America's urban religious milieu. I establish links with other contemporary movements and groups where appropriate, but this book is primarily a focused study of a Mexican American woman, her family, and her community in a particular place and time. Estela herself has commented on what she considers to be her family's place in society: "We're really just your average Hispanic family trying to make the world a better place for our children and grandchildren. We try to do what the Blessed Mother is calling us to do and we do everything we can to follow Her." This book is dedicated to exploring what Estela and her family consider their "calling," and to the study of contemporary lived Mexican American religion in the United States.

* I *

Estela Ruiz and the Virgin of the Americas
An Intimate Relationship

On the night of December 3, 1988, Estela Ruiz was deep in prayer. She was praying the rosary in her bedroom, accompanied by a small group of family members that consisted of her husband, Reyes; her son Fernando; and her daughter-in-law Leticia. Estela says that she was praying for three of her four sons and her two daughters, who were following the "ways of the world" and whose faith in God and Mary was lukewarm at best.[1] On this particular evening, Estela was praying especially hard for her youngest son, Reyes Jr., who was battling a drug addiction, and for a mending of Leticia's and Fernando's troubled marriage. Estela remembers clutching her rosary tightly as she stared at a print of the Sacred Heart of Mary that hung on the wall in front of her. She fingered the crystal beads, praying to the Blessed Mother to take care of her family.[2] As she was reciting the last decet of the rosary, she says, she saw a light emanating from the portrait; it grew brighter and brighter and she had to close her eyes. Estela describes this as a profoundly moving and life-altering moment:

> I began to see this cloud form around the bottom of the Blessed Mother, but before the cloud, a bright light appeared. I tried to let go of the rosary to rub my eyes but I couldn't; it's like it was stuck to my hand. I felt like I was paralyzed, but not in a bad way. . . . My heart was going bum bum, bum bum. . . . I *knew* that we were praying the rosary, I *knew* what was going on . . . then She spoke to me and said "don't you know that I am going to take care of your children?" I was praying for my children and She was listening *the whole time!* . . . After She spoke I knew it was Her. I

began to cry "*La mujer bonita!* She's here! Oh my God She's so beautiful!" I was crying and tears were rolling down my face. . . .[3]

This vision marked the first in a series of apparitions and locutions from Mary that would span more than twelve years.[4] These encounters with the Virgin started with Estela's experience as a visionary, and it is to the intimate relationship between Estela and Mary that this chapter turns. As the historian of Marian visions William Christian Jr. has written, "What people hear the saints say, or the way they see the saints, reveals their deepest preoccupations."[5] When we take a close look at Estela's life before and after the onset of the visions, we can understand more clearly the moods and motivations—the preoccupations—that led to her apparitions. Estela was a middle-aged Mexican American woman in a self-declared "crisis," and she desperately needed an intervention—which, according to her narrative, came in the form of the Virgin Mary.

Estela's apparitions are very real for her, and to reduce them to one overarching explanation (e.g., the psychological explanation offered by Carroll) would render her experiences and her interpretations of them unfairly simplistic and unsophisticated.[6] A multifaceted analysis, on the other hand, which melds sociology, psychology, anthropology, history, and theology can help illuminate Estela's relationship with the Virgin. Estela's experiences as a visionary are rich and complex, and they warrant and deserve an equally complex reading. In order to understand the familial visionary phenomenon that is an integral part of her own experiences and interpretations, we must start from the beginning—with Estela's story, her *historia*. When we take a close look at Estela's narrative, we can see that she grappled with ethnic in-betweenness and gendered expectations, and that her experiences with the Virgin enabled her to construct gendered, religious and ethnic identities that empowered her within the boundaries of her faith and her family.

"In and of the World": Estela's Life before the Visions

The Virgin Mary has been an integral part of Estela's life since that first apparition on December 3, 1988. The emotionally charged evening marks the boundary between Estela's old life and her new one, between profane and sacred time. She sees her old life/self in sharp contrast with her new life/self. Estela asserts that Mary arrived not a moment too soon, because

The Virgin of the Americas, center, as she appeared to Estela Ruiz. Painted by Reyes Ruiz in 1988. Photo by author.

her life was spinning out of control; she says that her desire for power and prestige in her career was taking her away from God and her family. Even though she was praying most earnestly for her children on that December night, Estela says that she was also praying for a more spiritual life for herself. What she calls her "conversion" had begun slowly in the months preceding her first vision, and Estela says that this is because she was being "prepared" by the Virgin Mary for her new role as visionary and communicator of the Blessed Mother's messages to the world. According to Estela, the life-altering event that took place in her bedroom that December evening did not occur randomly; she says she was specifically chosen to be one of Mary's messengers. Mary appeared to her, Estela says, because "She *had* to. I needed a radical conversion and to have my world turned upside down."[7]

Estela says that unlike her husband, Reyes, whom she describes as a "lifelong devoted Catholic," she was deeply involved in "the ways of the world" and was not a model of Catholic piety and maternity. After four of her six children had moved out of the house to attend college, Estela felt that she had made enough sacrifices and that it was time for her to start doing things for herself. In her early forties she returned to college and earned a bachelor's degree in education and a teaching certificate from the adult education–focused Ottawa University in Phoenix. Soon after, she enrolled in Northern Arizona University's Masters in Education program.[8] Estela remembers herself as "arrogant" and "distanced" from religion and spirituality while in graduate school. "Most academics are without God in their lives, they don't want to be in touch with God and are afraid of being spiritual," she once declared to me during an interview.[9]

During this time, Estela recalls that education was her "god," and she believed that she was in control of her life. "I was really into feminism and I bought all of the rhetoric. At the same time, I had what I call 'university faith,' I thought, '*I* can tell me what to do, *I'm* in charge.'"[10] When I asked Estela if she thought it was possible to be an academic and a spiritual person, she said, "yes, but it is very difficult and rare." Rare, indeed— Thomas Aquinas, Ignatius Loyola, and Augustine were the only examples she could think of.

Estela was hired by Phoenix's Murphy School District in the early 1970s, and she worked her way up the bureaucratic ladder until she became the administrator of bilingual programs for the district. In the mid-1980s, she was earning more than $40,000 a year, driving a new car, and wearing "fashionable clothes" and jewelry. "I was materially and physically vain: I had my prematurely gray hair professionally colored black and I never, I mean *never*, went outside without wearing makeup. I mean, I was a successful woman so I had to look and act the part." Estela says her family paid a price for her success and that she became "unavailable" to them. Her son, Armando, confirms his mother's personal assessment and adds that she was "not a very affectionate woman" at this time.

> Professionally, she was very sophisticated. I would call her a hatchet person, the kind of person who comes at you and takes your head off and you don't see it coming. A lot of times you didn't know it was her. She was very manipulative, very successful. She loved her children and grandchildren but there were conditions. There was an appropriate time.[11]

Estela has internalized her son's and her family's critical assessment of her and she agrees with Armando's unflattering characterization. When she recalls the woman she was before her apparitions, Estela makes a clear demarcation between the woman she was then and the woman she is today. The "old" Estela was a "driven" woman, bent on attaining academic degrees and career-related success to the detriment of her family, marriage, and religious life. Estela says that she chided Reyes for his fourth-grade education and that she was condescending toward him for making less than a fifth of what she made annually. Most of all, she says, she was angry at his devout love for the Virgin Mary.

According to Estela, she was envious of Reyes's love for the Virgin, whom, she says, was "the other woman" in Reyes's life. "I was so jealous of the Blessed Mother because Reyes spent a lot of time with Her. One time, I was so angry with him when he told me that he was thinking of dancing with the Blessed Mother—when he was dancing with *me* at a St. Catherine's dance!" Estela says she had "had enough" of Reyes's love and devotion to the Virgin of Guadalupe. In the Virgin of the Americas, she has her own Virgin, one who was not already claimed by her spouse, one in whom she can confide. Instead of a dark-skinned Mexican Virgin appearing to her, a fair-skinned, bilingual Virgin, with whom her husband did not have a relationship, told her she was her mother, friend, and confidante.

Before her apparitions began, Estela was what she calls a "Sunday morning Catholic," attending mass on Sundays with Reyes but nothing more. "I was in the mode of 'what can the priests tell me, I'm better off than them!'"[12] She says she was frustrated and embarrassed by her husband's behavior. Reyes, who had carried a rosary with him at all times since he was a child, described himself as "falling in love with Her when I was inside my mom; all of my family are Marianos, they've said millions of rosaries." A son of New Mexico farm workers, Reyes grew up praying daily in the field's Marian shrine. One of several jobs in his adult life was working for the diocese of Phoenix as a minister to farm workers throughout the 1960s, '70s, and '80s. He prayed with the workers, had them over to his and Estela's modest South Phoenix home, and said the rosary at his own home shrine several times a day.

In addition to his involvement with ministering to farmworkers, Reyes was also involved in the *encuentro* movement in the 1970s and '80s. These *encuentros*, "encounters," the Catholic theologian Moises Sandoval writes, were an integral part of Hispanics' struggle to be recognized within the American Catholic Church and were successful in organizing Hispanic Catholics and developing Hispanic leaders who assumed important roles in their dioceses.[13] In 1985 he was invited to the Tercero Encuentro held in Chicago—an "intense meeting," according to Reyes, that addressed the 1983 Bishop's Pastoral Letter on Hispanic Ministry. Reyes says that he was "frustrated" at this Encuentro because they did not address farmworkers.

I was so upset because it was like the farmworkers did not even exist; they were being ignored. I stood up at this meeting, I was *so nervous*, and I said that everyone was ignoring the common person. I said "what about the farmworkers?"

I mean, I had been sent to represent a large group of people who were being ignored here, at a conference that focused on Hispanic people![14]

After the four-day meeting, Reyes was made the new national farmworkers' representative, and he traveled to all of the Rocky Mountain area regional conferences, held in Wyoming, Utah, Arizona, New Mexico, and Nevada. Yet he still felt like a "token," he said, because there were no farmworkers besides him who attended the meetings. Reyes felt a "real sense of accomplishment" when farmworkers were a presence at the next national Encuentro.

Estela remembers being "annoyed" by her husband's involvement with the diocese and with the Encuentros, and with his overt devotion to the Virgin, which made her "extremely irritated." She didn't like the farmworkers in her house when she arrived home from work; she felt that she was "above them" as an educated middle-class Mexican American woman. She says that she used to call Reyes a "holy roller" and wanted nothing to do with his or his friends' piety. At work, she says, she was surrounded by educated men and women who were "cold and formal" in their dress, religion, and habits; the more she was around this subculture, the more she became like these people, as she admired their intelligence and power.[15] "I had been in school for so long that I thought Reyes was going insane. You see, I was the intellectual who thought the spirit world was crazy."[16]

Estela is one of many Mexican American women of her generation who have achieved high levels of success in education and work. In their lives and stories we are able to see the tensions between class, ethnicity, gender, and religion that arise as a result of this success. Estela, like other Hispano-Mexican American women, has internalized the familial and community pressures and critiques of her decision to have a career; the more involved she became outside of her home, the more she was accused of losing her ethnic identity. These critiques were compounded by her husband's "badgering" about her lack of Catholic devotion. Yet Hispano and Mexican American women throughout the twentieth century have had a history of working outside the home, both from economic necessity and for personal satisfaction.[17]

Estela says that she was "fortunate" to obtain an education, because many of her childhood friends did not graduate from high school, let alone earn a college degree. She says she realizes she had more opportunities than many Mexican American women her age and older, and her career parallels the 1980s increase in well-paying jobs for Hispanic women. According to Estela, Reyes was supportive of her career goals but did not like the fact that her Catholic faith suffered. A crusader for Mexican Americans' rights himself, Reyes understood his wife's passion for defending Mexican Americans' interests through education, though it was "very difficult at times," he admitted to me once, because "Stella worked all of the time."

Estela's discussion of Reyes as a supportive husband is echoed by other Mexican American women who cite their husbands as their biggest supporters, which highlights the one-dimensional and unnuanced character of the prevailing stereotype of the Mexican macho male. Of course, given the diversity of Mexican American women and their families, their opinions vary as to whether or not Mexican American men are generally supportive of successful wives. Some have talked about their supportive husbands and others about the difficulties their spouses had with their successes.[18]

Estela was achieving her goal of attaining a powerful position within education, and she claims to have had the support of her spouse. Oral narratives and history have shown that Mexican American women have always worked outside the home and have simultaneously been activists. Despite the limited opportunities available to them, these women pressed hard for more opportunities for themselves and their families. As the historian Sarah Deutsch shows, Hispanic women in the Southwest have a history of creating their own structures in response to their lack of power in Anglo society and culture. Hispanic women, according to Deutsch, became especially adept at generating "strategies of survival."[19]

Estela began moving up the bureaucratic ladder during the height of the Chicano movement in the 1970s, when recently politicized Mexican Americans were demanding better wages and services and more opportunities, and were finally starting to see some results.[20] An important figure in the city of Phoenix's bilingual movement, Estela campaigned heavily for the dual use of Spanish and English in classrooms. She received a government-funded grant for $100,000 and wrote the manual for bilingual education that was adopted by Phoenix's Murphy School District, and she

campaigned in the streets in support of bilingual education. She also publicly supported her son, then-State Representative Armando Ruiz, in his
ultimately successful campaign against the nativist Proposition 106. This
proposition, sponsored by Arizona Republicans in the mid-1980s, sought
to establish English as the official language of Arizona.[21]

Estela's entry into the workforce coincides with the Chicano movement, and, importantly, the parallel Chicana movement. As the historian
Vicki Ruiz writes, the Chicana movement found itself grappling with issues of feminism, familism, and the image of *soldaderas*—soldiers. Most
Chicanas dealt with the tensions that existed between the various repre-
sentations of the larger Chicano movement, and most opted to remain in
the Chicano movement. "At times biting their lips," Ruiz writes, Chicanas
dealt with the double standards of the Chicano movement because it at
least focused on Chicanos as a unit, in comparison to white Anglo feminism, which most Chicanas saw as dividing men and women.[22] Estela was
part of the larger Chicano movement through her education and activism,
and she fought alongside her husband and her children for a better life for
Mexican Americans. She fought hard, she says, for bilingual education in
schools because it was "the right thing to do." She was supportive of the
politics of the Chicano movement, but wanted "no part," she says, of the
"religious aspects" of the movement, such as the Encuentros.

In Estela's opinion, the Chicano movement involved "men and women
together," unlike "Anglo feminism," which she perceives as women distanc-
ing themselves from their spouses and families to flourish in their careers.
Ironically, this is exactly what her family thought she was doing—pursuing her own goals at the expense of the *familia*. Moreover, it is what she
later internalized. Estela was a deeply conflicted woman—she enjoyed her
career and embraced "Anglo feminism," yet she also rejected it in favor of
"Chicana feminism." Estela was experiencing a conflict of interests and a
profound sense of guilt for neglecting her family, and she was feeling pressures from the home front. Although Reyes was "supportive" of her career,
she still felt pressure from the *familia* to conform more closely to gendered
ideas of womanhood and women's roles.

Estela's narrative illustrates the complexities of lived Mexican American
experience. She is a woman who was, by her own admission, betwixt and
between her Mexican and her American identities, torn by her concomi-
tant pride and shame. Her story challenges the *mestizaje* thesis that pur-
ports an easy blending of cultures. Prior to her apparitions, Estela experienced shame over her ethnic and religious heritage; she was outwardly

embarrassed by her husband's devotions and the dark-skinned Mexicans, the farmworkers, with whom he associated. Yet despite her mixed feelings about her ethnic identity and despite her class-based shame, she also felt compelled to help Mexican American children retain their Spanish language in her work as a school administrator. Estela saw language as a cultural linchpin and devoted many years to developing bilingual programs. She was a woman in-between cultural worlds and comfortable in neither.

Suffering and the Psychology of Apparitions

Estela credits her work ethic and her motivation to succeed to her childhood and her relationship with her mother. Delfina Aguilera, Estela's mother, was a businesswoman who managed to support her daughter and three sons by her entrepreneurial savvy, while her husband, Mañuel, before his "conversion" in his fifties, spent most of his paycheck on alcohol. As a young girl growing up in Lordesburg, New Mexico, in the home of an alcoholic, Estela experienced an environment rife with emotional tension and outbursts.

> This was . . . not a good time in my life. My dad was an alcoholic and there was a lot of turbulence and chaos in our lives. It was a crazy house. When I was growing up, I remember my mom used to scream and yell and faint. She would sometimes "lose it." Even though I don't remember my father actually hitting her, he was extremely verbally abusive to her. His mouth was really bad.[23]

Estela's narrative of her childhood with an alcoholic parent parallels those of other adults who were children of alcoholics and highlights similar themes, particularly that of survival.[24] The psychologist Clare Wilson argues that children of alcoholics generally feel their rejection by their non-alcoholic mothers more keenly than their rejection by their alcoholic fathers. The alcoholic father is seen as having a "handicap," something he can't help. Moreover, wives of male alcoholics do not necessarily show "any especially close emotional relationships with their children." Girls, Wilson asserts, usually have the heaviest burdens placed on them.[25]

Estela, the oldest of three children and the only daughter, felt the brunt of emotional and verbal abuse from her mother, the co-dependent wife of an alcoholic; and even though she was just a young girl, Estela was expected to be a primary source of emotional support for her mother. Despite the fact that her alcoholic father was violent toward her mother at times, Estela does not recall being afraid of him as she was of her mother. She remembers, as a young girl, being acutely aware of offending her mother, who was under constant financial and emotional strain because of her husband's alcoholism.

Estela emphasizes that despite her father's disease, Delfina, a survivor herself, was able to take charge of the family and became increasingly resilient as the years passed. Estela describes her mother as a strong woman whose own mother had died when she was twelve. As a young girl, Delfina had helped her father raise her sister, who came to call her "mother." Later in life, as the dominant personality in the Aguilera household, Delfina dealt with her husband's drunken anger and periodic unemployment as a form of penance. Estela remembers her mother talking about the "cross" that she had to bear for Jesus and of her willingness to suffer. In addition to her marital burdens, Delfina experienced physical discomfort before and after she was diagnosed with uterine cancer in her early thirties; she had to undergo radium treatments for months and was very sick. This world of suffering, pain, and resilience deeply affected Estela, who spent the better part of her childhood and adolescence with a mother who was overprotective and watchful of her only daughter. Delfina's physical and marital suffering—her "cross to bear"—was enacted publicly for her family, as well as privately, in her own relationship with Jesus and with the Virgin of Guadalupe. When Estela was sixteen, Delfina petitioned the Virgin of Guadalupe to save her son Inocensio, Estela's oldest sibling, who was gravely ill. After he was cured, Estela and her mother climbed "Christ the King" mountain to fulfill Delfina's promise.[26] Estela recalls both her fatigue during this steep and strenuous climb and the "mysterious force" that lifted her up the mountain. She realized at the time, she says, that it was God.[27] Estela says she was surrounded as a child by religious icons of the Mexican Virgin of Guadalupe that decorated her family's home. The Aguileras attended mass only occasionally, primarily to participate in the sacraments of baptism, first communion, and confirmation. All four children had been baptized and had received Holy Communion and confirmation, and even though they were not regular churchgoers, the Aguileras were proud Catholics—what Richard Rodriguez terms *muy católico*. Theirs was a Catholicism of the home, and in it *la Virgen* and Jesus were honored on their home altar, their *altarcito*. The Virgin of Guadalupe reigned in their home, and after Inocencio's recovery devotions to her increased. And even though Estela did not attend mass regularly, her mother expected her to go to her confirmation classes and she was warned against associating with non-Catholics.

Estela says she loved and feared her mother. Delfina verbally and physically vented many of her fears and her anguish on her daughter. Estela once painfully recalled to me a time when her mother flew into a physical rage when Estela returned home from a dance later than her brother. He was supposed to have accompanied her back to the house but had left early without her. Rather than getting angry with her son, Delfina started to hit Estela for coming home by herself, unchaperoned. As the Chicana historian Vicki Ruiz writes, chaperonage was a traditional instrument of social control for Mexican American women in the 1920s and '30s: "Indeed, the presence of *la dueña* was the prerequisite for attendance at a dance, a movie, or even church-related events. Chaperonage existed for centuries on both sides of the border separating Mexico and the United States, and is best understood as a manifestation of familial oligarchy whereby elders attempted to dictate the activities of youth for the sake of family honor." And further: "A family's standing in the community depended, in part, on women's purity. Loss of virginity not only tainted the reputation of an individual, but of her kin as well." The Chicano historian George J. Sánchez also writes about how public dances, the "dance craze" in the 1930s, offended the sensibilities of and did not "sit well" with Mexican immigrant parents. Even when Mexican youths' participation was closely chaperoned, their parents did not approve of the public displays.[28]

Estela's solo return home after the dance violated the carefully constructed gendered system by which her mother abided. Delfina's worries over her daughter's reputation, combined with her frustrations over her own married life, came crashing down on her daughter that night. Thankfully, Estela says, before her mother could inflict any harm on her, Mañuel intervened and stopped the beating. Estela recalls her mother as a constant and at times overbearing presence in her life, who never let her only daughter out of her sight. Her mother was "always there. Always."

According to Sánchez, it was a common cultural practice for women of Mexican descent to be chaperoned and accompanied by a family member when they went out in public in the early to mid-twentieth century. "From the start," he writes, "women's orientation toward the United States was formed in the confines of a Mexican family, not as single, independent migrants living alone." Relatives were always watchful of a young woman's behavior, forming a network intended to protect a woman's honor. This focus in Mexican American culture on protecting Mexican women's honor is the focus of the anthropologist Ruth Horowitz's work. Horowitz argues that young male gang members defend their girlfriends', sisters', and mothers' honor by their willingness to become physically violent with those doing the insulting. According to Horowitz, a girl who has a "bad rep," a bad reputation that is predicated on rumors and stories in relation to her sexuality, brings shame to her family. Vicki Ruiz writes about the public nature of Mexican American women's sexuality, and the penalties they pay for transgressing gendered expectations; "Since family honor rested, to some degree, on the preservation of female chastity (or *vergüenza*), women were to be controlled for the collective good, with older relatives assuming unquestioned responsibility in this regard."[29]

While Estela was growing up, her actions were always accounted for. After school, she would walk straight home to help her mother prepare meals and do the housework. She was not around her brothers very much, she says, because of the gendered worlds of Mexican men and women:

> In the Hispanic, Mexican American, and Mexican cultures, my mother always used to tell me that men are looked at as being of the streets, and women are of the house. So the men came and went, whenever they wanted to. I had to stay home unless my mother was with me, and even then, she was with me.[30]

Estela's childhood experiences parallel those of other Mexican and Mexican American women, and of daughters of the immigrants from southern and eastern Europe in general.[31] The women in these ethnic immigrant families were constantly monitored and chaperoned, since a woman's honor was of utmost importance. The tensions in the relationship between Estela and her mother attest to the intergenerational struggles between mothers and daughters and to daughters' attempts to maintain a sense of their own boundaries and control over their lives. Stories of conflict with one's mother and struggles for independence are almost universal among women of Estela's age and younger, women whose parents were closely bound to their ethnic enclaves and identities. Their experiences illustrate the struggles the children of immigrants in the early to mid-twentieth century had in adapting to American lifestyles as their parents tried to keep them grounded in familial, ethnic ways.[32] Tensions arose in the home as children began to pull away in a desire to be free of the constraints placed on them. Women, whose actions were carefully watched by their families, had it harder than their brothers, who were free to roam the streets.

The gendered difficulties of being a Mexican American female were compounded, in Estela's case, by her father's alcoholism and its effects on her mother. Yet Estela's recollections are filled with and are ultimately overcome by tender moments. These fond recollections are indicative of her great love and admiration for her mother or of a selective memory. Darker memories give way to happier ones, in which her mother is remembered as a hardworking woman who gave her children "tough love," but love nonetheless. Delfina is also remembered as a talented woman who made Estela clothes just as lovely as those that hung in store windows. Estela recalls Delfina's skill as a seamstress: no matter what dress Estela saw in a store window, Delfina was able to replicate it without a pattern. Estela says that even though she was "a little bit chunky" as a girl, her clothes always fit her "just beautifully."

When Estela was in her forties, Delfina began to experience health problems from the radiation treatments she had undergone years earlier. During her mother's physical deterioration, Estela drove back and forth from the hospital in Lordesburg to her job in Phoenix. Estela says that she eventually "broke" under the tremendous physical and emotional anguish she was experiencing during her mother's terminal illness. She internalized her mother's suffering and took it on as her own:

> It is a strange situation where our minds work in relationship to what we're going through and how our bodies react to the same thing. I got the same symptoms that my mom had—stomach problems, etc., and I couldn't eat. She couldn't eat either and I lost sixty pounds in two months . . . like my mom lost a lot of weight. . . . I couldn't go to work anymore because I felt like I was dying.[33]

Seeing her mother in a condition of physical deterioration overwhelmed Estela, who entered counseling and stress management at St. Luke's hospital in Phoenix. She suffered from a "terrible, terrible guilt" that she was somehow responsible for her mother's suffering and impending death. Long before this time, Mañuel had quit drinking: twenty-five years before his wife's final illness, he had been struck by a car and had had a "miraculous recovery," according to Estela. He took care of Delfina during her physical decline and until her death. Yet most of Estela's narrative revolves around his drinking and her mother's anger and later terminal illness;

Mañuel's recovery and his life after Delfina's ultimate death were a small part of the narrative Estela told to me. She did mention that he was a "wonderful grandpa" to her children and that they have fond memories of him.

According to the psychotherapist Barbara L. Wood, adult children of alcoholics "have little or no sense of themselves as individuals, possessed of a unique self and a purpose that transcends family need."[34] Estela says that she was angry at her mom for dying. Delfina had had an enormous effect on Estela's development as a person, and Estela realized how dependent she was on her. "When I was losing my mother I thought, 'my God! Who am I going to depend on?' She was my rock, she was my everything, and now she's going to be gone and I won't have anybody."[35] Yet, when her mother died, Estela experienced a sense of physical and emotional relief.

> They [the hospital staff] knew that I had been sick so they told Reyes that my mom had died. Reyes said to me "let's go run," and as we were running, he told me. I usually ran three to four laps, but that day I ran eleven or twelve. I felt like I was dying with my mom. . . . I had always depended on her. I told Reyes "just let me run." I was finally so tired that I collapsed and began to cry. I felt a sense of relief that she had died and that I didn't die with her. I thought, "Wow! I didn't die!"[36]

After her mother's death, Estela became even more determined to succeed in her career. She continued taking the assertiveness training courses at the hospital that her therapist had recommended, and she began to feel in control of her life for the first time.

The courses Estela took at St. Luke's hospital come out of the feminist movement, what Estela refers to as "the 1980s movement of individualism." These courses enabled Estela to build her self-esteem and to feel as though she was in charge of her life; during this time she met each week with a counselor to work on her self-image and to project goals for her future. According to Estela, the positive aspect of these courses was that she realized she did not have to die with her mother; but the negative aspect of them was that she started to feel she was "in control" of her life and "that I didn't need anybody else." According to Estela, the courses she took were part of the excesses of feminism, the "me decade" of the 1980s, and contributed to many Americans' (herself included) growing distance from God. Estela now thinks that she took the training courses "way too seriously," for she began to think that her successes were based on her own merits and not, as she believes today, on God's help. This feeling of control was illusory, Estela believes, because she based her feelings of self-worth on how others perceived her and on the praise she received from coworkers. Estela says that she must have appeared a success story, an ethnic woman who had "arrived" and who had achieved success by her own merit. But Estela knows that she was just "kidding myself. . . . I didn't realize that it was God who was in control, I actually thought *I* was the one in control, can you believe it?!"

From "Feminist" to "Faithful" Woman

According to Estela, before her apparitions of Mary, she was a "true American."

> I was truly in the world. I desired all the things America wanted. I tried to get prestige through knowledge . . . the knowledge of the world. I pushed my family and God to the side but I didn't push God totally away because I thought I might need Him! [laugh] I was in the women's liberation movement. I loved it and wanted to be liberated; I don't know *what from*, but I wanted to be liberated.[37]

Estela describes herself in unflattering terms here, as greedy, headstrong, and confused. Her involvement with the "women's liberation movement," as she refers to it, created distance between herself and her family, and any "liberation" she may have experienced was illusory at best. She began to worry about her own mortality, she recalls, and about what would happen to her if she died;

> I was *woman*—I was "liberating" myself, so I thought, and had just begun to live. But I also saw my hair turning gray and my face starting to droop. I feared death and didn't know where I'd go if I died.[38]

Estela was reaching a "crisis" in her life—her salary and career successes were starting to lose their appeal and she was beginning to think about "the state of my soul." She missed her mother terribly and felt like her life was "empty." As the historian David Blackbourn indicates, the absence of a mother, feelings of intense emotional loss, and the reality of an unhappy family are common threads that link Marian visionaries. In addition, "long-term anxiety and a sense of neglect" are common among visionaries, the majority of whom have been girls and women.[39] Estela's narrative fits Blackbourn's description of visionaries, and her anxieties, her aching at the loss of her mother, and her awareness that she was not connecting with her family led to what she calls a "real emotional breakdown, I guess you could technically call it a nervous breakdown, but it was more than that—it reached into the depths of my soul."

Estela refers to the year 1988 as the time when her "soul was formed and her heart melted" by the Virgin Mary.[40] According to Estela, her distant relationship with God and the Blessed Mother began to change late in 1987, because Reyes had been so excited since his return from Medjugorje in October.[41] She says that before he left, she finally capitulated to his request that she write a petition to the Virgin of Medjugorje. She asked Mary, she says, "to take away my fear of death." According to Estela, "After he pestered me, I couldn't take it any more and I wrote it down on a piece of paper and gave it to him. I didn't really take it seriously at the time—I just did it."

Upon Reyes's return to South Phoenix from Medjugorje, he and Estela encountered some tough family problems and they both describe the year 1988 as an "emotionally draining" time. Their youngest son, Reyes Jr., was going through drug and alcohol rehabilitation; another son, Armando, was going through his second divorce. According to Estela, it was the suffering she witnessed in the words and actions of the men and women in Rey Junior's rehabilitation program that deeply affected her and made her look "outside of herself":

> I saw these tough biker men cry like babies. I began to listen to them from my heart, and my heart began to break. That day in rehab, I began to have compassion; my heart opened up, and it's because the Blessed Mother had already started to work on me and it was a change, a new beginning.[42]

Her acknowledgment of Rey Junior's addictions forced Estela to realize that she and her family were not immune to the problems that affected other families. She had been in denial about her son's drug addiction because she thought her family, well-educated at universities, was "above" such problems. Estela says that she and her family members "weren't bad people, just into the 'ways of the world,' and we were arrogant."[43]

But her heart "continued to soften," she says. By the time Reyes departed for his second Medjugorje pilgrimage in October 1988, Estela was not as hostile to religion as she had been in the past. By this time she was involved with *Cursillos de Cristianidad* with Reyes and was helping to lead *cursillos* for Mexican American Catholic women in Phoenix.[44] She was also helping her son Armando with the teen retreats he held through the South Phoenix YMCA. Yet Estela says that she vacillated at the time between wanting to be immersed "in the world" and wanting to be free from its seductive powers. Even though a struggle was going on within Estela's mind, she says, she was still not willing to accept that God and the Virgin Mary were starting to change her life.

Estela points to two experiences that forced her to come to grips with what was happening to her. One morning while Reyes was away on his second Medjugorje pilgrimage, Estela remembers walking to the kitchen to pour some coffee and hearing a sweet, soothing voice say "good morning my daughter" as she passed by the large picture of the Virgin of Guadalupe in the living room.

Her first reaction was that she was "just plain crazy!" Uneasy, she continued to go about her weekend tasks. By the following Monday, she had pushed the incident to the back of her consciousness. She was still consumed with her career, she remembers, and didn't have time "for this kind of thing." She was also worried, she says, about what her coworkers would think if she told them about what had happened. She recalls, "I had worked so hard to gain their respect and I didn't want them to think I was a nut! You know they put people away for hearing little voices!"

Estela says she was greeted again the following week by the same voice coming from the picture. This time, she had a revelation that the voice was indeed that of the Virgin Mary. "I don't know why exactly I knew that it was, I just knew it in my heart that it was indeed Her."[45] These locutionary experiences, however brief, helped to prepare her for the multisensory encounter she had in her bedroom in December. Throughout the fall, Estela says she began to receive signals from the Blessed Mother "in her heart." She would wake up early in the morning with an urgent desire to attend 6 A.M. mass at St. Catherine of Siena, her home parish, even though attending daily mass was not a regular part of her routine. "It was something I just could not control—I know now that the Blessed Mother was working Her way into my life."

When Reyes returned from his pilgrimage, Estela says she was "more open" to his spirituality. She told him she would help him take their children

The painting of the Virgin of Guadalupe that
Estela says spoke to her in the fall of 1988.
Photo by author.

to "a higher spiritual level." Reyes said he had "consecrated my family to
the Blessed Mother" while he was on his pilgrimage, and he begged his
wife for her help in "getting our family back on track." Reyes was as-
tounded by the "changes" he saw in his wife upon his return; "I expected
that she would be angry with my request, but she was not, and I could not
believe it." The night after she said "yes" to her husband's tearful request to
help him in his quest for their family, Estela had a dream of what was yet
to come:

It was about 3:30 A.M., and Reyes had just gotten back into bed after praying. I fell back asleep and had a dream that our Blessed Mother had come
to us. We were in the same room, our bedroom, and I saw a bright
light. . . . I then saw a small boy come in and dart across the room.

I woke Reyes up and told him that our Blessed Mother is coming. . . .
The bright light came into our room and lit up the whole room and then
I saw Her.

I was in ecstasy and kept crying, "Oh She's here, She's so beautiful,
there She is." Reyes said, "Yeah, I know She's here." When I came back
from that feeling I saw Her talking to Reyes. I tried to touch Her, and
then I stretched out my hand. I kept pulling and pulling but couldn't get
to Her to touch Her. All of a sudden She just left and I woke up. I
turned around and went to sleep. It didn't bother me, it wasn't scary or
anything like that.

In the morning when I woke up I felt a good, good feeling.[46]

Estela thinks that the boy may have represented her oldest grandson, Ser-
gio, but she says she is not sure. What she *is* certain of, she says, is that the
Blessed Mother was "warming up her soul," preparing her, little by little,
for her future status as a visionary. From the next morning on, Estela
began to believe that the Blessed Mother was in her home. Estela says that
whereas once she barely noticed them, she now grew attached to the images of Mary in her home and would greet them throughout the day, secure in the knowledge that her home was inhabited by the Mother of God.
When Reyes announced one morning at breakfast that he was "called" to
give away a painting of the Blessed Mother that he had just bought in
Medjugorje to the bishop, Estela says that she just "cried and cried." " I
asked him, 'do you have to give it away?' I was bawling and was just devastated. I felt like She wasn't going to be here anymore, it was like he [Reyes]
just tore my heart away."

Estela had a second dream of the Virgin, and this time she appeared
just as she would in December;

I had a dream where there was a light coming from the hall and I told
Reyes that the Blessed Mother was coming to see us. I was frantic and he
[Reyes] was calm. The Blessed Mother was talking to Reyes. She was so
beautiful, like Our Lady of Grace, and I began to call to her "you are so
beautiful!" I then felt like a bolt of lightening went through me . . . the

Blessed Mother extended her hand to me and I was trying to reach up but woke up instead.[47]

This dream marked the boundary between Estela's "old life" and her "new life," according to husband Reyes. "When Stella told me the morning after the dream that the Blessed Mother would appear to us, I told her that it might not be a dream. On that night, the old Stella died and the new Stella was born." Estela remembers that she felt like she was starting to change: "I felt my heart begin to get warmer, softer. I couldn't wait to see what the Blessed Mother would do."

What Estela describes as a "softening" and "warming" of her soul and heart signals the process of her conversion experience. Her narrative is echoed by some other Mexican American Catholic conversion stories we will consider in subsequent chapters, and shows the overlap of Catholic and evangelical language. Conversion narratives all differentiate a life "before" conversion from the life "after," and all assert the Virgin Mary's and Jesus' central roles in causing them to "change their lives."[48] Estela says that her conversion was more gradual than all at once, because the Blessed Mother was "working on me"; but she also recalls that she was later "shook to the ground" by Mary's appearance to her. Mary literally *had* to appear to her, Estela believes, because she was "too much of a skeptic."

> She *had* to appear to me if I was going to believe in Her. She knows me too well! Some people I know tell me that they see her in an "interior vision." I say, "A WHAT?!" Interior vision, hmmph. I have a hard time dealing with that stuff.[49]

This is a fascinating self-examination by Estela where she claims that her visions cured her of her skepticism—yet another layer is added to the healings she and her family claim took place because of the Virgin. Because of Mary's intervention in her life, Estela has been "cured" of her feminism; skepticism; painful longing for her mother; tensions between her work and family life; and non-Catholicity. In one powerful moment on December 3, the Virgin's visit to her enabled her to reconcile—at least on the surface—the contradictions and constraints that were tearing away at her self, her identity, and her place within *la familia*.

Estela firmly maintains that Mary did not appear to Reyes, a lifelong devotee, because "no one would have believed him! But when people would hear that I was seeing Her, they would believe because I was the biggest skeptic, the biggest nonbeliever you ever saw!"[50]

Estela sees herself as an instrument of Mary, being used for Mary's greater purpose. Because she was a nonbeliever before her apparitions, she felt her conversion would be taken more seriously, and it was, she says, because she was "so much like other Americans—self-centered, aggressive, and arrogant. People could relate to me because they were like me." Estela's nonbeliever status prior to the apparitions was frequently mentioned at the backyard rosary sessions and continues to be a focus of the annual December retreats. "If Estela could turn her heart over to the Blessed Mother, anyone can" is a kind of catchall phrase I have heard repeatedly at shrine gatherings. So because of, and not in spite of, her earlier "skepticism," Estela began to thrive under, and came to eagerly anticipate, the weekly visits from the Virgin. In the first five years of the apparitions, Mary appeared to her each Tuesday and Saturday morning with messages for the community and "the Americas." According to Estela, when the Virgin visited her with a message, she provided it a little at a time and patiently waited for Estela to type it into her computer. Sometimes the message was given in Spanish, at other times in English. Estela always translates the messages into the two languages with the help of her family and some close friends, and family members distribute the typed messages at the backyard rosaries. In addition to these more official visits, the Blessed Mother also visits Estela for her own religious and personal edification, and will give her messages to relay to family members as well. The Virgin has become Estela's "best friend" and is her most reliable and closest confidante. To Estela, the Virgin is the perfect mother and friend:

> She just brings joy to my heart. She's that perfect mother, the one we all wish we would have had, you know, but can't because they were human mothers in this world. With Our Blessed Mother you can't see her faults. As far as I'm concerned, She has none.[51]

As a mother, the Virgin filled the gulf created by Delfina's death and, according to Estela, she perfected the act of mothering—she offered what Delfina was unable to offer herself. Estela could not sever her own identity from her mother's—she needed a maternal figure and symbol in her life. As she had once merged her identity with that of her mother, Estela now identifies with the Virgin of the Americas, who serves as her role model, mentor, spiritual guide, best friend, liberator, and mother.

She is the ideal mother that we would all like to have, that we think of in our dreams. Even the most perfect mother on earth encounters anger from her children. She also has to be a friend because that's what we want out of our mothers, all of us.[52]

The Virgin is the ideal Delfina and the kind of mother Estela herself wants to be. In addition, the kind of relationship Estela has with the Virgin of the Americas is an exclusive mothering one, much like her relationship with Delfina. As Nancy Chodorow writes, "at some levels mothers and daughters tend to remain emotionally bound up with each other in what might be called a semisymbiotic relationship, in which neither ever quite sees herself or the other as a separate person."[53] Estela had this kind of relationship with Delfina, her biological mother, and now she has it with the Virgin of the Americas. When her mother died, Estela felt a profound sense of loss, felt as though she had died. She also experienced feelings of profound loss when the Virgin told her that she would be "cutting back" on her visits and messages because, according to Estela, "She felt as though I was doing her work and didn't need Her as much." Then, in 1998, she was "devastated" when the Virgin told her that she would no longer be appearing with messages for the public. "I just crawled into my bed that day and cried like a baby" is what she told me. Just as Estela had become emotionally dependent on her mother, so too had she become dependent on the Blessed Mother. She agonized over her visions of Mary and tearfully asked the Virgin *why* she had appeared to her, a "sinner" who had not been a "good Catholic":

I used to cry a lot in the beginning, "Why did you pick me?" I'd cry this over and over. I felt this terrible guilt that I had rejected Her for so long. One time, She told me that the person She chose had to have a visible conversion. . . . I wasn't a prayerful person before She came. I went to mass on Sundays, as many Catholics do, but I didn't know why, what, or anything. There really *was* a visible conversion on my part.[54]

Estela's own spiritual and existential questioning was calmed by the "loving presence" of the Virgin, who assured Estela that she was worthy enough to be her messenger. Estela was also distraught because she thought that the Virgin should be appearing to Reyes and not to her. According to Estela, the Blessed Mother became her spiritual tutor, leading her to read the Scriptures and to pray and meditate daily. Estela was instructed by Mary to work on her own spiritual life before she could become a public spokeswoman for the Virgin Mary.

When I asked Estela if the Virgin had asked her to resign from her administrative position she said no, on the contrary, the Blessed Mother had encouraged her to stay with her job until the end of the contract year and that she had also instructed her to finish her Masters in Education:

> I wanted to quit my job and my Master's program too, but the Blessed Mother told me that I had to finish what I had started . . . that I would never know when the experience and the degree might come in handy. She also told me that finishing my Masters was a way of honoring Her. See, She *knew* that it would . . . I am at the school now and am doing Her work all of the time.[55]

Estela says that the Virgin "worked on my soul" and on her family's faith for almost a year before the visions were made public—then Mary began to bring messages for "the world."

Balancing Familia and Self

Through the medium of her Marian visions, and drawing on her relationship with the Blessed Mother, Estela challenges assumptions that the Virgin can somehow be disempowering for women in that she represents female passivity.[56] Estela's Virgin and her experiences with her do not encourage what Martha Cotera calls Marianismo, an ideology that encourages women's passivity, submissiveness, and virtuousness and that sets a double sexual and moral standard for women.[57] In her personal messages to Estela, the Virgin acts as mother, counselor, and spiritual guide and has not, according to Estela, encouraged passivity or meekness on any level. "She has always encouraged me to go out there and be the best I can be, no matter what I do," Estela once told me. Indeed, for Estela as well as for other women in the community, this Virgin takes on the multiple roles of counselor, mother, spiritual role model, and example of Catholic womanhood. Under the guidance and tutelage of the Virgin of the Americas, Estela is able to maximize her roles as wife, mother, educator, public visionary, and evangelizer, and it is the Virgin herself who gives her encouragement and approval to thrive in all these capacities.

Because of her relationship with the Virgin of the Americas, Estela has been able to overcome past fears and insecurities and is now ensconced in a world of devotion that honors her motherhood and family life as it respects her role as a Marian visionary. With the onset of the visions Estela was able to feel good about being a wife, mother, and grandmother as well as a "career woman." The latter role, repositioned within acceptable cultural and religious boundaries, is seen as enhancing her maternal and wifely roles. Estela has been the principal of Mary's Ministries' charter school for the past several years and says that "I just love working with the children, especially the little Hispanos." Her work now is not much different from her work before her self-proclaimed conversion; the main difference is that it is now carried out and validated within a family-run enterprise, Mary's Ministries and its subsidiary, ESPIRITU. Her previous career was away from the family, and her prestige was a separate entity. "The children call me grandma and they call Reyes grandpa and I just love that!" When I have visited the school's campus, the truth of these proclamations has been evident; the children run up to her and throw their arms around her. Estela says that she loves to hug the children, "especially because many of them don't get any affection at home." Estela's new career complements her wifely and motherly roles, and when she talks about it she emphasizes her nurturing qualities. But when she talks about her early days as an administrator, it is evident that she enjoyed those years thoroughly, and her eyes gleam with pride. "You know that the manual that I wrote on bilingual education was used for many years in the Phoenix school system and still is in many schools," she proudly told me.

Her roles as a Marian visionary, wife, and mother complement her work at the school and in Mary's Ministries—all are deeply entwined. Estela sees her career before the visions as "a job" but her new occupation as a vocation, a "calling." "When I work with the children at the school and the teachers I am doing the Blessed Mother's work, just as when I help organize a faith course for Mary's Ministries—this is all for the Blessed Mother." As a woman who says she was "chosen" by the Virgin Mary herself to do this important work in her community, Estela is what the Latina theologian Gloria Ines-Loya calls a *pasionaria* and *pastora* in her community: as a visionary and evangelizer with Mary's Ministries she "takes responsibility" for the evangelization of her community and seeks to change the way the Church perceives Hispanics, and specifically Mexican Americans.[58]

Estela has been able to liberate herself from the contesting powers and demands of *la familia* and her own desires for success and individualism because of her relationship with the Virgin. Though she claims she is no longer a feminist, Estela holds fast to feminist principles that women are fulfilled human beings and that their concerns are deeply entwined with their communities and their families. Estela's narrative is much like those of the evangelical women in Judith Stacey's sociological study of late twentieth-century American families; Estela and these women point to a complex feminism, a "postfeminism" that makes room for competing interests and demands.[59] Estela, like the women Stacey portrays in her book, blends political and social liberalism with religious and gendered conservatism— which makes for a complex blend of positions. On some issues, such as her strong advocacy of women's higher education, Estela would be considered "liberal," yet on others, such as her stance against birth control and abortion, she would be called "conservative," Women like Estela and those Stacey interviewed challenge our perceptions of the boundaries of feminism because they make the boundaries malleable. The term "postfeminism" is an attempt to put into language the inherent contradictions within women's lives.

Through and because of her apparitions, Estela has been able to create a space for herself within traditional expectations of Mexican American women and womanhood. Her apparitions have enabled her to bridge the gulf that separated her from her society's and her family's expectations, and she has forged an even more legitimized status in her family and community. The Virgin, like Estela, balances "feminist" with more "traditional" demands and concerns. She tells Estela to achieve her educational goals but at the same time she encourages a kind of submission to her husband and her family—much like she takes a back seat to her father and son, Jesus. After all, it was the Virgin, Estela claims, who told her to finish her Master's degree and her term as school administrator before "devoting myself to Her one hundred percent." The Virgin wanted a well-educated, well-connected Mexican American woman to deliver her messages to South Phoenix and "to the world," and in Estela she found that kind of messenger.

These apparitions have not only given Estela more acceptable power in her family and community, but on a larger scale, they have placed her on the national stage, giving her the legitimacy and acceptance that she "craved" in her "unconverted life" before the visions. Her status as a Marian visionary gives her the moral weight that effectively legitimizes her fame. In the early 1990s, Estela was a guest on the nationally televised Sally Jesse Raphael and Geraldo Rivera shows, and she was actively sought out as a keynote speaker by numerous Catholic church groups and Marian-focused organizations throughout the 1990s and into the present millennium. And Estela, accompanied by Reyes, has been an invited special guest on several Marian cruises which she has "thoroughly enjoyed." When I asked Estela if any of these appearances was more meaningful for her and why, she said that the Geraldo Rivera show was "very special" because its theme was "Christmas Miracles" and she was "very touched" by the other guests on the show. Estela mentioned that she was "especially happy" because the Rivera special was aired on subsequent Christmases.

Estela's occupation as a visionary is a prestigious one that has accorded her moral and spiritual authority, and she has reveled in the many hugs, kisses, and accolades she has received from believers and devotees. Many pilgrims to her backyard shrine saw one of her television appearances and were intrigued; one young Anglo Catholic, Jeannie, went so far as to move to Phoenix from her home on the East Coast to join Mary's Ministries and to "just be around" Estela. And John, a Mexican American man in his forties at the time, saw Estela give a talk at an Anaheim Marian conference; a year later he moved to South Phoenix to join Mary's Ministries. Like Jeannie, he felt "called" to follow Estela because he was "so impressed with her." In my years of interviewing men and women at the shrine, I have encountered many who claim to have received "inspiration" from Estela; many of these pilgrims have joined Mary's Ministries and have become active members of the organization. Those who have not committed themselves to the organization still claim to be "in awe of" Estela as a visionary, and they treat her with utmost respect. Over the years, Estela has been accorded celebrity status and has received numerous cards, flowers, and small gifts from her admirers and supporters, both men and women.

Yet not all of this attention and outpouring of love is welcome. Estela has talked about the "crazies" who believe that she is a saint and who "won't leave me alone." Some devotees have been what Estela has referred to as "way out there, if you know what I mean," and she has made a decision to not respond to their letters and pleading messages. Father Jack Spaulding, a close friend of Estela and Reyes and a high-profile Marian locutionary in the 1980s (who will be discussed in the next chapter), has also spoken about the "crazies" who wouldn't leave him alone—he calls them the "groupies who just go from shrine to shrine." For Estela, at one point the phone calls were so overwhelming that she and Reyes considered making their phone number unlisted, but ultimately they decided against it because they would have screened out many devotees' calls.

Estela finds her status as a visionary a difficult, demanding job. The Virgin, she says, is a demanding boss, one who expects her to be her stalwart "soldier." Estela has jokingly referred to the Virgin of the Americas as "a real go-getter; I mean, she has worked me so hard and sometimes I just don't feel that I can do everything that she wants. I try very hard to do everything that She asks." This Virgin, according to Estela, is a "tough woman" who makes demands of herself, her family, and the Mary's Ministries community, and is seen as a liberator for the poor and the oppressed.

Estela and her family members acknowledge that, in contrast to the pious Reyes, she had been a dyed-in-the-wool "feminist" who was "far removed from God" prior to the first of her visions. The apparitions and the ensuing Marian phenomena were a way for Estela to reform her family; to borrow the anthropologist Elizabeth Brusco's phrase, Estela's visions were a "strategic movement" on her part. She used her apparitions as a way to bring her family together, as did many other Hispano-Mexican American women who became devoted to the Virgin of the Americas.[60] Estela's apparitions have been a way for her to negotiate the demands of motherhood and career. Estela reclaimed her motherhood, became an important religious figure in her community, and embarked on a new career. Through her narrative, we are able to see the very real contestations of ethnic identity and gendered tensions, and how Estela demonstrated agency through her conversion experience. While she ultimately made concessions to satisfy cultural and familial expectations, in her new role as a Marian visionary Estela was able to construct an even more powerful role within her family and community. Yet there is an important qualifier to Estela's empowerment: although she may be the one who sees and hears the Virgin, it is her family's experiences that have legitimated her claims.

* 2 *

From the Devil to Mary

The Ruiz Family Narratives

Estela's visions and their interpretations were interconnected with others' lives from the beginning. Her visions were and still are her children's and her husband's visions, and an inseparable bond links her, the visionary, her visions, and the public witnesses, who were from the start her spouse, sons and daughters, and their significant others.[1] By taking a close look at Estela's narrative in the context of her family, we can see how the visionary is influenced by those who surround her. Recent studies of Marian visionaries have focused on how the visionary is influenced and affected by her family and culture, and Estela is no different. She, like other visionaries, has been influenced by her family and by the public and their perceptions, and it is these interactions that shape the contours of her visions.[2]

Estela's apparitions of Mary obtain their ultimate meaning from the family context in which they are placed and shared. Her experiences are informed by her past and present family history; her visions and her interpretation of them have become a foundation on which her family adds their own narratives. Estela may have been the first in her family to experience the Virgin of the Americas, but soon after she revealed her experiences to her husband and children, they enriched her story with theirs and made her narrative part of a complex story with interwoven, overlapping parts.

While it is possible to separate Estela's experiences of her apparitions from her family's, it is difficult to separate her interpretation from the context of the *familia*. There has never been just one story of the apparitions; instead, multiple narratives converge to form an overarching, familial experience with the Virgin. Like Estela, her husband, her grown children, and their spouses were all searching for spiritual renewal in their lives. They were all, each in his or her own way, desiring to shed old habits and to become new both as individuals and as a more cohesive family unit. Estela's apparitions gave them a chance to meet and to attempt to collectively "heal" the past tensions, frustrations, and hurts they had individually and collectively gone through.

Estela knew that her family needed "healing," from "all kinds of pain," and her apparitions of this Virgin gave her the legitimation as a visionary, wife, and mother to reform her children. In addition to the spiritual, emotional, and ethnic healing the Virgin brought to this family, the visions provided a means for the Ruizes to forge closer ties with the Catholic faith and church—most clearly through their connections with a local priest, Father Jack Spaulding, and his wealthy Scottsdale visionary group. Ultimately, this Marian phenomenon guaranteed Estela and her family a special place within Catholicism, allowing them to expand the boundaries of official and popular piety. The visions provided the necessary venue for the Ruizes to address their ethnic and spiritual angst, and the vehicle through which they could define, on their terms, what it means to be Catholic.

Kitchen-Table Talks and the Virgin

The apparitions gave Estela a reason to call her family together for a series of kitchen-table talks, beginning December 10, 1988, and for her children and their spouses to share their responses to her news. Within days of having her first vision, Estela and Reyes went to meet with Reyes's friend and spiritual confidant, Father Jack Spaulding, then of Scottsdale's St. Maria Goretti parish church. Reyes and Father Jack had become quite close during their Medjugorje pilgrimage in October 1987, and when Estela had her first apparition, Reyes immediately thought to call Father Jack, because he was by that time a locutionary who had become well-known in Marian circles for hearing Mary and Jesus. Acting on Father Jack's advice, Estela and Reyes called the first family meeting on December 10. This was the first of several meetings, which developed a month later into "prayer sessions" at Father Jack's suggestion. These were emotional gatherings, evoking tears of happiness and sorrow among family members over their own self-described sinful ways. The family claims these sessions brought them closer together and eventually made them a working unit of Marian believers. This took some time, according to Estela and Reyes, because the more skeptical among them had to "face their own demons."

Armando taped these conversations, which spanned fifteen days and nights in the months of December and January. When I was staying with

Little Rey and Norma and conducting fieldwork, he gave me the unique opportunity to listen to and transcribe these tapes. I was the first person other than Armando, Reyes, and Estela to listen to these tapes in full; several of the Ruizes did not even know that the tapes still existed. On these mini-cassette tapes, Ruiz family members are heard discussing their reactions to Estela's news of the Virgin's appearances. These sessions allow the listener to hear what the historian of apparitions Paolo Apolito refers to as the "language of visions," and what we hear unfolding on these tapes is the "intense collective process" of apparitions.[3] According to Armando, the family agreed to his suggestion to tape these conversations so that they could listen to these first encounters years later to relive and recapture the thrill, wonder, and excitement. "We wanted to have our first meetings together documented somehow so that we could be taken back, you know, to those days." Yet Reyes, and perhaps some others, were clearly cautious and worried about how the conversations would later be interpreted, and at several points during the sessions Reyes sharply tells Armando to "turn it off." We can only speculate what the family discussed during these interludes; the conversations that are recorded are intensely personal, at times raw and riveting.

I was excited to be the first non-family member to know about and listen to these tapes. Yet I recall feeling more than a little strange—even perhaps voyeuristic —when Little Rey asked if he could listen to them when I was finished, since he had never listened to them before. I experienced a privileged and yet also uncomfortable anthropological moment, an important entryway to understanding the ecumenical visions and experiences of this family. Moreover, I was able to tap into a family's archived, firsthand accounts of their responses. These tapes are among their first reactions, their individual testimonies, before the family narrative overtook the individual narratives for the purposes of validating and authenticating the apparitions for the public. By comparing these earlier responses with more recent ones, we can learn much about the sociology and anthropology of visions and vision-making. The Ruizes' voices are raw with emotion, they break down crying and take pauses before they speak again. They interrupt each other in their excitement and they challenge each other's assessments. These tapes catalogue, as much as possible, a chronology of their individual experiences and their coming together in collective devotion.

Even though there are occasional gaps in the taping where Reyes tells Armando to turn off the recorder, Reyes, his wife, his children, and their spouses openly discuss their reactions to Estela's news and voice their opinions, fears, hopes, and concerns. These conversations are a unique opportunity to understand the complex process of collective religious experience; listening to them we can excavate a sociology of religious expression. In these tapes, against the sounds of their grandchildren playing and babies crying in the background, Estela and Reyes tell their family about what Estela experienced and the dreams and events leading up to her first apparition and locution. Estela speaks to her family about her first apparition experience:

> We had been saying the rosary for a long time. From the very beginning, I was facing the painting of the Blessed Mother—the one that Father Louitious gave to your dad. Now I had never paid any attention to that painting, *ever*, but as we started praying the rosary, I started looking at it . . . it was pulling me to it. It was calling me. I said to myself, "no, I'm not going to pay attention to it" and I closed my eyes, out of fear, and I kept them closed to the end of the rosary, toward the end of the last decet. But then I *had* to open my eyes, it's like somebody had said "open your eyes right now!" My eyes immediately opened and looked at the picture. I felt a real pull. I couldn't even say the rosary anymore, I couldn't breathe, I couldn't speak, I couldn't say anything! As I stared at it, my eyes wouldn't move from it. . . . I wanted them to but they wouldn't. Then I started seeing steam and my glasses were in this steam. All of a sudden I started to rationalize this thing, you know, the rational person that I am. I started seeing this haze and all of a sudden the *whole picture* was a haze and my eyes zeroed right in on the picture. I could only see the picture and there was smoke, a kind of smoke, all around it. Then, out of the picture I saw Her come out. I realized that our Blessed Mother had just come out and was *right there!* And She moved and She talked to me! And then I went bananas. I guess I started crying and yelling, I don't know what the heck I said. They [Leticia, Fernando, Reyes] were all sitting there and they saw me and watched me. Then I started saying "there She is!" "There She is!" "She's here!" and "how beautiful She is!" And she *was* beautiful, *God* She was beautiful.[4]

At that point, Reyes interjects and says to his wife "in Spanish," which Estela affirms: "yes, I said it in Spanish; 'Que linda! Que linda!' And I kept reaching out to Her, like I did in my dream."

In these taped kitchen table talks, Estela and Reyes take turns unraveling what they understood to be the chain of events that had led up to the first vision: Reyes's pilgrimage to Medjugorje; Mary speaking to Estela on two separate occasions from the painting of the Virgin of Guadalupe in the fall of 1988, Estela's prophetic dreams, and Reyes's ongoing discussions and consultations with Father Jack.

Armando, Leticia, and Estela's and Reyes's youngest daughter, Rosie, all declare in these sessions that they believed their mother "right away," while Armando's twin, Fernando, Leticia's husband, is openly skeptical. Little Rey, Estela's and Reyes's second youngest child, tells Estela that Mary would have to accept him "just as I am," meaning as a drug addict, and Becky is ambivalent—she wants to believe, she says, but is not as accepting as Armando and Rosie. Oldest son "Lolo," an evangelical Protestant living in Los Angeles with his wife and three young sons, later accepts the news from his mother and tells her that he believes her. But he is not and cannot be, given his Protestant fundamentalism, a Marian devotee. For his part, Reyes is ecstatic that his "beloved woman" is appearing to none other than his wife. When asked by her sons and daughters what message the Virgin has given her for Reyes, Estela laughs, saying that Mary told her to tell Reyes "*Dime hombre que es calme!*" (tell my man to be calm!) and that "when the time comes everything will work out." To this, Reyes, chuckling, replies, "I *am* calm!"

Estela and Reyes take turns at these kitchen-table meetings, speaking about their own experiences with the Virgin and leading the family forum. Reyes declares that he is "beside himself" with happiness; he tells his children that the Blessed Mother appearing to his wife was "the most beautiful thing," an "answer to my prayers." He goes on to talk about the rigorous praying regimen that he has recently undertaken in an effort to cleanse himself of his sins and to reach "a new level of prayer." After his return from Medjugorje, Reyes says that he would get up in the middle of night and pray until, exhausted, he would fall asleep again. This routine bothered Estela a great deal, and she would say, "ugh! There he goes again!" when she felt her husband get up out of bed each night. Reyes says that he was compelled to bring his family to a new spiritual level and knew that he had to do it through prayer. Now, after the first vision has occurred, Reyes addresses his family:

> When I do these things I go deep into meditation, a different kind of prayer. There's a lot of things you've done with your life that are too heavy, and there's no way that prayer alone can clean it. It was necessary to go to another stage of sacrifice, and I am telling you to go to this next

level, all of you, to a higher and harder level. A lot of times it's physical
hardness of the heart that we need to overcome.[5]

During the family gatherings Reyes challenges his two most skeptical children, Little Rey and Fernando, to allow their hearts to be "softened" by the
Virgin. Estela chimes in, telling her youngest son that the Blessed Mother
gave her a message for him that morning, that he should ask "with all of
your heart for your *complete* separation from your desire for drugs." Little
Rey acknowledges his reticence to turn himself over to the Blessed Mother.
"I know that I haven't done that yet—I haven't asked Her for help. I am
having a hard time with that." Estela counters his assertion and stresses to
her son that he must stop trying to rid himself of drugs on his own and
"turn your heart over to the Blessed Mother."

Armando talks at length about his belief in the visions, saying that the
Blessed Mother is "all-consuming. I dream about Her and when I wake up
it's a constant companionship. You can feel Her." He cites the love that he
sees in his family's eyes as proof that something "amazing" is happening.
"Yes," Reyes laughs, "it's amazing that no one is fighting!" Estela also acknowledges the change that she claims was already underway in her family: "I know that the Blessed Mother can see us here and I can just see the
pleasure in Her face because of the love that we are all having for each
other." Armando chimes in and tells his siblings and their spouses that
they must all see themselves as "a part of the same body" and that they
must start praying the rosary together. Estela and Reyes both speak about
the importance of praying as a family. Estela claims that it is what the
Blessed Mother wants—for the family to come together on a regular basis
to pray, in a calm manner.

Armando, who believes in his mother's visions based on his own "faith
and intuition," was rewarded soon after the first family meeting when he
experienced the Blessed Mother's presence. One night when he was praying the rosary, he says that he experienced the Virgin Mary's presence in
an "awesome" way:

All of a sudden the room got really glowing. I was conscious of what was
going on, everything was like a dull gold. What happened was I couldn't
turn away. I remember that around the edges there was a mist, it was
fuzzy. I couldn't see anything outside the cloud. Inside the cloud it was
gold. You know those crayons that are gold and colored . . . it was like that
. . . a misty gold. You ever ride the ride at Disneyland, the ghost ride? Well,

at the end of it you're told not to take anyone with you, and you see it three-dimensionally. That's how it was—what I saw last night was that she was changing real, real quickly. All of a sudden I saw Our Lady of Medjugorje, where She was holding the baby Jesus. I saw one of Her with roses . . . the Virgin of Guadalupe. She was three-dimensional and the last vision was of the Immaculate Heart of the Americas.[6]

Armando describes this multiple vision of Mary as an exhilarating awakening. As he tells his family about this experience the next night, he pauses for a moment and exclaims that Mary had *just* appeared to him:

She was pulsating, radiating . . . She did it *right now* . . . in gold. She did that, and everything got dark and then boom! She gave me that gift through Her whole rosary. I wasn't overwhelmed with crying or fear, but She borrowed a piece of my heart that I was asking for. . . . I know that she gave me, last night, peace. She stole my heart a long time ago, She broke me down and She knows that. She gave me peace. She gave me the faith that She will come for me the day I die. I told Her that I trust in Her completely.[7]

He acknowledges that it was his father's prayers that gave him the opportunity to see the Virgin. At the time of his mother's first visions, Armando was an Arizona state legislator, and he claimed that the Virgin gave him strength when he was in legislative session not to be afraid. "She doesn't talk to me, She just radiates and pulsates." During one of my interviews with Armando, he stressed that his devotion to the Virgin "took off" in the previous year when he was in Mexico on legislative business. It was when he made a pilgrimage to the Basilica of the Virgin of Guadalupe, four years after his mother's first vision, that he made the decision not to run for reelection and to follow "whatever She wanted me to do."

It was like being anywhere that She is. I was really overwhelmed by that and I kept thinking about the feeling of being at home. I had this overwhelming sense that I was home even though I was over two thousand miles away. It was there in Mexico that I began to change.[8]

When we spoke, Armando said that his mother's announcement of her apparitions had moved him deeply and that he believed her "one hundred percent," but that he just wasn't ready at that point to "give myself over to Her." He compared himself to his mother as "she was before her apparitions" in that he, too, desired power and prestige and had gained wide-spread popularity in Phoenix for his work with youth, for his opposition to the English-Only Proposition 106, and for his YMCA youth programs. It was when he came face to face with Guadalupe's image in the Basilica that his ambitions "no longer seemed as important as what She desired me to do."

Like her brother Armando, Rosie talks in the tapes about how she believes her mother's announcement because she "just knows" the Blessed Mother was appearing to her mother. Rosie says she had been "looking for meaning in my life" in the months preceding her mother's apparition, and she takes Estela's news to be a "sign" that she needs to start changing her life around and to devote herself to the Blessed Mother. When Rosie and I talked about her life before Estela broke the news to them, she admitted that she had been "a little wild, a little crazy," and that she felt "aimless" and based her self-worth on how others perceived her.

In the tapes, Rosie emphasizes the painful process of conversion: literally, her own body was taking on the pain of Jesus and the suffering of Mary. In the months and weeks preceding her mother's first vision, Rosie experienced extreme physical discomforts and received messages from Jesus and Mary that she later understood were "preparing me" for her mother's announcement of her own visions and locutions. Along with her father, Rosie had been joining in the Scottsdale nine's prayer sessions at St. Maria Goretti in the months preceding her mother's experience. In the tapes, Rosie emphasizes her experiences with praying to Mary and Jesus, which she describes as incredibly exhausting and cathartic. She admits to her family that she needs a lot of cleansing, and that she has a lot of penance to do for her past sins. Ever since her internship in Washington, D.C., that year (1988), she knew, she says, that she was "being called to heal myself and my family." During her internship year, a deeply unhappy and lonely time for her, Rosie visited the National Cathedral frequently and stared at the Piéta. "I would just cry and cry in the pew," she tells her family with a shaking voice. It was when she returned to South Phoenix in September that year, she says, shortly before her mother's first visions, that she began to attend the St. Maria Goretti young adult prayer groups with the visionaries and Father Jack. It was at these meetings that she began to feel Christ's pain and his passion, she explains to her family:

Everything that has concerned His passion has been shown to me, placed in my hands. I see his passion and the first thing I notice is His hands.

That day I got sick at St. Maria's, Father Jack told me that if I get any passions, not to get scared about it, but to just go from there. . . . When we went to the prayer meeting on Friday, during the rosary I felt a pain in my back on my right side. It came to the front and was a pain that I had *never* before in my life felt. It felt like somebody was stabbing me, right through me. I was just clenching my hands because it hurt so bad. I just kept asking for the strength to deal with it. The pain was through the whole rosary. Our Lord told me to lie down for the last Mystery. I was lying down, on the carpet, and then I felt that I had to lie on the marble. Once we finished the rosary my pain was gone.[9]

Rosie continues to discuss in detail how she felt Christ's passion, and that she knew that it was necessary "to understand the pain that He went through." She realized, she says, that she had to endure her own painful times in order to get closer to Jesus and the Blessed Mother. The pain she had experienced and continued to experience on several occasions was rewarded, she says, by her own visions of Mary and locutions from Christ and Mary.

As with her mother, the Virgin became her dear friend and confidante. Rosie told me that one day, about a month after Estela's first vision, as she was driving to pick up some lunch at her favorite restaurant, Knock Kneed Lobster, she got behind a diesel semi truck that was moving slowly. She grew frustrated, she recalls, and then she heard, "Be patient, my child." Rosie asked, "Is that you, Blessed Mother?" She received the answer, "Yes, it is." Rosie said that she walked into the restaurant with "a big smile on my face" because she knew that Jesus and Mary were both communicating with her. Rosie went on to be one of three family members besides Estela to see the Virgin of the Americas.

Like her brother Armando and her father, Rosie felt responsible at the time of the visions for "getting the family together," and she tells her family that she was explicitly told so by Jesus while she was praying with the St. Maria Goretti prayer group a month before her mother's first vision:

I remember that I really didn't want to be there—I kept looking at my watch—"Is it time for me to go yet?" I kept wondering. Then I started praying, I just shut my eyes and all of a sudden He was telling me that I had to get my family together. He was speaking to me in my heart. It really didn't hit me . . . I mean, I didn't know what was going on and the next day I was crying to mom and dad. I kept saying, "I don't want us to go the wrong way! I don't know what I have to do. I just know I have to do it."[10]

Rosie, Armando, and Reyes had, each in their own way, begun to work toward inner healing, which they would then bring to their family in the wake of the visions. All three felt a sense of urgency regarding the Ruiz family's spiritual health, and the signs from Mary and Jesus confirmed their fears and prompted them to take action. Individually and unbeknownst to each other, they say, they prayed, meditated, deprived themselves of sleep, and abstained from bodily pleasures in order to begin the process of healing their family.

Leticia, who was in the room with Estela the night of the first apparition, also says that she believed in Estela's visions immediately. She, too, says in the tapes that she had been receiving signs from the Virgin Mary that something was going to start happening in her life. She had been praying for a long time, she says, for her husband, Fernando, to "come around" and start being a husband to her. Her love for him was great, yet she suffered because of his friendships with other women, his long absences from home, and the awkwardness that had developed between them as a married couple. A devout believer in the Virgin of Guadalupe, Leticia had gone to the Basilica in Mexico City several months before Estela's first vision and had gotten down on her knees, sobbing, and begged Guadalupe to "bring back my husband." Ever since the Virgin appeared to Estela, Leticia says, she started to see a change in Fernando, "little by little." She kept praying to Guadalupe, she says, to help her and her husband, and she was "called over to Her" while praying at St. Catherine of Siena church one morning a month or so before Estela's first vision.

> This morning the Virgin of Guadalupe was calling me over to pray to Her. I had gone to mass by myself and She was calling me over. I never go up to pray to Her because She is so far away from where we sit. I went up to Her and started crying. I was praying to Her and crying, just crying. I was all alone, nobody was around me, not even the Hispanics who are always around her. I felt really good that day, it's mind-boggling, all of it.[11]

During a conversation I had with her ten years after the family's first meeting, Leticia told me that a few weeks after Estela's first apparition she saw the statue of the Virgin Mary in Peggy and Armando's house "light up and show the Blessed Mother's beauty. The face on the statue was not pretty—it was ugly compared to the beautiful face that I saw. I had my glasses on, so I know what I saw."

When she was sitting alongside her husband and in-laws on the night of Estela's first vision, Leticia said she "prayed so hard" to Guadalupe to bring her husband back to her, "not just physically, just to bring him back to me as a person." As she prayed, Leticia says, she became very uncomfortable and was "real warm and sweating." She grew increasingly hot and cried; "I couldn't get myself together again." Leticia says that as she was saying the last decet of the rosary in Spanish, Estela began to shout out, "Que bonita, que *bonita!*" "You could feel the presence of Her there, and when She left, it was cool again, and I wasn't sweating or crying anymore. It was like someone just bopped Estela and she was just stunned."[12] Leticia says that she immediately felt that things were going to get better, as she had a strong and enduring faith in *la Virgen.*

Leticia's and Fernando's daughter, Xochitli, who was ten years old at the time, was the only Ruiz besides Estela who saw the Virgin in the form of the Virgin of the Americas. During one of the family gatherings following Estela's first vision, Estela, watching the intensity of Xochitli's prayers to the Virgin, asks the Virgin to "please show Yourself to little Xochitli," who "wants to see You so badly." When she sees Xochitli's body tense up and her eyes light up, Estela tells her family that she knows the Blessed Mother has appeared to her oldest granddaughter. "The Blessed Mother just told her that Xochitli prays so beautifully" and that "She is very impressed with her behavior and devoutness." The Virgin wants to encourage Xochitli, Estela says, to keep praying and to continue being a "good girl."

For his part, Fernando, Leticia's husband and Xochitli's father, says that his story is not all "cupcakes and roses." For years before the exciting events of his family, he had been going through "spiritual and personal turmoil" because of the things that he had done in his past and that he continued to do at the time of his mother's vision. He had reached a point where he was "wallowing in the mud with the pigs." He had done very little to give his wife reason to trust him, he soberly declares, and all he wanted was to "get rid of the garbage and to get peace back in my life." Before his mother had her first vision, Fernando went to afternoon mass and "cried through the whole thing." Afterwards, he went home to ask Leticia for forgiveness, which is when the healing began, he says. He was ready for his life to change and was prepared for what happened to his mother soon after, yet it was difficult for him to accept that the Virgin Mary was appearing to his mother.

A few nights later, on the night of the first vision, he and Leticia went to talk with his parents. Fernando tried his hardest to "come clean" with them, telling them about his sins and sorrows. "Believe me, it wasn't an easy thing to do, to go in there with my mom. I covered my face the whole time we talked. I couldn't look at my dad, I just couldn't." Fernando acknowledges that he has a very difficult time expressing his feelings and that he knew his uncommunicative stance was ruining his marriage. He wanted so badly to be cleansed, he says.

> I said, "you know what Holy Spirit? Come talk to me. Clean me, let me talk and have peace in my life." I started telling my parents everything and I cried like people do . . . when they're dying. . . . When I was done, Leticia told me to look at them [Estela and Reyes] and I knew that I had been cleaned. Not by them, but by the Virgin Mary who forgave me. I didn't think I could do it, but I looked to them for forgiveness.[13]

After his confession, the foursome began praying the rosary, and it was during the last decet that the Virgin of the Americas appeared to Estela for the first time. The Virgin, Estela says, answered her prayers to help her children. "I was so worried about Fernando's and Leticia's marriage and the Blessed Mother *just knew that;* she came to help me take care of my children!"

> Around the time I had my dreams of the Blessed Mother I could see changes in all of you. I could see in Armando, when his eyes shone when he talked about Her . . . I could see that something was *moving* him. I could see it happening and I could see Leticia, already into it. I said "my God, something is happening with my kids but I don't know exactly what." By that time I was kind of having conversations with the Blessed Mother but I hadn't yet seen her. I said to Her, "Blessed Mother, You've *got to do* something with them. I'm just a mother here on earth. I can only talk with them, but if they don't want to listen to me they won't." So I started praying to Her *a lot* . . . especially for Fernando and Little Rey. I told your dad that I had begun to pray the rosary every day for Her to soften your hearts! It was that evening that Fernando came to me and it was that night that She appeared to me.[14]

Estela was also worried about her daughter Becky, who was having her own marital problems. Like her siblings, Becky talks on the tapes about experiencing the Virgin Mary before her mother's first apparitions. The mother of a young son and infant daughter at the time, Becky was in turmoil because of her then husband's marital infidelities. She had been having frightening dreams of evil and chaos, and when she drove to work in the mornings at the time of the vision, she prayed the rosary more vigorously than ever.

> When I was in the car I kept thinking of my dream. What happened was that there was this big hole of evil that had opened up in the world . . . it was literally a hole and chaos was just like blowing out, like in a movie. There were lots of people and there was the hole, and I started to pray the rosary over the hole, the Hail Mary, and I kept saying it over and over and got louder and louder.[15]

As she thought about the significance of her dream, driving to work, Becky started saying the rosary "louder and louder, like in my dream." She started to feel "dumb," but then began to feel a "presence" inside her. Although she was not sure if it was Jesus or the Blessed Mother, Becky "offered up" all of her feelings to the presence she felt. When she arrived at work, she "walked around all happy."

After her mother announced that the Virgin had appeared to her, Becky began to experience the Virgin Mary in a more intense and powerful way, like Armando, Rosie, and Reyes. She says she was filled with an overwhelming love for the Virgin and that the Virgin's eyes penetrated her, making her "faint from weakness." At home one evening during the time of the family sessions, Becky saw a "glow around Mary's head and saw Her cry," something that made her realize that she "belonged to Her." Yet despite her joyful experiences, Becky's journey to the Virgin Mary was difficult and full of fear. Just as Estela had been afraid in the beginning that it was the "evil one" and not the Blessed Mother appearing to her, Becky was fearful that she was being tricked by the Devil into thinking that it was Mary appearing to her. Becky says that she was scared—afraid that she was misinterpreting what was happening to her. What she had thought to be a "beautiful feeling" of being "pulled out of my body" during her vision of the Virgin became questionable and frightening to her later when she thought back on the experience. Becky says that her experience with Mary during the family rosary at one of the post-vision sessions was strenuous.

It was very physical . . . somebody was actually *grabbing me,* and trying to pull me out of my body. I talked with Father Doug and he told me that *I* should be able to tell the difference. But I was still afraid that it was the Evil One behind it all.[16]

Acting on the advice of her father and Father Doug Nohava of her home parish of St. Catherine of Siena, Becky began to sprinkle holy water inside her home, to protect it from the "evil one," should he be behind her visions and feelings. She also experienced physical pain, like Rosie, and felt "like a crown of thorns" was on her head. To ward off the pain and evil that may have been a part of it, Becky says, she repeated the rosary over and over. Soon after she began to pray, the pain stopped. Becky says that although she knew that her siblings believed in Estela's visions, she was just not as sure. She was influenced, she says, by her then husband's skepticism and his unwillingness to attend the prayer meetings. She was torn between her love for her family and her love and loyalty toward her husband, which was constantly being tested because of his infidelities. Although she was having parallel visions and experiences with the Virgin, Becky felt as though embracing the visions was equivalent to choosing her family over her husband.

The one child Estela was worried about perhaps the most was her oldest son, Inocensio, "Lolo," an evangelical Protestant living in Los Angeles with his wife and their three sons. Estela was afraid that he and his wife would not accept the visions because of their Protestant fundamentalism and would not want to be around the family because of its growing faith in the visions. Before Lolo and his family visited the family for Christmas in the December of the first visions, Estela spent "a lot of time" talking with the Virgin about her concerns and worries. Estela told the Virgin that she was afraid because "Lolo and Luisa have already given their hearts to Jesus, and I don't know if they have any more room for You." The Blessed Mother reassured her, Estela says, that she wanted all Estela's children to take the same road, the road to Jesus, and that the Virgin's role was to make their journey easier. She also told Estela that she was "very happy" because "She knows how much Lolo and Luisa love Jesus." According to Estela, the Virgin told her that because Lolo and Luisa have so much faith in Jesus it is "up to them" whether or not they say the rosary, because "their faith will lead them to Jesus, with or without My help." Just before Christmas 1988, the Virgin gave Estela a message that the behavior of Lolo and his wife "pleased Me very much" because they "gave up worldly things long ago for the greater glory of God." When Estela confided her worries to Mary, the Virgin told her that the glory is "My Son's and not Mine" and affirmed Lolo and Luisa's actions.

While they did not embrace the news of the apparitions, Lolo and Luisa did accept Estela's news about her experiences, much to her relief, and at the Virgin of the Americas' request, Lolo read from the Bible Christmas Eve at his parents' house during his Christmas visit. While he was reading about the birth of Christ, Estela says, she had a vision of Mary.

> I saw Her whole body this time, and her dress turned to gold. Light emanated from her, beautiful, beautiful light . . . the most luminous you could ever imagine. Her Son appeared behind Her, as an adult, but I could only see His shadow. She told me that She is pleased that my firstborn praises Jesus. She spoke to me about how the path is to Her Son . . . not to Her.[17]

According to Estela, Lolo was the least troubled by the visions because it was clear to him that the Virgin was going to lead his parents and siblings to Jesus and God. When I spoke with Lolo at an annual retreat to the Virgin of the Americas, he told me that he had "come around" in the years since his mother's first apparition and now was more involved with his family because he realized that the messages were meant to "glorify Her Son Jesus, and that is what is most important, so I don't have a problem with my mother having messages from the Virgin Mary."

When we met again two years later, Lolo focused on the more apocalyptic elements in the Virgin's messages and talked about the "end times that are to come." He did not seem to share the rest of his family's optimism for social and religious reform and when I asked him some pointed questions about whether he thought his family's efforts were useless, he replied, "well, I won't go that far, but I will say that there is nothing that we can do to avert the destruction that lies ahead. What my family is doing now is helping in the present, yes, but it will not have a lasting effect because that is out of our control." Lolo's Protestant fundamentalism and its premillennialist leanings clearly distinguish him from the rest of his family, whose language conveys postmillennial hope that they can indeed make a difference through their organizations and efforts.

Lolo says that he has been "let down" by Catholicism, and specifically by Catholic priests "who don't walk the talk, if you know what I mean." He specifically mentioned how Luisa was penalized by her Catholic faith as a young girl: "her priest actually told her that her mother's cancer was her 'cross to bear.' Now, that is ridiculous and just plain wrong." Lolo, disillusioned with the "religion of my youth," dabbled in many different faiths when he was in college at Loyola Marymount in Los Angeles. He says that he is more comfortable with his family now that they are "more into Scriptures." He is pleased with their greater emphasis on the Bible now, he says, because "as Catholics, they didn't always focus on it as much as they should have." Lolo says that he tries "to distance myself, my wife, and my sons from the visions," and when he is with his family in South Phoenix, he chooses to share his knowledge of the Scriptures and to "focus on Jesus." Lolo's stance toward and interpretation of the visions have had a direct impact in his family and its interpretations of the apparitions—especially his mother, Estela, who longed for his acceptance. Estela's and her family's increasingly evangelical perspective was certainly affected by his views.

Estela's visionary experiences enabled her to attain equal footing and prestige in her family. In the tapes, we hear powerful evidence that Estela's story overlapped with her husband's; Reyes adds to her story, and she to his. They were finally partners with equal spiritual footing, and they reveled in their shared experiences and stories. It is especially significant that Estela did not see the Virgin of Guadalupe but a fairer-skinned bilingual Virgin. It was Guadalupe who initially spoke to her, she says, out of her living room painting, but it was *not* the brown-skinned Virgin, her husband's *"mujer bonita,"* who ultimately visited her—it was a Virgin to whom her husband and children did not already have a strong devotion. Like their father, most of the children had a longstanding devotion to Guadalupe. Seeing a fair-skinned Virgin was a way for Estela to break away from her husband's influence and devotional stronghold on the family; yet it also enabled her to connect with him in a way she had not been able to before, and to have a partnership in her marriage. The Virgin brought them together in a new way. They were a Mexican American family—middle-class, well educated—and the Virgin who appeared to Estela was herself in-between, neither Mexican nor American but both.

Recall that it was the Virgin, according to Estela, who "told me to finish my Master's degree." Estela's education and the economic benefits of her status had distanced her from her husband, who had a third-grade education and was sensitive about his lack of schooling. Reyes told me on numerous occasions that he always felt a "great shame" for his lack of education and that he "feels badly" because he was the least educated in his entire family. Their children followed in Estela's footsteps and all, except for Little Rey, received college degrees; most of them, they say, were "arrogant" like their mother. Estela says that she was insensitive to Reyes's feelings before her apparitions, and now they can join together in a common cause—devotion to the Virgin of the Americas and dedication to the spiritual conversion of their family. Their marriage has been refreshed, renewed, because they now have a common cause, to spread their love for Mary and to promote her messages. Their voices have become almost giddy with this knowledge. Reyes is now able to talk about his "great, great love" for the Virgin and not fear ridicule from his wife and embarrassment in his family. For her part, Estela no longer feels that she is competing with the Virgin for Reyes's affections. In the tapes we can hear the joy and excitement both Estela and Reyes are experiencing as they tell their stories and their story; they are like a young couple on a first date together, full of adventure. Their life together after December 3, 1988, keeps "getting better and better," they both say, as they work together as a team. Estela's sightings and conversations with the Virgin of the Americas, instead of Guadalupe, enabled her to start a new family tradition while remaining in her husband's devotional patterns. She still deferred to his longstanding devotion to Guadalupe, but she was also able to be one with him in her devotion and through her new status, which also gave her her own identity and her own "*mujer.*"

Just as Estela's interpretations of her visions are deeply informed by her childhood and by her relationships with her mother, husband, and family, they are also influenced by her connections to Father Jack Spaulding and the group of nine Scottsdale visionaries. Estela's visions occurred in the midst of a Marian revival in Paradise Valley, the home of St. Maria Goretti church, as well as within the context of the Medjugorje apparitions, and we are able to see many similarities among Estela's visions and those of the young Scottsdale and Medjugorje seers. Establishing ties with the St. Maria Goretti Marian group, the "Scottsdale nine," further legitimated her and her family's experiences as Catholic, and prepared Estela to go public with her messages.

Father Jack and the Scottsdale Nine

At the time of Estela's first vision, Father Jack Spaulding was both an established locutionary of Jesus and Mary, and also the spiritual director

and overseer of the "Scottsdale nine," a group of young visionaries and locutionaries at the wealthy St. Maria Goretti parish church in Scottsdale,
where he had been head pastor since 1982. Each of the nine visionaries, according to Father Jack, had come to him separately and "unbeknownst to
each other," in the summer of 1988 to tell him of their encounters with the
Virgin Mary and Jesus, and each of them was "pretty amazed by it all."[18]
By the time Estela claimed to have had her first Marian experience, St.
Maria Goretti had become an active pilgrimage site and Father Jack and
his flock of six young women and three young men had become highly
sought after as prayer leaders and guest speakers. They were celebrities on
the Marian pilgrimage network that included the United States, western
Europe (primarily Lourdes and Fatima), Mexico, and Medjugorje in the
former Yugoslavia.

The Scottsdale nine were and are considered by many Marian devotees
to be the American version of the Medjugorje visionaries, the group of
seven young adult Bosnians, two young men and five young women, all of
whom claimed to have seen the Virgin, the *Gospa,* from 1981 to 1998. The
Scottsdale visions and locutions lasted from 1988 to approximately 1992,
when the group disbanded, apparently at Mary's initiative. All but Gianna
Talone, the primary Scottsdale seer who went on to become the well-pub-
licized Emmitsburg, Maryland visionary (1993–1999), ended their public
careers as visionaries in 1992. They did so, they say, because they had already fulfilled the Virgin's request of three full years of devotion. They all
claim they were profoundly changed by their experiences and that their
lives after their experiences were more spiritual and more meaningful than
before their Marian encounters.

Members of the Ruiz family were aware of the Scottsdale phenomenon
and were actively involved in it. Reyes, daughter Rosie, and Armando were
among those who attended the Scottsdale gatherings; Rosie was especially
enthusiastic about the prayer sessions and became actively involved in the
fall of 1988. Reyes and Gianna were on the same Medjugorje pilgrimage
with Father Jack, and although neither has spoken about having conversations there, it is likely that Reyes had some time to talk with Gianna about
her Marian piety.

While on pilgrimage, Reyes said that he "poured [his] heart out to Father Jack" about his nagging concerns over his family's lack of spirituality.
Reyes was especially distraught because Estela, unlike himself, had "no devotion" to the Virgin Mary, and he says that he knew "if Estela didn't have
faith then my kids wouldn't and I was worried about them, too." Reyes

told Father Jack that he was having a difficult time talking with his wife about his love for the Virgin because she dismissed his piety as "lunacy." Father Jack empathized with Reyes, assuring him that things would get better. A few days after their discussion, Father Jack found Reyes, who was praying to the Virgin, and told him that the Virgin Mary had spoken to him while he was walking outside on the small mountain near St. James parish. Father Jack didn't realize it at the time, he says, but Mary was telling him that he would be an integral part of the Marian phenomenon when he returned to Scottsdale.

The first time Estela met Father Jack Spaulding, in the fall of 1988 when she was coaxed by Reyes into attending a prayer session, she says that she was "not impressed" and thought him to be "arrogant, full of himself." She was skeptical of his locutionary claims and his group of visionaries, she says, and she thought he was grandstanding when she saw him relate his message from Jesus. She was angry, even, she says, because he seemed "so out there." Despite this negative first impression, Father Jack would turn out to be the first non-family member to know about Estela's apparitions, a loyal supporter who would be one of the speakers at the annual celebrations of the apparitions.

Father Jack told me during an interview in his office at St. Thomas the Apostle rectory that although he was unable to see the Virgin in Medjugorje, he was "overwhelmed by Her presence" and knew immediately that it was "Her next to him." The Virgin instructed him to "walk by faith, not by sight" and to prepare himself for the events that were going to happen at his parish when he returned.[19] He was also told, he says, that someone else in Phoenix would both see *and* hear Her. Although the Mother of God was not specific in her message, Father Jack told Reyes that he "knew deep inside" that something out of the ordinary was going to start happening upon his return to Scottsdale. He says that he prayed continuously during the remainder of his pilgrimage for the strength for whatever God and Mary had planned for him. He realized "soon enough," he says, what she had in store for him.

Late in the summer of 1988, Father Jack says, several months before Estela's first vision, he was approached by six young women and three men, all separately and each unaware of the others' visits. They all reported experiencing their own locutions and visions of Jesus. Father Jack says that he was "shocked and amazed" because he too was receiving locutions on a regular basis from the Blessed Mother and Jesus, although he had not yet publicly divulged the news.[20] Within a few weeks of being visited by all nine young adults, Father Jack and the visionaries formed a prayer group at St. Maria Goretti; as word got out of these events thousands of pilgrims traveled from across the United States and abroad to hear the messages.[21]

When in the winter of 1988 Estela claimed to be having Marian apparitions, Father Jack was the likely choice as the Ruizes' spiritual advisor and confidant. He acted as the family's spiritual advisor during the first year of Estela's visions, from December 3, 1988 to December 1989, before they were made public, and would have liked to remain their spiritual advisor, he says, "but Bishop Thomas O'Brien of Phoenix told me to step down as their advisor. He said I had conflicting interests, because both Estela and I were being investigated by the diocesan committee at that time." Father Jack said that he was "not happy" when he heard the bishop's request, but he had to obey. By that time, the Scottsdale nine and the Ruiz family had grown quite close, according to both Father Jack and Estela, as they had been meeting for group prayer sessions since early January 1989—soon after Estela met with Father Jack to tell him about her experiences and to get advice from him.

It took me several years to understand the depth of intimacy of the connection between the Scottsdale group and Estela's family. The only other scholar who has written about Estela's and the Scottsdale nine's experiences is the religious historian Sandra Zimdars-Swartz; she includes a brief description of the two groups in an article on contemporary American Marian visions. In the article she summarizes what she considers to be the conservative bent of contemporary American visionary phenomena, but she draws no connection between the Scottsdale seers and Estela, and writes about them as two distinct and separate phenomena.[22] In missing the connection between the two groups, Zimdars-Swartz overlooks an important component of Marian apparitions—that each group draws on and refers, however implicitly or explicitly, to other seers' experiences. Even if Estela and her family had not been meeting with the Scottsdale group, surely they would have been in some kind of contact, however informal, given that they are located only ten miles or so apart. They are not simply "Hispanic" and "Anglo" groups, as Zimdars-Swartz portrays them; they are much more complex—Estela's family is distinctly middle-class and reaches out to Anglo groups, both at their shrine and in their everyday lives. And the Scottsdale seers all prided themselves on leaving their "yuppie" lives behind and embarking on new cultural encounters. Like Estela, each of the Scottsdale seers claims to have been not particularly religious before their experiences, and if they did go to church it was just "going through the motions," according to one of the visionaries, Steve Nelson. This is almost the exact wording Estela used to describe her church attendance before her apparitions. These former "yuppies" and the self-described "career woman" were much more alike than different. In one sense, Estela's own legitimation as a visionary was bolstered by her connection with the Anglo Scottsdale group, but on the other hand, she wanted to remain distinct.

Shared Experiences: Visions as a Social, Familial Phenomenon

The same diocesan committee that investigated the apparitions and messages to Estela examined Father Jack and the Scottsdale visionaries in 1990, and published almost identical reports on the two phenomena. While Estela's assessment of the committee is at least outwardly positive, Father Jack says he is "very disappointed" in the three members of the investigating team, "a priest, a sister, and a psychiatrist" who he says never spoke individually with the visionaries and who spent very little time observing the visionaries and the prayer meetings. Father Jack was especially perturbed and even insulted, he says, "because they only attended about half of a prayer meeting, as if they are going to have enough evidence to adequately discern!" Father Jack says that he understands and fully supports the Church's need to have strict requirements and to use discernment, but he argues that the committee that investigated both his own group and Estela was not rigorous in its investigation. "The three members told me that I am not crazy or delusional, but that the visions were not happening; this is a contradictory statement, is it not?"

Ever since he went public with his locutions, life has been difficult for Father Jack, who was once chancellor of the diocese of Phoenix and served as one of Mother Teresa's bodyguards during her visit to Phoenix in the mid-1980s. He was pastor for fourteen years at the wealthy Scottsdale St. Maria Goretti church (1982–1996) before he was transferred by the bishop to St. Thomas the Apostle, where he was head pastor from 1996 to 2002. He is currently the head priest at St. Gabriel parish, forty-five minutes north of Phoenix in Cave Creek, Arizona; he has been there since the fall of 2002. During our 1998 interview, Father Jack said that he prepared himself for the events that occurred, including his transfer, as he is aware of the bishop's disapproval of visions. "I knew that my career with the Church would stop where it is now because the bishop doesn't approve [of the visions and locutions]." It took him awhile, he says, to "get used to" the number of priests who "would just ignore me," as well as those priests "who came to St. Maria Goretti and St. Thomas just to see a spectacle." Father Jack insists that he has always been careful, from the beginning, not to make a "circus" out of his locutions and the Scottsdale group's experiences.

On one occasion, Reyes was able to talk Estela into accompanying him to one of these prayer meetings. Her reactions were mixed. Even though she felt God's presence, she was also angered by what she perceived to be Father Jack's "arrogance." What bothered Estela this night is what Reyes believed and wanted her to hear and see—that Father Jack was a locutionary of the Virgin Mary. Although Estela had her doubts as to Father Jack's authenticity, other family members, also in attendance that night, did not. In addition to Reyes Sr., son Armando and daughter Rosie were also impressed by what they saw in Father Jack. At the time, Armando was especially amazed by Father Jack's humility, saying "the little priest was not always so humble." Rosie, deeply moved by what she saw, had already been attending the public prayer meetings on a weekly basis.

Despite her reluctance to entertain the idea that the Virgin Mary was speaking through Father Jack and the young locutionaries, Estela began to have her own visions and locutions of the Virgin a month and a half later and was told by the Blessed Mother, she says, to form a prayer group with them. In the tapes, Reyes asks Estela, "what about Father Jack, is he invited too?" to which Estela responds,

> Of course he is invited. She told me to invite them all. The girls who are communicating with Her and Father Jack are to come pray with us in front of Her. She wants them to come over here to pray and She said that it has to be a calm meeting . . . no rushing. . . . She wants us to use the time for prayer to Her and Her Son. She kept saying that it *has* to be calm, without rushing the rosaries. She wants beautiful prayers for Her and Her Son . . . beautiful prayers from the heart.[23]

After Estela tells her family about the Virgin's desires, Reyes says excitedly, "*That's* what I was asked in Medjugorje—to pray from the heart!"

Estela says that even though she was excited about her apparitions and messages from the Virgin, she still was not sure if it was the Virgin and not an imposter. She thought that it might be the "evil one" trying to "trick me." Perplexed and confused, she went to talk with Father Jack about her fears and concerns. Estela says that she did not allow herself to enjoy her first vision fully because she was worried that she was crazy. The day after the visions she remembers being cranky, tired, and full of doubts and worry. She kept thinking about her colleagues at work and what their reactions would be to her news. Estela says that she was so full of doubts that she exhausted herself from worrying. When she went to see Father Jack, he told her that she could either accept or decline the visions:

> I talked with Father Jack and he told me to enjoy it because it's beautiful. He also told me that if I didn't want to feel it, to say "no" and that I would still be loved the same by Her; he told me that I have a choice.[24]

Estela says that she vacillated between "saying yes" to more visions and saying "no." She went through "trials and tribulations." She felt tremendous guilt that the Virgin was appearing to her and not Reyes, and she felt unworthy of the visions. She was afraid that she was being deluded by the Devil and she was concerned because the "evil one," or Satan, as she refers to him, tormented her in her dreams. Estela recalls one particular dream she had in the fall before she started having visions of the Blessed Mother. In this dream, Satan was physically aggressive with her:

> He came into my dream. I was dreaming that we were in the kitchen, talking about the Blessed Mother, and I covered myself with a blanket. Now I know I covered myself with Her mantle . . . She covered me. I went outside with the blanket on and I got close to a little shelter. All of a sudden, I felt someone grabbing me . . . it was the evil one, laughing. He was saying, "I'm going to take you into *my* room." I was afraid at first, but then I had a thought: "You don't have to be afraid of him . . . you have authority over this evil thing." I thought, "*I'm* going to show you who *I* am!" And then I went YAAAAAA![25]

Estela believes that she was tempted by Satan into thinking that it was not the Blessed Mother appearing to her but an imposter. The Devil showed his cunning with her, Estela believes, when he tried to trick her. He was "messing with my mind," she says, and trying to make her think that she was crazy and that the Blessed Mother wasn't appearing to her at all. Soon after the first vision, Estela went to buy flowers for the Virgin, which she arranged in a vase on her home altar. As soon as Mary appeared to her, Estela was "looking into Her eyes" and was suddenly afraid that it was not

Mary at all. She asked the Blessed Mother several times who she was and who sent her, and even though Mary told her that she was the Immaculate Heart of Mary, sent by her son Jesus Christ, Estela's fears did not go away. Estela began cleaning her house and then had a revelation that the fear "was my *own* fear in *my* head—I had to get rid of Satan who was tempting me. I then asked Her to help me get rid of all of these thoughts."[26]

Estela says that Father Jack put her fears to rest, telling her that she had "nothing to fear" because it *was* the mother of God appearing to her and that she could resist Satan's wiles by believing in the Virgin Mary. For his part, Father Jack knew intuitively that Estela was the one the Virgin spoke to him about in Medjugorje—the one who would both "see and hear" Her. It was after her meeting with Father Jack, Estela says, that the Virgin told her "to invite the girls that are communicating with Me over to this house."

During one of the joint prayer meetings at Estela's and Reyes's home, Stefanie, one of the Scottsdale visionaries, had a vision in which Mary told her that Estela was to be the spiritual mother of the group. These weekly rosaries and get-togethers helped to strengthen the visionaries' resolve to carry forth the messages they were receiving from Jesus and Mary. These gatherings legitimated Estela's status as the "mother" to all of them, including Father Jack. That evening, Estela addressed her family and the Scottsdale group, telling them that the Blessed Mother told her that the Ruiz children have a "big responsibility."

> She has told me that you will be Father Jack's supporters, his angels, and will pray for him and with him. You have been called to be his angels . . . this is just the beginning of something so big, as She has told me that it will blow our minds. This is not just a plan for South Phoenix, but for all of the Americas, as She has told me. You children really, really have to prepare . . . it will be difficult, God knows. I have said yes and I mean yes, and now I know that she is calling you too. Be strong, it will be necessary that you are strong for Her.

Yet despite their favored status with Mary, family members still fell into what Estela described as their "old ways of sinning." One day, after she had appeared to Estela, apparently the Virgin was angry with the family because they had not prayed enough to her, and she penalized them as a result. Estela recalled that "terrible day" to her family and the Scottsdale group when they met in January:

She was *very angry* and wouldn't even speak to me that day. She told me not to forget to pray. I had watched TV all day and was cocky. You were all doing your own thing. But She was listening to everything and was watching our every move and boy, was She upset! The Blessed Mother told me "My army is NOT going to be like that! My army is going to be of humility and obedience above everything else." She has expressed Her anger and Her sorrow and we are *never* to act that way again. *Never.*

Through her apparitions and locutions of the Virgin of the Americas, Estela claims maternal authority over her family and the Scottsdale group, including Father Jack. She is able to dole out praise and punishment at the Virgin's behest, and she is obeyed by all in her family, even Reyes, who said, when he heard Estela's message that the Virgin had been very unhappy with their behavior, "It scares me that *She* can get so mad!" Because she is recognized as a visionary and locutionary, Estela's status as the *madre* in her family is secure and she has gained a new respect and authority, for she is backed by the one they all acknowledge to be the primary mother of all.

As we analyze the taped family sessions and the St. Maria Goretti story, we are able to witness the unfolding of a family's collective narrative. As the anthropologist Paolo Apolito shows in his study of contemporary apparitions in southern Italy, language is a key determinant in the production of vision discourse, and one person's story is rarely, if ever, the sole factor in making a vision a public reality. Stories overlap and make what may initially have been a single visionary's experience a shared reality and public discourse. As we see with Estela's visions, the apparitions moved from a subjective event (Estela's experience) to an objective one that was supported by family members' own experiences with Mary. Parallel visions, feelings of warmth, and various "signs" as shared by various Ruizes served dual purposes: to legitimate their own experiences, and to validate their mother's encounters with Mary. The family tapes illustrate the "cyclical feedback" process of apparitions: Estela's story is embellished and made more credible by her family's and the Scottsdale visionaries' parallel experiences.[27]

Yet this feedback takes a new turn with the Ruiz family because, unlike family members of other visionaries, Estela's family members claim to *actually experience* the Virgin. Their narratives move beyond supporting their mother's claims and their own belief in the Virgin Mary; they, too, see and feel the Virgin's presence. Stories told by the Ruizes move away from the traditional model of Marian apparitions in which one family member has visions and others promote them. As Ruiz family members' stories unfold on the tapes, it is clear that in South Phoenix, the Ruiz *family* has visions. Although Estela is the only one with whom the Virgin of the Americas speaks, the only one to whom She gives messages for the family and the public, other family members had, and continue to have to this day, powerful experiences with her. They see her glow, wink, and pulsate; they dream about her and feel her presence. To my knowledge, no other visionary's family has had such experiences or has made such comprehensive claims. As their own encounters with Mary overlap with their mother's dominant experiences, the interpretation that predominates among the Ruizes and the Marian devotees and pilgrims who go to South Phoenix is that this is a family specifically chosen by the Virgin to spread her messages to South Phoenix and beyond.

The experiences of Estela and her family support the thesis that visions are an eminently social, collective enterprise, an argument that has been well supported by such historians of religion as William Christian Jr., Paolo Apolito, David Blackbourn, and Sandra Zimdars-Swartz.[28] Estela may have been the one who saw and heard Mary, but her family's embellishments of her visions through their stories have made hers all the more credible to those outside the family, including the Church, pilgrims, and those who have become members of Mary's Ministries. The Ruiz family's stories and belief in Estela's Marian encounters support the reality of the visions and safeguard against what Apolito calls the "hazard of personal subjectivity." When Estela's family added their own compelling and personal stories to hers, they made her story more credible and facilitated the apparitions' move from subjective to objective reality. The family's horizontal speech, the narratives that overlapped on the tapes and evolved into public testimonies, paved the way for the official version of the arrival of the Lady of the Americas.

Yet a gap exists between the personal family revelations on the tapes and the public testimonies that were and are told years after Estela's and the family's first encounters with the Virgin. The voiced struggles to make sense of what was happening within the family, the anguish and exhilaration we are able to catch on the 1988 and 1989 tapes, is toned down and streamlined for public consumption in the months and years following these family gatherings. The Ruiz family's eventual public testimonies of the Virgin's reality and her power end up conforming to an official description of what happened. The intense personal anguish heard on the family tapes is not available to the public; instead, carefully worded and thought-out testimonies are the public versions that replace the private experiences. A possible explanation for this unwillingness to share private revelations and experiences with the public is that the intensely personal, wrenching information could be misconstrued and even used to argue for the falsity of the apparitions. The family's detailing of its problems, dysfunctions, and misunderstandings, offered in depth on the tapes, could damage not only the visions' chances of meeting with public approval but also the family's respectability. The family's frank and personal discussions, conducted as a way of uncovering shared experiences, became for the family a powder keg of information that could cause considerable damage.

In anticipation of the potential ramifications and repercussions, what became the family's normative reading, and subsequently the public's understanding, of the apparition phenomenon focused on the "events" more than on the individual narratives.[29] Estela's and her family's histories eventually receded into the public background to make room for the concise, official version of how the Virgin appeared and how the family responded, which is much less colorful than the version on the tapes. The Ruizes, who are openly self-conscious of how the Phoenix Catholic diocese perceives them, have emphasized the official rendition of the experience most vigorously since the early 1990s, when the diocese began its investigations into the visions. Although family members remain for the most part forthright about their past sins and indiscretions, the elaborate details of their lives prior to the visionary experiences have remained private, as have their vivid, emotionally wrenching descriptions of their encounters with Mary. That the Ruiz tapes were never revealed to anyone outside of the family underlines the careful and mindful handling of events surrounding the apparitions and the desire to have a unified, official version that would allow for greater credibility. Yet it is these tapes, which Armando has kept hidden away in an old dresser drawer, that reveal the inherently social production of apparitions. Exploring them offers an opportunity to see the process of vision-making and world-creating as it unfolds.

Suffering and the Devil

Estela and her immediate family experienced anxiety, emotional loss, and unhappiness that in some cases had accumulated over many years. It is now acknowledged by family members that prior to the conversions that began under the Virgin's influence, they were on the "Devil's side." As we have seen in the family's individual and collective narratives, classic evangelical language of sin/salvation and conversion are used. As evangelicals, family members see an ongoing battle between good and evil, and as Catholics they turn to Mary for inspiration and hope—they are both evangelical and Catholic. Estela was "fooled" into believing that education held the answers she was seeking, Little Rey had thought that he needed drugs to feel powerful, and Armando had thought politics would give him the power he needed. The family's use of binary oppositions in their everyday language—good/bad; God, Virgin Mary, Jesus, Holy Spirit/Devil; life before conversion/life after conversion—all illuminate the polar opposites that exist in their lives. Their language, through the years, becomes more and more like that of Lolo, the oldest Ruiz son and a proud fundamentalist Christian whose influence on his family's interpretations of the apparitions is important and should not be overlooked. The Ruizes now say that their suffering was caused by their commitment to the "ways of the evil one" and not the "way of the Lord and the Blessed Mother." The family now speaks openly of its quest to become saint-like. Reyes Sr., in particular, encouraged his children to "live the lives of saints" and to "seek sanctification." Working toward sainthood is held up as the way to defeat Satan.

An evangelical theology of predetermination informs the Ruizes' interpretations of their visionary experiences. Shared experiences are understood as miraculous and preordained occurrences, as "everything happens for a reason." The prayers of family members (Rosie, Armando, Reyes, Leticia) before Estela's experiences are interpreted as laying the groundwork for Estela's visions and apparitions, and those that began in earnest afterward are seen as further proof of Mary's arrival. Before Estela's experiences, both Reyes Sr. and Rosie had taken it upon themselves to "save" the Ruiz family from its sin. Becky too suffered physically and felt the "crown of thorns" on her head. Their efforts to fight evil in themselves and in their families are seen as laying the groundwork for the Virgin's arrival, as is Father Jack's encounter with the Virgin in Medjugorje. Armando's and Becky's visions and perceptions of Mary are interpreted as proving the validity of their mother's claims, and Leticia's prayers to Guadalupe to "bring back my husband" are understood as foreshadowing Estela's apparition and locutionary experiences. Individual family member's prayers are seen as preparing Estela and the family both for the apparitions and for their continued existence. These prayers make Estela's experience more meaningful, as they have a profound effect on others.

For Estela, her spouse, and her children, the Virgin led them to the Scottsdale group and to the prestige that it afforded as a well-known visionary group. By connecting with this other group of visionaries, Estela could shed her jealousy over Father Jack's experiences and, going back to the feelings of ethnic shame she had that were explored in chapter 1, could find a way to reconcile her admiration for Anglo culture with her ethnic guilt. What Estela's and her family's narratives and the St. Maria Goretti narrative illuminate is that Marian visions are experienced as a group, with each individual member adding to the larger narrative. Estela, her husband, her sons, and her daughters recount their experiences with the Virgin Mary, creating a shared composite of the Virgin. Their relationships with the Virgin of the Americas are based on a combined effort to share family experiences with her, as well as on their intimate knowledge of the Scottsdale group and of Medjugorje. Each family member adds to the narrative and to the overarching experience with her or his own story. Although Estela is the one who receives the visions and locutions, their meaning would be greatly diminished were it not for the integral participation of her family. Estela's motivation to beseech the Virgin's help stemmed from her concern for the well-being of her family. The Lady of the Americas acknowledged her pleas for help in the message she delivered to Estela when she appeared for the first time. The visions and locutions themselves are predicated on the concept of a larger social network.

Estela's visions have also been influenced by her relationship with Father Jack Spaulding and the visionaries from St. Maria Goretti church, whose visionary experiences began soon after Reyes and Father Jack formed a friendship in Medjugorje. Estela's visions, like those of Father Jack and his group, are directly informed by the messages given to the visionaries of Medjugorje. The visions of Medjugorje are the "spiritual touchstone" of twentieth-century Marian culture, much like the visions of nineteenth-century Lourdes.[30] These messages of hope and love from the Virgin to her "children" are repeated in the messages to Estela and to Father Jack and the St. Maria Goretti visionaries.[31] The similarity of their experiences to those of Estela and her family show the circuitous nature of visions and the shared realities of those who experience and who believe in them.

Visions influence other visions, and the power of visions for visionaries and those who believe in them is a "new version of a power very old indeed, the everyday power of God among them."[32] This power of God and the Virgin is felt in very real, sensory ways—Estela, her family, Father Jack, and the Scottsdale nine all claim to have seen, heard, and experienced the Virgin in ways that are outside everyday experience. The blinding light of Mary, her blue eyes dancing, and her moving image in the portrait of the Virgin of the Americas are very real for those who experience her. She speaks to Estela and to Estela's family, to Father Jack, and to the St. Maria Goretti visionaries in a way that no one else can and she gives them hope. The Virgin does this not as a distant, removed saint, but as a concerned mother who talks to her children and who gives them signs of her presence by letting them know that she is here, with them. Unlike other contemporary Marian messages, the ones given to Estela Ruiz by the Virgin of the Americas are more hopeful and postmillennial than apocalyptic, and stress men's and women's ability to make changes in themselves and in their communities.

✳ 3 ✳

Battling Satan

The Blessed Mother's Messages of
Healing, Hope, and Urgency

According to Estela, the Virgin Mary delivered this message to her while she was praying fervently in her living room on September 7, 1996:

> I have come to bring My love to My children in the world, but more importantly, I have come to speak about God's love for His children in the world because it is His love that saves souls. It is His saving grace that you must turn to. It is His profound love for you that you must open your hearts to. My earthly children have allowed that the knowledge of God's great love for mankind be erased from man's head and heart, yet that knowledge is what is greatly needed in these days of chaos and violence.

The contents of this passage are typical of the hundreds of messages Estela believes she has been given by the Virgin of the Americas since December 3, 1988. As we saw in chapter 2, Estela and her family strongly believe that the Virgin appeared in order to "convert" their family to Mary and God.

The Virgin said to appear to Estela is a bilingual *mestiza,* a Mexican American Virgin who combines the hope Estela speaks of with more sobering information about the current state of the world, much like another recent Marian apparition, the Virgin or *Gospa* of Medjugorje. To Estela and to the other Hispanos and Mexican Americans who honor the Virgin of the Americas, the Virgin's genealogy has a syncretic racial, Marian, and Catholic heritage—she is a Mexican American Virgin. Recall that according to Estela, it was Guadalupe who initially "spoke" to her from a painting, and who appeared to her in dreams; and that a few months later it was the Virgin of the Americas who arose out of a painting of the Sacred Heart of Mary on the night Estela had her first apparition and locution.

The Virgin of the Americas was, from the start, a combination of dreams and voices of Guadalupe as well as the image of the Sacred Heart of Mary. The nine years of public messages from Our Lady of the Americas to Estela show that the Virgin is ultimately hopeful that her children will embrace God. But as Estela asserts, this "Blessed Mother" also realizes that there are many who have been "seduced by Satan," which tempers her hope.[1]

This Lady defies stereotypes of a passive, sweet Virgin and definitely shows her displeasure to Estela when her children are misbehaving, as we saw in chapter 2. She issues stern warnings that draw attention to the rampant evil in the modern world. Her messages have apocalyptic overtones and reflect millennial themes of twentieth-century Marian visions. In this way the Virgin of the Americas connects contemporary Catholicism with evangelicalism—she demands that her followers do more than pray the rosary, she tells them to evangelize in their community. Estela's apparitions are also specific to her South Phoenix community, particularly in the Lady's concern for the social welfare of the urban world of South Phoenix where she appeared to Estela with messages for the public for nine years, and where she continues to give Estela messages for personal and familial spiritual edification. But even more important than their geographic specificity is that Estela's visions clearly participate in the broader international culture of Marian apparitions that has taken shape over the last several decades, with roots deep in the nineteenth century. Her apparitions to Estela tie this Mexican American woman, her family, and her community in with larger Marian discourse and apparitional culture and can tell us much about the hopes and desires of a group of contemporary Catholics.

Although there have been several excellent studies of European Marian apparitions in the eighteenth and nineteenth centuries, there have been far fewer academic studies of contemporary, specifically American, Marian apparitions.[2] Yet when we compare Estela's experiences with those of other European and American visionaries, we are able to see threads of continuity as well as similarities with the visionaries of Lourdes, Fatima, Eskioga, Marpingen, and the more recent Medjugorje. How Estela's visions are and are not like these other visionaries' experiences as well as those of other American visionaries helps us understand what is happening in this twentieth- and twenty-first-century South Phoenix barrio, and on a larger scale, what issues are important for many contemporary American Catholics who are embracing a devotional, conservative Catholicism.

A close look at Estela Ruiz's apparitions of the Virgin Mary can help us better understand the interworkings of evangelicalism and Catholicism, and official and popular Catholic piety. It is only by exploring and analyzing the apocalyptic messages and their interpretations that we can make real the fusion of Catholicism and evangelicalism, and popular and official Catholicism. Mary's messages to Estela provide her, her family, and her community with the means to nurture their own personal, "popular" devotions even as they encourage links with the Catholic Church and its hierarchy.

The Lady of the Americas' Messages

Our Lady of the Americas' messages to Estela, like other contemporary Marian messages, promote an apocalypticism that is close to what the folklorist Daniel Wojcik calls "catastrophic speculation," a millennial perspective distinguished by its belief in the prospect of successful human intervention.[3] An excerpt of the Virgin's message to Estela of September 15, 1990, expresses these sentiments:

> I continue to thank you for your commitment in coming here to pray with me for the conversion of the world, especially your continent of the Americas. I invite and urge you to unite yourself to my work and in prayer so that *together* we can help all my children to return to God's love. . . . I come to warn you, my little ones, that the world is at a crossroad. It will either cross into the path of destruction, or allow Our Lord to reign in the hearts of men. Time is running short. I am here to beg all who will listen to turn to God. [Italics mine][4]

The Virgin makes her sorrow known, for she knows that her children will enter upon the "path of destruction" if they do not change their wicked ways. Although Estela's messages contain bleak imagery, the most prominent theme, and ultimately the dominant one, is that the children in the Americas are dearly loved and have the *choice and capacity* to follow Mary and God. There is a reason to be hopeful, Mary assures Estela and her listeners, because men and women can defeat the evil threatening the world. When they find themselves at the fork in the road that separates good from evil, the Lady's messages assert, the devout *can* choose the right and good road. The world is worth saving, Mary's messages to Estela emphasize, but men and women need to turn their "hearts" over to God in order for a new era to be ushered in. This Catholic community activism, taken up by the women and men of Mary's Ministries, reflects the messages' optimistic and exhortative spirit. Satan's influence on men and women and their tendency to sin is fully acknowledged in the messages, but no precise and violent end is predicted. Satan can be overcome, but it will take a battalion of Mary's "soldiers" to wipe clean the stain of sin. There are many "battles," however, and Mary's children are told not to take satisfaction in those that they have already won.[5] Estela says that Mary constantly reiterates men's and women's ability to overcome sin and to avert evil; the Lady tells her "it is only through the work of people like you that I have chosen, that this country will have a chance of surviving the horror that has overtaken the world."[6] Abortion is one of the horrors cited by Mary, who implores her children to discontinue the sinful practice.[7] The messages against abortion illustrate the premillennial and postmillennial themes that characterize the Lady of the Americas' messages. They reflect God's wrath and judgment, "the destruction of the children of God," which is typical of premillennialism; and they ackowledge the potential of human intervention that is emphasized in postmillennialism ("My children . . . can begin to stop the destruction"). The Marian devotee and author Tom Petrisko emphasizes these coexisting millennial strains of Estela's visions, writing that the visions to Estela show that the day of judgment will be brought about "gradually and noncatastrophically by human beings acting according to a divine plan that will transform the world into a place worthy of Christ's Second Coming."[8]

I asked Estela outright during one of our interviews if she thought that Our Lady of the Americas' messages were apocalyptic, and she answered that they are not:

> The messages of the Blessed Mother are *not* messages of despair; rather, they are of hope. She teaches us that God is more merciful than just, and that we are not to fear God. She tells us that God is a god of pure love, mercy, forgiveness, and awesomeness. The Blessed Mother has described God in beautiful ways. No, I do not think it is the apocalypse that we hear from the Blessed Mother. I think that the Blessed Mother is preparing us for something beautiful. I think that the world will be changed sometime soon; I think that people will be more loving. I don't think that the Blessed Mother is preaching or telling us about the end of the world. I think She's telling us about the beginning of beautiful things. God is love and this is what the Blessed Mother tells us.[9]

Here we are able to see that Estela emphasizes the postmillennial thrust of the Virgin's messages to her, interpreting the messages as affirming that with work, a more godly place can be made of the world, a new and more positive era ushered in by God. Messages that are full of "gloom and doom," Estela says, are not really from the Blessed Mother because messages like those are not constructive, but cause people instead to despair and to worry about themselves and their future. Estela's interpretation focuses on how Mary's messages encourage a community of spiritual soldiers to work toward purging the Americas of evil and godlessness. According to Estela, Mary does not want "weaklings."

The Lady who appears to Estela is a tough Mary, a Virgin of the streets, a divine *chola* who gives Estela messages of personal, social, and religious reform. She warns her "children" about what can happen if they fail to wage war on Satan, but she also displays an optimism that her children can make the world a better place. The Ruizes believe that the Virgin chose them and their community purposely—that appearing in South Phoenix to a Mexican American woman was no accident. At the time the Virgin appeared to Estela the community of South Phoenix was like a "war zone," according to Little Rey; gang warfare was at a high point and was propelled by the dire socioeconomic conditions of the area. The Virgin came to Estela in the midst of urban blight and economic recession and her messages, though they do not *specifically* address the challenges facing South Phoenix, are *understood* by Estela, her family, and members of Mary's Ministries as telling them that they need to reform their own lives and the health of their community before tackling the rest of "the world," as stated in the Virgin's messages. While the conservatism and the pre- and postmillennial themes link Estela's visions to other modern and contemporary apparitions, what distinguishes them from the rest is the Catholic evangelizing organization, Mary's Ministries, that was founded to "do what She wants us to do," according to Little Rey.

The Virgin of the Americas' messages to Estela, like other modern and contemporary apparitions, depict a sense of apocalyptic urgency in that she wants her children to pray and embrace Jesus in order to defeat the rampant "evil" in the world. Mary's Ministries' members pepper their evangelical speech with a sense of God's governing love, saying such things as "nothing happens by chance," "everything happens for a reason." There is no random act; everything is determined by God's directing influence. The religious worldviews of Mary's Ministries members have an intrinsic sense of meaning and moral order. My own presence as an ethnographer, for example, was understood as being predetermined by Mary and Jesus themselves, and my research was more about my being "called to Mary and Her Son" than about my research interests. My acquaintances and friends in Mary's Ministries cited my Protestant background and my presence in their conservative Catholic community as further proof that Mary was "guiding me." Although the Virgin declares her love for her earthly children to be unconditional, there are conditions for their entrance to heaven. They must not stand idly by and be "of the world." Accepting God as their savior is necessary in a world that is seen starkly as a struggle between good and evil, a classical millennial theme. Although the Virgin sees that many of her children have embraced God, she frets because most of them are still mired in the "ways of the world."

Estela received messages from the Blessed Mother for her "earthly children" beginning December 1, 1989, and ending December 5, 1998. In the months before the messages became public, Estela and her family were spiritually coached by Mary, who prepared them to engage in public ministry. In the messages she gives to Estela, the Virgin of the Americas displays a sweet and caring side, but she can also show her anger. When the Ruizes are not praying hard enough or not working up to their spiritual potential, Mary sends verbal chastisements to Estela for the family. Mary also shows her displeasure and anger in other ways, such as by ignoring the family. Estela says that once, before the messages were made public, the Blessed Mother was "so mad at us that she didn't talk to me all day." According to Estela, she had gone shopping that day and had "ignored" the Blessed Mother, as had her family.

The 277 public messages given to Estela during the nine-year span emphasize Mary's role as mother, intercessor, and warrior for God; the need to "change hearts" by turning to God; the "evil in the world," especially in the United States; and the possibility of healing. In these respects, the Lady's messages to Estela closely resemble other modern Marian apparitions. Mary does not mince words with Estela and her "children"; she tells them that they have a choice to make between evil and goodness, Satan and God. Mary renders evil particularly clear in her message to Estela of October 1, 1994:

Satan has unleashed all the demons in hell, and I have come to help you, each and every one of you, resist this evil which is so powerful throughout the world. You, my children, are not blind and you can see this evil that is so evident all over. You can feel him trying to destroy you and thus overtake all whom he can. Many of you do not know how to fight him. I am here to help all those who desire to be helped, but you must open your hearts and allow me to touch them, that through My guidance and love you may turn to your God who is your salvation.[10]

What distinguishes Estela's messages from other Marian apparitions is the evangelizing group, Mary's Ministries, that Estela, her family, and members of her barrio formed in 1993 to spread the messages in South Phoenix and beyond. This group of conservative Catholics take Mary's messages of social praxis to several cities in the United States with high Mexican American populations, and since 2000, to locations in South and Central America, Africa, and western Europe. Mary's Ministries takes seriously the Virgin's insistence that the powers of evil can be averted through hard work, a diligent, introspective spiritual life, and prayer. Not everyone has the ability to do this, Mary admits in her messages to Estela, because "Satan's charms" are powerful:

I came awhile back with messages of warning of imminent destruction of the world and to call you to conversion that this destruction might be avoided. Many heard My words, heeded them and became My warriors ready to fight off this evil destruction with prayers and lives of holiness. Many others heard My call, attempted to change their lives for a period of time but were tempted back into a world of frigidity toward God's ways, seeking more the comfort of materialism that the world offers than the salvation of the soul that God offers.[11]

As this message indicates, the Virgin has given up hope for those who may have once committed their lives to God but who are now back in Satan's grasp. Rather than engage in a futile battle, the Virgin now shores up her strength and focuses on her "chosen ones," those men and women who are actively living lives of holiness. In her message to Estela of September 6, 1997, Mary asserts this theme: "God has begun the great call to the chosen, that He may raise holy people, great saints to be models of goodness and faithfulness. It is to these faithful believers that God is entrusting the salvation of His children on earth. This call to holiness is a formidable call, a hard but joyous journey."[12]

Estela, her family, and the group of Marian devotees, primarily of Mary's Ministries, are all acutely aware of what they see as their daunting role as "chosen ones," but they have accepted their tasks willingly because they believe they are playing a part in saving the world from Satan's destruction. Although their journeys may be "joyous," they are physically, emotionally, and spiritually taxing. The Virgin's spiritual rhetoric is a battle cry for God's presence in the world. Members of Mary's Ministries wear their rosaries, scapulars, and T-shirts of the Virgin of the Americas less as a fashion statement and more as protection in a world full of evil. The Lady of the Americas' messages have inspired a group of dedicated men and women who see themselves as announcing Mary's messages to the rest of the world. These Catholic activists also point to the "fruits" of the visions—the faith courses, community activism and service, and conversions—as proof of the Lady of the Americas' authenticity.

The Church's Search for "Fruits"

According to the Marian devotee and theologian Fr. René Laurentin, "authentic visions" are determined by Church representatives, and Mary is seen as a spokesperson for God who focuses on the necessity of embracing God. Authentic visions are, he writes, "an invitation to evangelisation which is characterised by a dynamic and joyful urgency."[13] This litmus test for judging apparitions has been encouraged by the Church, especially since the 1974 Fourth Synod, and has been used most recently by Pope John Paul II.[14] Throughout the twentieth century, the Catholic Church has played an integral role in the Marian vision phenomena. The Vatican II Dogmatic Constitution *Lumen Gentium* clarified Mary's role in the church, linking her significance to the history of the Catholic Church itself. Efforts to consider Mary as her own person, apart from her relation to the Church, were denied.[15] Church fathers were careful not to inflate Mary's significance, for it was feared that this would widen the divide that separated Protestants from Catholics. The language of *Lumen Gentium* was designed to be ecumenical, stressing Mary's role as mother to everyone: "We proclaim Mary most holy *Mother of the Church,* i.e., of all the people of God, faithful and shepherds alike, who name her Mother most loving."[16] The document expanded the definition of the Virgin Mary and made Mary relevant to non-Catholics. In *Lumen Gentium,* Mary's role also expanded in terms of her relationship with the Church: she was now perceived as an integral, central part of the Church.

Marian apparitions are regarded, for the most part, with initial skepticism by Church authorities, because the visions can detract from official dogma and can pose a challenge to the Church, as the visions of Necedah, Wisconsin, and Bayside, New York, ultimately did.[17] When a person claims to be having apparitions, the local bishop forms an investigating committee, which submits an official report based on interviews and observations to the bishop. The basic criteria established by the Church adhere to the Congregation for the Doctrine of Faith, the criteria of discernment for visions established by Cardinal Seper on February 25, 1978.[18] This concise four-page document is rendered *sub secreto,* which means it can only be read by bishops who need it to assess apparitions under their jurisdiction. The Congregation sends a copy to a bishop only when he requests it to pass judgment on apparitions.[19]

The last positive criterion, that of "good fruits," is the one most often cited by Marian devotees, including Estela and members of Mary's Ministries, as proof of an apparition's authenticity. Such fruits include conversions, spiritual healing, physical healing, miraculous events such as the sun dancing, the scent of roses, and crosses turning gold. Mary is believed to be present when her children embrace God and are willing to be her spiritual soldiers.[20] Based on the committee's report, the bishop issues a statement that indicates his opinion and that will, in turn, serve to encourage the continuance of the devotion that has arisen at the apparition site or to condemn the apparitions as false and harmful to the Church.[21] Bishops proceed very carefully in such matters because they do not want to bring discredit to the Church. Based on these stringent and careful criteria, only a small number of Marian apparitions have been approved by the Church in recent times.

Only four twentieth-century Marian visions have been officially approved by the Church: those of Fatima, Portugal; Beauraing, Belgium; Banneux, Belgium; and Betania, Venezuela. Bishop Pio Bello Ricardo of Los Teques, Venezuela, recognized the apparitions of Finca Betania that had been occurring since March 26, 1976.[22] The visionary, Maria Esperanza Bianchini, a middle-aged Venezuelan Catholic woman, continues to have apparitions to this day, and her shrine site continues to be one of the most active in the world. Bianchini stands out from the majority of post–Vatican II visionaries for being a pious, churchgoing Catholic prior to her visions, for not having to undergo the same kind of radical "conversion" her contemporaries claim to have experienced. Like the majority of Marian visionaries, Bianchini has worked closely with and cooperated with church officials.

The majority of apparitions are judged to be non-miraculous and are neither accepted nor condemned by church authorities. The declaration made by former Bishop of Phoenix Thomas O'Brien in regard to the Scottsdale and South Phoenix phenomena represents this middle-ground position. A three-person committee of "experts," two theologians and a psychologist, was assigned to investigate Estela's visions and the shrine phenomena in her backyard. In addition, the "experts" also investigated another local Marian phenomenon that had gained international attention—the visions and locutions at St. Maria Goretti church in Scottsdale. Father Jack Spaulding, along with six young adults, claimed to be having individual and group visions and locutions of Mary and Jesus.[23] Bishop O'Brien received the Scottsdale report from Fr. Ernest Larkin, O. Carm., Sr. Therese Sedlock, O.S.F, and Dr. James Lange, Ph.D., at the end of October 1989 and, based on their findings, commended Father Jack and the visionaries' deep faith and their "spirit of prayerful cooperation."[24] He also noted that "even authentic devotions do not add anything new to our faith, but only recall what we have always believed."[25] Recall from chapter 2 that Father Spaulding reported that he had a hard time accepting the decree because the committee barely spent any time with the visionaries. The three members, Spaulding says, sat in on only one of the prayer groups, did not speak with all of the visionaries, and seemed to be in a hurry. Spaulding was also "very disappointed" by the committee's line of questioning, which he says was "self-contradictory": "On the one hand, they told me that I am not receiving messages from Our Lord and Our Lady, yet on the other, they assure me that I am not crazy! I said to them, 'how can you say that I am not crazy if you do not believe that I am really receiving messages?'"[26]

The Bishop's decree in regard to Estela's apparitions is similar to the one written about Father Jack's apparitions and adopts the same middle stance. After reviewing the committee's April 10, 1990, report to him, O'Brien wrote an assessment that was almost a verbatim replica of the Scottsdale judgment. Neither approving nor condemning the visions, the Bishop permitted them to continue as long as specific steps were taken to ensure their adherence to Catholic doctrine. In his report, Bishop O'Brien commended the Ruiz family for their devotion and for "adding greatly to the devotion of the people of God to their Church," and declared that the prayer services could continue for the "spiritual welfare of the Ruiz family and the people who attend the devotional services."[27] The bishop also appointed a new spiritual director, bypassing Father Jack. As we have seen, Father Jack is a close family friend of the Ruizes, who had asked him well before the committee investigated the visions to serve as their advisor. Father Jack says that he was told by O'Brien that his role as spiritual director was "inappropriate." Despite the bishop's resistance to Father Jack, the committee's judgment of Estela's claims was generally favorable. Told to find a new spiritual director, the Ruizes asked Father Doug Nohava, then of the South Phoenix parish St. Catherine of Siena; he agreed and eventually became a trusted family friend and advocate of the apparitions.

Estela says that she was "very relieved" when the investigation was over and was glad that the committee was scrupulous, because, in her words, "the Church has to be careful because there are a lot of crazies out there." Because the committee did not see any "visible miracles" like the mass healings at Lourdes, the miraculous image of Guadalupe in Juan Diego's cactus fiber *tilma,* or the "dancing sun" at Fatima, the messages and apparitions to Estela were not deemed supernatural. This judgment by the three members of the committee in no way dampened the enthusiasm of the Ruizes or the thousands of pilgrims who visit the Marian shrine each year and who are convinced of Mary's presence. Men and women who go to Estela's shrine have experienced or witnessed what they refer to as "fruits." Many conversions are reported each year in addition to various "joys," "gifts," and "miracles."

The public revelations to Estela, like those of other twentieth-century Marian apparitions, point to the second coming of Christ and to the choices people will have to make in order to have what Estela refers to as a "better world" for those who have "turned their hearts over to Mary and Jesus." Estela looked to the new millennium with hopeful anticipation for those who have converted to God's love and with trepidation for those who have not. To fulfill her part of the relationship with her children on earth, the Virgin of the Americas promises her followers a healing such as they have never known before, by her son, Jesus Christ, a conversion of their hearts and souls to God, and an assuaging of their pains and anguish. To honor their part of their contract with Mary and to permit the "healing to begin," men and women, according to the Virgin, need to "open their hearts to God." If we examine the apparitions in South Phoenix in the context of contemporary Marian culture, we will see both what is distinctive about Estela's visions and, at the same time, how profoundly they have been shaped by developments in Catholic Marian culture over the last thirty years.

Visions Influence Visions

That Estela, her family, and the group of Marian devotees say the Virgin Mary has been appearing for more than ten years is nothing new; men, women, and children have been claiming to have apparitions and locutions of Mary for hundreds of years.[28] The Virgin has appeared primarily to women and children, usually uneducated and poor; but these characteristics have changed in the late twentieth century. Contemporary Marian visionaries in the United States are most often middle-aged, middle-class, educated women. The Virgin is said to choose her messengers deliberately and to give them revelations for their personal benefit as well as for the larger public.[29]

Contemporary Marian visionaries and their followers make clear connections between themselves and earlier visions and visionaries, understanding themselves to be part of a circulation of visions mandated by heaven. Devotees of Marian apparitions say that each vision is a distinct expression of the one Mary. Each vision of Mary is like a strand of a web that links the seer and believers to the strands of other visions.

Late nineteenth-century and twentieth-century visions combine the worlds of popular and official piety, complicating strict definitions of "popular" and "official" religion. The seers maintain the authority of their visions while remaining faithful to the teachings of the Catholic Church. The Catholic theologian Robert E. Wright notes this coming together of popular and official realms and asserts that standard definitions of popular religiosity throughout academia have missed this complexity. The majority of descriptions of Marian phenomena have been based on separatist notions of "popular" that define it as distinct from more formal, "official" religiosity.[30] Post–Vatican II apparitions show a working relationship between popular and official piety. Mary's Ministries has courted the support of priests in its far-flung locations in Latin America and at home in Phoenix. Since 1999, priests' involvement at the annual December retreats to celebrate the apparitions of the Virgin of the Americas has been strong.[31]

The Virgin Mary, in all of her manifestations, makes inclusive references to church matters and to the personal faith of men and women. She appears to laity and offers them hope and healing; she asks her followers to be true to their religious beliefs; and she helps form a community that has a relationship with the local church but maintains a separate and distinct identity. The Virgin also asks that a shrine be built for her, almost always outside of the Church, as in the case of Estela's backyard shrine.

Mary's contemporary messengers are all faithful to the Church, as were those of the nineteenth century. Most visionaries over the past two hundred years have claimed that they underwent a "conversion"—to God and to the Catholic Church—as a result of their apparitions. Contemporaries Estela Ruiz and Nancy Fowler, the Marian visionary of Conyers, Georgia, believe that they were "chosen" because they were skeptics. They juxtapose their spiritual vacuity prior to the visions with their religious fervor afterwards as additional proof of Mary's power. Fowler, who has described herself as a "bench-warmer Catholic" before her visions, and Estela, a "Sunday-morning Catholic," both believe that Mary chose them specifically because their conversions would be more convincing than if the Virgin had appeared to a devout Catholic.[32] Although many visionaries claim to have been "fallen away" Catholics at some point in their lives, all had at least some exposure, usually in early childhood, to the Catholic faith, and became faithful, churchgoing Catholics after the onset of their visions.[33] In short, Mary makes them better Catholics.

Knowledge of the social networks of visionaries makes it easier to understand the proliferation of Marian apparitions that has occurred since the nineteenth and early twentieth centuries. Apparitions during the nineteenth century occurred primarily in western Europe, while more recent apparitions have taken place in the United States, Korea, Japan, Venezuela, Nicaragua, Argentina, Egypt, Syria, and the former Yugoslavia. A direct and powerful relationship has formed between the earlier, nineteenth-century and early-twentieth-century visions and the more recent apparitions, which make conscious references to and model themselves after their famous predecessors. The visions of Mary to Bernadette Soubirous in Lourdes, France, beginning in 1858, for example, are nowhere near being "dated," and are continually invoked by contemporary Marian devotees.[34]

Marian devout have been, and continue to be, well aware of the significance of the Lourdes visions, and they strive to make "their" visions a new Lourdes. Blackbourn notes the efforts taken in the late nineteenth century to make the Marpingen, Germany, visions into the "new" Lourdes, and, more recently, in the twentieth century, to reinvigorate the visions and apparition site. The Ruiz shrine dedicated to the Virgin of the Americas is also situated in this shrine culture of healing, as the Virgin herself is said to have told Estela of the possibility of healing at the South Phoenix shrine. Pilgrims to the shrine of the Lady of the Americas talk openly about the Lourdes shrine and its reputation for healing and take home waters from the "blessed" fountain in hopes of curing themselves, their friends, and their loved ones.

The popularity of Lourdes visions has grown tremendously through the years, as stories of physical healing at the grotto have circulated throughout the world. Mary's instructions to Bernadette and her nineteenth-century devotees to pray the rosary are heeded by Marian devotees throughout the world today. The healing waters at Lourdes that sprang from what has come to be known as a miraculous well that Bernadette herself dug, are cited as proof of a divine gift from the Virgin.[35] The Virgin who appeared to Bernadette is remembered for her insistence that she was the "Immaculate Mother of God," for her benevolent gift of healing and graces, and for her ability to draw thousands to her grotto. Although this manifestation of Mary is not known to have given Bernadette substantial messages for the public, as with more recent manifestations, the Lourdes visions serve as a spiritual touchstone for twentieth-century Marian faithful, and the possibility of healing is important to contemporary Catholics who are searching for spiritual and physical health.[36]

Contemporary Marian visions are understood by devotees also with reference to apparitions at Fatima, Portugal, in 1917 to a group of three child seers. The primary seer, Lucia dos Santos, was given the famous "secrets" about the destruction of the world.[37] The Fatima visions, which are known for their apocalypticism, seem to stand in contrast to the Lourdes visions, which promote unconditional love, benevolence, and prayer requests. Mary gave Lucia stern warnings of chastisements to come if men and women did not begin to pray for the release of Portugal from socialism. These were the Virgin's first twentieth-century apocalyptic messages, representatives of a genre described by Wojcik as "those beliefs and discourses that the cataclysmic destruction of the world is inevitable and unalterable by human effort, and . . . [that] describe both redemptive and unredemptive visions of the end."[38] Subsequent apparitions offered warnings that portrayed Mary's sense of urgency for the state of the world and for her children's souls, which were seen to be in imminent danger.

Contemporary American Catholics who believe in Marian visions draw on both the hopeful visions of Lourdes and the apocalyptic visions of Fatima. Experiencing a sense of anxiety over what they see as the moral decay of America, American Catholic Marianists look to the Fatima prophesies as confirmation for the retribution they believe will surely come. The Fatima visions told of chastisements and impending retribution and invoked bleak imagery; they are believed by many contemporary

Marian devotees who see the world as a place full of sin. The Lourdes visions, with their emphasis on prayer and healing, are cited to ameliorate the harshness of Fatima. The thousands of healings that have been documented at Lourdes are cited as proof of the power of prayer and of Mary's intercession. In Estela Ruiz's backyard shrine, for example, hundreds of pilgrims since the early 1990s have scooped up water from the fountain that Mary supposedly blessed, to take home to family members and friends. Applying the lessons learned at Lourdes to those of Fatima, Marian faithful generally believe that it is possible to be healed, both in a physical and a spiritual sense, and that chastisements can be averted just as men and women can be healed and "convert their hearts" to Mary. This double millennial message characterizes the majority of contemporary Marian apparitions.

Evangelicalism and Marian Messages

Marian visionaries like Estela Ruiz share the perception common to conservatives across the religious world that contemporary American culture is in the grip of a dire moral and spiritual crisis; as Robert Wuthnow explains, conservative Protestants, Catholics, and Jews find more in common with each other than they do with their more liberal coreligionists. Not surprisingly, evangelicals have found their way to Estela's backyard shrine to Mary and the Ruiz family is not unaware of broader apocalyptic impulses in the United States. But Marian apocalypticism takes distinctive forms, in particular blurring the distinction between pre- and post-millennialism that analysts of Protestant eschatology have found so useful. Indeed, the fluidity and complexity of Catholic attitudes toward the end of the world may raise new questions about the construal of Protestant experience.

Conservative Catholics like Estela, her family, and devotees of the Virgin of the Americas constitute the majority of Marian devotees and believe in Marian apparitions and messages. They find common ground with their Protestant evangelical counterparts in apocalyptic, millennial language of post–Vatican II Marian messages. Conservative Catholics, like Protestant evangelicals, tend to see themselves as being under siege in a sinful world.[39] Like their evangelical Protestant counterparts, who experienced what Wuthnow calls a "political rebirth" in the 1970s, ushering in a renewed concern with public morality, abortion, and relations between church and state, conservative American Catholics began to espouse their own evangelical beliefs in the years after Vatican II.[40] A group that arose in the midst of the spiritual upheavals caused by the Council, these conservatives aimed to preserve what they saw as a distinct Catholic identity and at the same time became involved in the 1970s sweeping charismatic and Pentecostal religious movements that put them in touch with the Holy Spirit and Jesus Christ and with Protestant evangelicals. Conservative American Catholics, as they came to be known, generally took to defending the Catholic faith. They did so primarily by emphasizing post–Vatican II continuities with earlier, more Tridentine Catholic thought.[41] In response to the Council's *Gaudium et Spes* decree, which seeks a dialogue with the modern world, conservative Catholics pointed to the Council's emphasis on the modern world's spiritual deficiencies.[42]

The Virgin of the Americas' messages to Estela fit well within the conservative and charismatic Catholicism that arose in the post–Vatican II decades. This orientation is seen through the messages' incorporation of themes of Protestant mainstream evangelicalism, which is interpreted in the week-long faith courses offered by Mary's Ministries that emphasize developing a personal relationship with Jesus, starting a process of conversion, and giving one's testimony—all hallmarks of American evangelicalism. Conservative Catholics of the twentieth century share the belief with conservative Protestant evangelicals that there is a widespread moral crisis in the United States. Abortion, artificial means of birth control, drug use, lax religious faith, and violence are cited as evidence of America's moral and social decline. These Catholics adhere to what they believe to be the historical and traditional teachings of their faith, as do their more evangelical Protestant brothers and sisters. In addition to their conservative social and religious leanings, both groups lead a generally middle-class existence, what James Hitchcock summarizes as a widespread ecumenical consensus.[43]

Conservative Catholics' and Protestant evangelicals' commonalities also overshadowed their relationships with those who were more fundamentalist. Both traditionalist Catholics and Protestant fundamentalists eschew cross-denominational associations. Yet these traditionalists/fundamentalists share something with their conservative counterparts: the sentiment that "liberal" religionists have a weakened faith. By the end of the 1950s, the term "fundamentalist" had come to be associated with the hard-liners, the strict separatists, just as the term "traditionalist" had come to represent hard-line, separatist Catholics who were anti-*aggiornamento* by the end of the 1960s.[44]

Followers of the Virgin of the Americas do not belong in this community of hard-liners. While they are outspokenly conservative in their views and believe that Catholicism is the "true" religion of Christ, they do not eschew dialogue with people of other faiths. They are self-conscious about being perceived as close-minded to other faiths, and they regularly share stories at backyard shrine gatherings about their delight when non-Catholics make pilgrimages to the shrine. They believe that Mary appeared for everyone, Catholic or Protestant or other, and can make any person stronger in his/her own faith; as Reyes Ruiz Jr. once told me, "The Blessed Mother wants all of her children to return to their faith, whatever it might be, and to be better at it." While the Ruizes espoused their Catholic beliefs, they also acknowledged, both privately and publicly, that the "bottom line" is trust in "the Father, Son, and the Holy Spirit." They believe that Mary facilitates the "journey to God" and that the willingness to "grab ahold" of the Virgin's mantle greatly enhances and facilitates this process. They are outspoken and devout Catholics, yet their discourse also points to larger evangelical concerns.

These evangelical connections may seem ironic, as Protestants and Catholics have had polemical battles since the sixteenth century. The Virgin Mary has historically been one of many issues that have maintained divisions between these religions.[45] Yet despite the fact that the Virgin Mary does not occupy an important role in Protestantism, her messages, which emphasize saving *all* of her children from the "cup that is overflowing from all of the sin in the world," speak to contemporary evangelical concerns. Detailed, precise Catholic Marian doctrine is muted in favor of a more generalized, loving mother who cares deeply about the well-being of her children. Her messages condemning specific practices such as abortion and widespread materialism, and more generally, what she sees as rampant sin in the world, are in direct conversation with evangelical concerns and beliefs.

Healing, Hope, and the Golden Age

Since Vatican II, Marian visions such as those from the Virgin of the Americas have overwhelmingly drawn on millennialist and evangelical themes. Marian visionary phenomena are a prominent and ongoing example of how American Catholics have entered into an evangelical discourse, as both the Virgin's messages and Marian devotees' interpretations of them signal a desire for a better world and the willingness to work toward that goal. Like evangelical Protestants' insistence that the world is full of sin and needs to be reformed, the millennial themes in Marian messages issue warnings for Mary's children to work on their spiritual lives for the future of the world. Contemporary Marian messages throughout the world are linked to evangelical issues of personal healing and social reform. Among Catholic Marianists like the Ruizes and members of their organization, Mary's Ministries, the positive emphasis outweighs the negative, focusing on the ability to usher in a better era. This orientation is akin to the postmillennialism Wojcik describes as "an expectation of the gradual transformation of society brought about by Christian ideals, the belief in the idea of human progress and perfection, and a relatively liberal perspective."[46]

This motivation toward social and religious reform characterizes, to varying degrees, the majority of twentieth-century Marian visions. The visions at Conyers, Georgia; Medjugorje, Yugoslavia; Cold Spring, Kentucky; Hillside, Illinois; Belleville, Illinois; Batavia, Ohio; Cleveland, Ohio; Mesquite, Texas; San Bruno, California; Scottsdale, Arizona; and South Phoenix, Arizona, all emphasize group prayer, daily personal prayer, and commitment to Jesus and Mary as ways to bring about the dawn of a new and better era.[47] At each of these apparition sites, Mary emphasizes the power of prayer in defeating Satan and evil in the world. Prayer is a divine weapon against Satan and his "armies."

In South Phoenix, the Marian devotees of Mary's Ministries work toward the transformation of society more directly, choosing to bring about change sooner rather than later. Although the public messages Estela Ruiz receives from Mary are similar to those of contemporary Marian visions, she and her family have opted for an activist approach with more tangible, immediate results. In addition to daily prayer, these Marianists engage in intense labor. Through the Mary's Ministries organization, their community charter school, and urban revitalization efforts, the Ruizes pose a direct challenge to what they see as Satan running rampant in the world. This community embraces postmillennial beliefs that motivate them to work toward what Wojcik terms a "golden age," and they strongly believe that they are contributing to the eventual defeat of Satan. This community's hopefulness is tempered, however, by the sobering reality of what they perceive as the sinful world. Abortion, unmarried couples cohabitating, feminism, atheism, and violence are just some of the trends in the contemporary world that the Virgin of the Americas, like the *Gospa* of

Medjugorje, has spoken out against. This summons to respond to contemporary world problems is a common thread in Mary's messages throughout the world. Mary has made it clear, Estela says, that her "children" must be her "warriors" against Satan. This view is paired with the harsh belief that those who do not convert will die if the chastisements do indeed occur as Marian devotees, including members of Mary's Ministries, claim. Those who work toward the golden era of peace and love are saved, but those who do not accept Mary and Jesus will not live to see the days of Christ's glory.

The majority of twentieth-century Marian apparitions do have "apocalyptic overtones" but are not characterized by assertions that believers are unable to avert the coming destruction. Modern apparitions assert the ongoing struggle between good and evil; Satan's "hold" over the world in the form of materialism, atheism, violence, abortion, and other "crimes" is asserted. But in some, such as those to Estela Ruiz, there is also a glimmer of hope, because Jesus is seen as ultimately triumphant over the devil in the battle against Satan's "legions of devotees."

The "Battle" Continues

As with other contemporary apparitions, the public appearances and messages to Estela came to an end. The most common explanation for Mary's "stepping back" is that she has done everything she can, and now it is up to her children. Marian devotees also say the Virgin is paving the way for the coming of her Son, Jesus. Estela says that when the Blessed Mother told her on August 1, 1998, that her final public message to her would be December 5, after which there would be no more public messages, she was deeply distraught and "broke down" sobbing. Estela says she was in shock, deeply saddened because her "best friend" would be appearing to her less frequently. Although Mary assured her that the private messages and visits would continue, these too would decrease in frequency. Estela says that Mary told her that this was happening because she and her family were spiritually stronger and, most important, because they had started a community of evangelizers who were actively spreading Mary's messages across the United States and Latin America. Estela was told by the Lady of the Americas that she had already said all that needed to be said in her ten year's worth of messages and that now it would be up to her devotees to continue working for the conversion of souls in the world. In her message to Estela this first day of August the Virgin announced:

> I came to set up communities of faith and hope and I pray that these, My communities, will learn the true meaning of love. Remember that love is unconditional and this love is open to others who may have yet not found God's peace. Those who follow My guidance, please continue to walk in faith and trust in God, with great love in your hearts so that the peace of God in you can be contagious and win many souls for God. I walk with you always and love you.

Estela says it took her several days to accustom herself to the news, but she now understands and accepts what the Blessed Mother told her. She announced the news in a memo that was distributed at the shrine November 7 and wrote that although she was saddened by the end of the public messages, she and her family had been privileged "to see thousands of conversions in front of our eyes, the greatest being our own and our family's." In this one-page handout, Estela went on to emphasize Mary's request, asking everyone to "continue to be soldiers for our beautiful Blessed Mother."

In the final public message, tearfully read by Estela in her backyard shrine on the evening of December 5, 1998, to more than a thousand pilgrims who filled every inch of the small backyard, Mary further entreated her "soldiers" to fight her battles with their "faith and sacramentals."

Mary's Ministries is a response to Mary's call, and these Catholic evangelizers believe that they are continuing "Mary's work," both in the barrios of South Phoenix and throughout Latin America. The "battle against Satan" is not over, and Estela and her family of urban Catholic reformers are committed to fulfilling their part of their covenant with Mary. It is only through love, the kind of unconditional love demonstrated to her by Mary, Estela says, that the "battle against Satan and his legions" can be won.

What sets Estela's apparitions and shrine site apart from the others discussed here, as well as some visions not mentioned here, is that the Virgin Mary's messages have been the catalyst for Catholic evangelization and social justice, a clearly demonstrated social reform that physically engages in the "battle against good and evil in the world." No evangelizing organization like Mary's Ministries, no urban and social reform efforts like those of the Ruiz family and their network of believers, have appeared at any other

Marian apparition site in the United States, the Americas, or Europe. Although prayer groups have been established at virtually all apparition sites, nothing has arisen that is even close to the kind of widespread reform that has taken root in South Phoenix. In addition to evangelization, the Lady of the Americas is especially concerned with social justice and is well aware of the social problems that plague South Phoenix. Both in her personal messages to Estela and in her public messages, the Virgin challenges her followers to undertake a spiritual renewal of the city and beyond. "She has *heard* the ambulances outside, guns and violence. She said 'that's what I want you to pray for, you *have* to pray. I want you to conquer evil out there.'" What the messages of the Virgin of the Americas to Estela Ruiz, her family, and her community ultimately tell us is that apparitions never exist within a historical or cultural vacuum. Indeed, Estela's own experiences are deeply informed by a rich history of apparitions in European and American cultures, and by her family's and community's responses to them.

Estela and her family believe that the Virgin of the Americas specifically chose them and their context, the poverty of urban blight–stricken South Phoenix, because their spiritual and urban reform there would speak volumes to "the world." They have all undergone what they call "conversions" to Mary and God, and they believe that the Virgin Mary is calling them to have a positive effect on others' lives, too. Their evangelizing efforts and the Mary's Ministries organization blend popular and official Catholicism and Protestant evangelicalism, and promote the postmillennialism found in the Virgin of the Americas' messages.

* 4 *

"On Fire for Mary and Jesus!"
Becoming New Men and Women in Mary's Ministries

At a Mary's Ministries faith course held in Estela's and Reyes's backyard Marian shrine space, Abel, a member of Mary's Ministries, gave his testimony to a crowd of thirty mostly Mexican American women and men. During an impassioned speech delivered in a voice that remained steady, he detailed his admittedly sordid past of coveting other women and committing adultery. Abel's voice trembled with emotion, as he proclaimed: "I was like King David in the Bible! I was *muy hombre*. I thought I had to prove myself as a man and I went around with other women, even though I was married and had children." Abel said that he had a loving wife and daughters at home, but that he continued to frequent the bars each night and to live the "life of a bachelor." His wife suffered, he said, from his late-night partying with loose women and fast friends. Abel said he hit an "all-time low" when he failed to visit his wife when she was in the hospital recovering from surgery because he didn't want to leave the bar or the woman he was with at the time. His "conversion," he admitted, was a slow process. "It took God a while to put me on the road back to Him," Abel said, "but I finally came around and embraced God, and my life 'began again.'" According to Abel, his conversion back to God started when he was out driving his semi truck and felt a powerful urge to pray the rosary, something he rarely did. He said it was as if God wanted him to pray: "It was like someone was picking my head up . . . [I felt like I was] flying." Abel went on to say that slowly but surely, he went from being a "servant of Satan" to a "son of God." He ended his testimony in a strong voice, proclaiming "Now, like a new King David, I dance for God without shame and with joy."

When he finished his tearful testimony, Abel handed over the microphone to Terésa, who went on to describe her life before she was "saved" by the Virgin Mary. For the next ten minutes or so, Terésa gave a powerful anthropological and sociological thick description of her life before her "conversion to Mary and Christ." She talked about living in a drug- and gang-infested apartment complex in South Phoenix, and about facing death threats from apartment residents, in addition to the everyday problems of sewage backup and cockroaches. She proclaimed: "I couldn't fight the battles all on my own." Terésa says that in the midst of her suffering she was "touched" by the Virgin while praying to her in Estela and Reyes Ruiz's back yard, which was a mere hundred yards from her apartment. She said that she felt a "wave of peace" wash over her and that she "just knew" that everything would work itself out in her life. Soon after this experience, Terésa took a Mary's Ministries faith course and became involved in evangelizing her community.

Rosa María, who spoke next, said that unlike Abel, she had always been close with the Blessed Mother. Her devotion was so strong that as a girl she would fall asleep with her arms encircling a small statue of the Virgin Mary. Yet this childhood trust in Mary and God was tested most strenuously when she was left alone to raise her two babies, ages six months and two years, after her divorce. Rosa María tried very hard to discern God's will for her; she began a fasting regimen to bring her closer to God, until one day she felt Jesus in the form of a "ray of light" touching her. She remembered feeling "nothing but pure love," and from that day she was "full inside," unable to be depressed because, as she put it, she "knew Jesus." After this experience, Rosa María began to talk about Mary and Jesus whenever the opportunity arose, because she wanted to share her deep love of her "mother" and "father" with others.

Rosa María, Terésa, and Abel are Catholic evangelizers, faith course "graduates" who gave their testimonies, their "witness," at this Mary's Ministries faith course, a week-long set of interactive sessions in which participants are schooled in Catholic doctrine and popular Marian piety. The sessions last from four to five hours each day for the first five days (Monday through Friday) and all day the sixth and seventh days (Saturday and Sunday). And for those who make it through the course and graduate, the work has only begun. Being a member of God's family of Catholic evangelizers requires a lifelong commitment to the principles promulgated in the faith course and a willingness to evangelize in the names of God and Mary.

The organization's Marian piety is based on apparitions of the Virgin of the Americas to Estela and her family, and Mary's Ministries members believe that Mary is calling them to clean up their barrio, spiritually and physically, as well as the rest of the Americas. As Little Rey told the candidates this particular evening, "We are all here for a reason because we were all called by God." Speaking about the imperative to "get out and evangelize," he continued to encourage the crowd: "we should not be selfish and keep God all to ourselves." "We can't get to heaven with our sins," longtime Mary's Ministries member Mañuel emphasizes, "we have to work hard on our faith, because the Devil is always there, waiting for us to let our guard down." He stresses that kerygma, the "proclamation of the message, the good news," must come from our heart; it is not something that can be learned, it has to be *experienced and lived.*

These Mary's Ministries members believe that the Blessed Mother appeared to Estela with this good news to save the Americas from a host of "evils," including corruption, materialism, atheism, racism, poverty, and violence. *La Virgen,* they say, has given them messages of religious and social reform and they, as her "warriors," are to battle Satan and his "legions" in the streets of South Phoenix and in homes and schools throughout the Americas. Members are optimistic that they will overcome the "evil of the world" and the battles that the Virgin has prepared them for in her numerous messages to Estela. The Virgin of the Americas' sense of millennial urgency provides an important link between Mary's Ministries and Hispanic Pentecostalism, with its focus on apocalyptic end times. In a message Estela says she received in February 1995, the Virgin declared: "Evil is loose all over the world and Satan devours My children who do not have God in their lives. My words are now to those who have heard Me and who continue to be My warriors, ready to work with me against this evil, with rosaries in hand, God in your hearts, and prayer in your mouths."

Support from the Catholic Church has been instrumental in the success of Mary's Ministries. From its founding in 1993, Mary's Ministries has had the support of parish priests in Arizona and in the greater Southwest, and of priests in Central and South America.[1] Local and international parish support of the apparitions and the organization remains strong, despite the former bishop of Phoenix's reluctance to approve the apparitions officially. Letters of support from these church representatives have helped give Mary's Ministries a credible reputation, primarily in the Southwest and increasingly in Latin America. The organization's "Project Americas" has been supported by Father Tom Forrest, C.S.R., International Director of the Vatican's evangelization initiatives.[2] Mary's Ministries indicates the new direction Catholicism is taking in the Americas,

one defined by grassroots movements and by laity who cultivate relationships with priests and bishops and who complicate rigid ideas of what it
means and does not mean to be Catholic.[3]

Specifically, the Ruizes and members of Mary's Ministries fuse what
scholars have long referred to as "official" Catholicism of the Catholic
Church with "popular" Catholicism of the people. The Ruizes confound
this "division" by faithfully following the church hierarchy, including the
Pope's messages, the Vatican's evangelization initiatives, and conservative
teachings on birth control, while still creating their own kind of Catholicism. Their Marian-inspired Catholicism is a countercultural and profoundly grassroots faith, one born out of the realities of racism, ethnocen-
trism, and poverty that are reflected in their urban barrio. Mary's Ministries addresses the in-between existence of Mexican Americans like the
Ruizes and other members who are searching for and are constructing
meaningful identities. These men and women by and large choose to remain in the barrio but are economically in the middle class. They meet in
the backyard shrine and honor *la Virgen,* and they attend mass at St.
Catherine of Siena parish, thus maintaining a dual Catholic existence.
They also use Pentecostal language of healing and embody the blending of
Catholicism and evangelicalism in the United States. Mary's Ministries
reflects the complex and ever-changing world of Mexican Americans who
are situated in the United States, and offers them hope for a better life
through a connection with Mary, the Holy Spirit, and Jesus. Through their
involvement in Mary's Ministries, faith course graduates become "new"
men and women who shed past devil-influenced lives for present and future Marian-inspired ones.

Faith and Fun for the Lord

It is six o'clock on a warm Arizona evening. Faith course candidates are
filling out their name tags and have begun to introduce themselves to one
another. A booth is set up in the driveway where participants can register
for faith course number forty-six and pick up information on Mary's
Ministries and a schedule of the week's events. A group of twenty-five men
and women, all but three of them Mexican or Mexican American, find
seats on folding chairs and wait for the Ruizes and Mary's Ministries
members to begin. Candidates talk above the Christian music that plays in
the background from oversized speakers. At last, Norma Ruiz, Estela and

Reyes Ruiz's daughter-in-law and Little Rey's wife, walks onto the stage in front of the shrine of the Virgin of the Americas with a microphone and greets the audience. Blonde and gregarious, Norma flashes a big smile to the candidates. She is comfortable speaking before audiences, displaying a confidence that has come, she tells me, from "lots of practice" and is a "gift from God." Norma feels "called" to work with people and to help to bring them to a closer relationship with "Our Lord and Our Lady."

Norma introduces herself and her husband to the group as "servant leaders" for the week and then gestures to indicate people to the right of the stage and shrine altar, identifying them as graduates of past faith courses who will be helping out as course "servants" this week. The latter have tasks ranging from giving testimonies and reading from Scripture to cooking meals for the faith course participants. Norma reminds the audience that the course is free except for a nominal fee for food that adds up to thirty dollars for the entire week. She tells faith course candidates not to worry if they cannot afford the fee, because "everyone who wants to be here should be able to." She thanks everyone for coming and says that there is a "reason for us all being here this week, it is God calling us to Him."

Norma briefly discusses the week's agenda: Candidates are to arrive a little before 6 P.M. for the next four evenings and should expect to stay until around 10 P.M., sometimes later. Candidates are also told to commit their weekend to the course and to bring "sleep-over items" for Saturday evening, when they will spend the night. Fernando and Leticia Ruiz have a large home and will make accommodations for the women; the men will sleep in the auditorium of the charter school next door. Norma acknowledges that the course does require a significant time commitment but tells the audience that they will be "amazed by the gifts" they receive, promising that the faith course will offer each person a deeper understanding of the Holy Spirit, Mary, God, and Jesus. "I like to think of each night as a sweet dessert with each night getting sweeter, this night is rocky road ice cream as it is always a little bit rough starting the program, but is *so sweet* as we will learn more about our Lord, and will deepen our relationship with Him and Our Lady."

After her introduction, Reyes Jr., also known as "Little Rey" or "Rey," walks up and takes the microphone. A big part of the course, he announces, is having fun, "rejoicing for the Lord"; part of it is "serious," in that candidates learn about Scripture and the tenets of evangelization. But the overall objective is to have a "truly joyous" week. The Ruiz family has designed what they call "dynamics," hands-on ways of learning Scripture that incorporate fun into the course. "We don't want you to be bored, and this is not a catechism course," Little Rey tells the candidates. The best way to learn, he asserts, is by acting out what one has learned, which is the "whole point to the dynamics, you may feel a little bit strange or uncomfortable at first, but little by little you will start to have fun for the Lord." Little Rey warms up the crowd by telling a few jokes and then asks everyone to stand up and form two circles as an ice breaker. The mood shifts from nervousness, giggles, and anticipation to a more serious tone in which men and women share with one another their thoughts about their relationship with Mary and Jesus.

Next, those with green stars on their name tags are told that they are "pigs" and that to find fellow "pigs" they have to start oinking. Within minutes, the "pigs"/"green stars" are in a small group. Next, those with gold stars are told to begin roaring since they are the lions. Then the red-starred people are told they are donkeys and have to make donkey noises. The silver stars are the camels; the blue stars, parrots; and the brown stars are the dogs. After about ten minutes all of the "animals" are in their respective groups, and they are instructed to sit with their groups for the rest of the week. Norma asks the groups to find their seats to watch a presentation on the "conditions of being an evangelizer." Reaching into a bag full of small stuffed animals, Norma chooses a pink pig. As she holds it, she explains that like a pig, evangelizers must have strong stomachs and that as evangelizers, we must "accept any food that is offered to us." She tells a story of how Reyes Sr. ate lasagna, which he hates, for four days straight in New York with Estela. The two had been invited to give a series of talks and when the evangelized served Reyes lasagna, Norma said he "didn't say a word," just cleaned his plate. With that, Norma throws the pig out to the audience and pulls from the bag a teddy bear wearing a jester hat. Like the jester, she says, evangelizers must "be fools for God." After the jester is tossed to an audience member, Norma picks a donkey and observes that like the donkey, we must "all carry burdens on our backs." Next come the camel, the parrot, and the dog: evangelizers all have to have strong knees like the camel because they have to "pray, pray, pray"; like the parrot, they have to "talk, talk, talk"; and they have to "have feet like a dog for we will walk, walk, walk." The presentation receives lots of laughs and each person who has caught a stuffed animal is asked to make the animal's sound before tossing it back to Norma. The presentation has the intended consequences—the messages come across simply and effectively and participants "don't have to have evangelization shoved down their throats," according to Little Rey. The stuffed animal dynamic underscores how the organization values "simplicity" over "complex theology"—a distinction I heard many times during my fieldwork. The Ruizes pride themselves on breaking down Catholic theology into understandable—and, more importantly, "fun"—dynamics for the candidates. Rather than provide the participants with detailed Catholic and evangelical theology, Mary's Ministries offers them easily digested nuggets of information.

The mood then turns more serious as Reyes Sr. speaks about Mary's Ministries' involvement in the Catholic Church's evangelization efforts. Reyes emphasizes Mary's Ministries' strong ties to the Catholic Church and the importance of institutional Church support for Project Americas. According to Reyes Sr., the goal of the Church's evangelization efforts is no different from that of Mary's Ministries: the "conversion and the renewal of the Catholic faith by inviting all people to hear the salvation of Jesus." He goes on to emphasize the evangelical identity of Mary's Ministries, affirming that the goal of the faith courses is to bring men and women closer to God and to let them "know Jesus," whatever their faith. Even though the faith course is decidedly Catholic, it is broadly evangelical in orientation. "We are all here for a reason," Reyes continues, "because we were called by God." After Reyes's talk, two hours of "dynamics," Scriptural teachings, and testimonies, the candidates are released to the charter school's cafeteria for supper. Everyone is hungry, and the spaghetti, garlic bread, salad, cookies, and fruit punch that await them are eagerly consumed. Peggy and Leticia Ruiz, along with four of their children, dole out the food and beverages to the participants and clean up. Various "animal" groups sit together during the meal, getting better acquainted with one another and sharing their love for the Virgin Mary, the Holy Spirit, Jesus, and God.

Deacon George, a friend of the Ruizes from their home parish of St. Catherine of Siena, awaits the candidates when they return to their seats. A Hungarian American who has lived in South Phoenix for most of his life, Deacon George has embraced Mary's Ministries' evangelicalism. With the energy of a fiery preacher, Deacon George asks members of the crowd why they came. He receives various responses from the men and women: "for my love of the Blessed Mother," "to bring the Holy Spirit into my heart," "to learn more about God the Father." Deacon George responds like an enthusiastic evangelical minister, with a vigorous "JESUS is the answer, the answer inside us all. JESUS put his hand on your shoulder and will let the

Holy Spirit burn inside us all. Praise JESUS!" He continues to talk about the power of Jesus Christ, how Jesus has called the candidates to be evangelizers. It is not necessary to stand in front of stores or on street corners, he says, "we are just asked to evangelize in our daily lives by incorporating JESUS in our lives. JESUS will tell us in our hearts to do good things, and when people see this example and our good deeds they will know that there is something special going on. We have to *live* Jesus and not just *talk* about him!" The deacon continues to talk to his attentive audience about the summons to "live the life of love through Jesus and his mother Mary."

As he is talking, faith course graduates distribute slips of paper and pencils to the new candidates. Deacon George places a clay pot on the stage of the shrine and asks everyone to write down a problem they are having, something that is troubling them. Then he asks the candidates to come up to the pot one by one and light their pieces of paper on fire with a lighter he offers. Each candidate is to place the burning paper into the pot, and after everyone's paper has been added and burned, the Deacon extinguishes the fire. He continues, "Incense is one of the many symbols in the Catholic Church . . . but the rising smoke from our paper didn't smell like incense. It smelled because it was a *problem*. It stank." He breaks the smoldering pot with a hammer, and asks everyone to take a piece, "for this piece symbolizes your problem and what has been keeping you from Jesus." The Deacon asserts that it is not necessary to travel to faraway pilgrimages, for healing can happen "right here . . . the Blessed Mother and Jesus are one and are right here." As the candidates hold their warm pieces of clay pot, the atmosphere is quiet, and the smell of burned paper is in the air.

After this "dynamic," all are called to gather around the fountain in the far right corner of the yard, where a large wooden crucifix stands. A large statue of the Virgin of Guadalupe is to the right, and several votive candles have been placed in front of her. Next to these images of Mary and Christ, Reyes Sr. has set up a table covered in a bright Mexican blanket, on which Deacon George leads the Exposition of the Sacrament.

Let the Healing Begin

All but two people return the next night, putting the class at twenty-three candidates. This pleases the Ruizes, who say that it is "better to not come back if you're not sure" than to go through the course half-heartedly because candidates should only "do the course if you feel that it is what the Blessed Mother and our Lord want you to do right now." This evening's theme is "coming out of the cocoon," and participants are told the story of King David. They, too, are encouraged to "not feel ashamed" and to "rejoice for the Lord." Like Abel, who witnessed that he now "dances for God," the twenty-three candidates are asked to get up from their seats and dance, to "lose themselves" for God. Each person is given a crown made of yellow construction paper and is asked to move around to lively Mexican music. A band across the crown reads "Fool for Jesus" in black magic marker. Laughing and linking arms, the faith course candidates weave their way across the backyard. This dynamic continues for about ten minutes. A call and response pattern of praising God, a hallmark of the week-long course, is issued by Little Rey, who calls out, "Who's your Savior?" The participants respond, yelling, "JESUS!" Little Rey tells the crowd that everyone needs to "have fun and be silly"; he reads from Matthew 18:3, and emphasizes that it is necessary to become like children to enter the kingdom of God. As with Norma's animal presentation, the paper crowns are meant to signify being "like children"; the message conveyed is that the best evangelizers lose their adult seriousness and become "simpler."

After this session of enthusiastic praising, Norma introduces on a posterboard the concept of "NEWS," a kind of acrostic that stands for "experieNce of salvation," "zEal for the Gospel," "live the Word," and "analySis of reality." Norma emphasizes that to be an evangelizer, one must have an experience of salvation. One must have real excitement for the Gospel. She also stresses that evangelizers are to be aware of boundaries; different situations require different evangelizing tactics. Like Jesus, Norma says, "by living the word, we have to have kerygma, a bold preoccupation to preach what we believe." But this boldness does not mean that evangelizers should be "pushy." On the contrary, Norma says that it is necessary to "go with the flow" and to "just be yourselves" when evangelizing. Norma then introduces a peculiarly gendered interpretation of II Timothy 2:2, and "two Timothies in a tutu," Johnny and Ricky, men of substantial girth, run out on cue, wearing pink tutus. Performing a little jig to a laughing crowd, they present a short skit, emphasizing the necessity of "going out and spreading the Word." "Now you won't forget Second Timothy chapter two, verse two," Little Rey jokes.

The course again switches from playfulness to a more serious tone when Mañuel gives a "kerygma talk." He says, "we have to keep our minds on Jesus constantly because the Devil wants us to lose the kingdom that he once had but lost; as long as the Devil bothers us we're with Jesus, but as soon as he leaves us alone, he's got us." We can't get to heaven with our sins, Manuel emphasizes, and we have to work hard on our faith, because the Devil "is always there, waiting for us to let our guard down." He stresses that kerygma must "come from our heart," it is not something that can be learned but has to be *experienced and lived*. "Fernie," Reyes Sr.'s younger brother, joins in and elaborates on "the heart" in his testimony, saying that everyone must work on forgiveness.

"When we have anger," Fernie stresses, "we are not able to live a life of Christ"; when we are able to let go of the anger, "we are healed." Fernie talks of his "mission from Mary," which he says has been to learn to love his black son-in-law and his black/Mexican grandson, and essentially to "forgive" his child of miscegenation. He has also had to learn how to accept the loss of loved ones and has had to "let go" of his anger with God. He concludes, "if you have lost someone put him in Jesus's arms." An evangelical Christian song, "I Will Raise Him Up," immediately follows Fernie's testimony, and everyone is asked to stand and to raise their arms in the air to witness to the saving powers of Jesus. As the candidates sway back and forth, arms held high, Fernie, dressed in a "Jesus costume," holds a large wooden cross with one hand and moves to the music up on the shrine's stage. When the song ends, Johnny, dressed up as Satan, jumps out and begins to taunt Fernie. Fernie/Jesus turns to the crowd, saying, "it is through Jesus that we must evangelize, because the Devil is always out there."

Yet another dynamic follows Fernie's talk. Each candidate is given cotton balls to put in his or her ears and a black cloth blindfold to wrap around his or her eyes. After several minutes, the blindfolded participants are led by the hand through the yard by a graduate. The purpose of this exercise, says Little Rey after everyone can see and hear again, is to demonstrate that Jesus will lead us and that we are saved. All we need to do, Little Rey says, is to "open our hearts" and "let the healing begin."

The next testimony capitalizes on the ever-present Devil theme. With her voice straining under the weight of emotion, Margaret, Manuel's wife, begins to speak about the "living hell" she and her spouse have had to endure. Their son, who has been incarcerated off and on since he was in his teens, has caused them a tremendous amount of grief and suffering. "It has taken me a long time to heal and it is still happening," she says. Margaret talks about the trials her son put them through with gang activity and drugs and says she is "so grateful" to the Virgin Mary for helping her cope with her son's waywardness. She reads aloud the story of the mustard seed, Mark 4:30–33, and comments, "We're all the mustard seeds and Mary asks us to close our eyes and to put our trust in Jesus . . . all it takes is to have faith." After her talk, each candidate is given a mustard seed said to "symbolize the beginning of your renewed faith in Jesus."

"High" Off the Lord

Following Margaret's talk this evening is Rey Jr.'s testimony, one that he has been giving for more than ten years. In this evening's version, Rey incorporates the powerful language of renewal and makes sharp comparisons between his pre- and his post-conversion life. He describes his conversion in these words: "My god was drugs, I believed in drugs, depended on them, and had faith in them." He says he hit a "real low point" when he smoked an entire eight-ball of cocaine in one evening. His body shaking, his lips burning with blisters, and his lungs on fire, Rey cried to God and promised that he would throw out all his pipes and smoking paraphernalia. Frightened by his "close call," he told God that he would never smoke crack cocaine again. "I told God, I will *never ever do that again;* I will only *snort* it from now on!" says Rey, laughing at himself. Shortly thereafter Rey Sr. disowned him after finding a cocaine bottle in his car. It took the Virgin Mary, in the form of the Lady of the Americas, to tell him that she "would take me as I was," and Jesus, who "had to come at me like Paul and knock me off my horse." Instead of drugs, Rey says, he became "chemically dependent," "hooked" on Jesus and Mary. He began wearing multiple strands of colored plastic rosaries around his neck and T-shirts emblazoned with Christ's image. Rey evangelized his former "drug buddies," all of whom thought he had gone "off the deep end."

Rey creatively uses drug terminology to describe his conversion experience; he is now "addicted" to Jesus and Mary instead of the toxic substances that harmed his mind and his body. Rey chooses his words carefully and is aware of their effect on audiences; he has, after all, been fine-tuning his testimony for the past ten years. He uses terms like being "chemically dependent" on Jesus, "high" off of Jesus, and "hooked" on Jesus and Mary because that is the language he knows, and because it is a language familiar to residents of South Phoenix. He knows that his troubled youth will resonate with Mexican American parents who have children involved in gangs and the accompanying drugs and alcohol, and he hopes that his story reaches young men who think, like he did, that there is "no hope." Rey borrows from and mocks treatment center language— real recovery, he stresses, comes through a dependence on Jesus. During one of my many discussions with Rey, he emphasized that the "problem" with Alcoholics Anonymous is that it doesn't rely on Jesus—it looks to God but not "His Son." Alcoholics who rely on AA, he says, are not truly recovered until they have found Jesus.

An atmosphere of sharing and spiritual healing is present during the recitation of the testimony, enabling the one giving the testimony to reenter society as a new person; the testimony serves as a "commitment and re-socialization mechanism." Testimonies, at least those given at the faith courses, are usually full of passion, melodrama, and emotion, and involve the listeners, asking them to examine their own lives. Little Rey's and Abel's testimonies touch on all of these key aspects of giving a testimony; the narrative of transformation provided in a testimony asks others to do some soul-searching and to lead a life of self-examination. As each Mary's Ministries graduate gave a testimony during the week, the candidates listened attentively; some cried, others nodded their heads vigorously, identifying with the story.

During the third night of the faith course, the "night of meditation," candidates are told that all they have to do is to say "yes" to Jesus. John, a faith course graduate and servant, urges the candidates to hand themselves over to Jesus, saying, "I'm trying and that's all I have to do. . . . He will guide you, protect you, anything and everything to make sure that you end up with Him." The Blessed Mother "is to be our model," John says, because she said "yes" and followed the "will of the Father." He talks about the youth group he used to lead in southern California and about the youth group members who were baptized in the Holy Spirit. "They told me, 'Oh John! It was so good. . . . Jesus was there and he was motioning for us to go play. He wanted us to be like children.'" In order to be like children again, John asserts that "we must trust our Father and our Mother because they know what is right."

Next, each candidate is given a candle and is told to take as much time as necessary to reflect on the Holy Spirit. The candidates are asked to take their candles up to the shrine when they are finished and then to proceed to the cafeteria for dinner; they are told to refrain from talking until they are back in their seats at the shrine. Little Rey then greets everyone and reviews what has been taught: the four conditions of being an evangelizer, the seven characteristics of an evangelizer (the animals), and the meaning of kerygma. The apostles, he emphasizes, lived in unity and community, received the Holy Spirit, acted with boldness, loved others, and were unified because they all "believed in the same thing, JESUS as their savior." The four Gospels, Rey asserts, are the "keys to heaven": "The apostles' kerygma was that they preached Jesus and had the fire of the Holy Spirit." He holds up a posterboard with the image of an equilateral triangle with "BELIEVE," "TRUST," and "DEPEND" written on the sides. "As apostles," he says, "we have to have faith, we need to believe, and we must depend on God; and if we don't, then we won't have a conversion."

This night of silent meditation, review, and testimonies ends with Abel's wife's gripping testimony. She introduces herself: "Yes, I am the one who suffered and I am also the one who forgave" Abel. She talks about her many heartaches: pregnant at fifteen, she married Abel, only to have their marriage plagued by his philandering and verbal abuse. She grew to hate her husband, she says, and after his conversion she would torment him. "I would make him miserable when he tried so hard to get back together with me. I just *couldn't* forgive him. One night I fell to the ground and begged God to change him and to allow me to heal." She started to attend the rosaries in Estela's and Reyes's back yard with her mother and there began to be "healed of her anger" toward her husband. They reconciled and together joined Mary's Ministries, and her husband has been faithful ever since. "This community helps you when you're down, they pick you up. . . . It is very important to be part of a community, because without one the light inside can turn off." After this tearful, emotive testimony, several women rise to give her hugs, and shortly thereafter the group disperses for the evening.

"Divine Plan of Salvation"

When the candidates return the next night, they are greeted by Norma, who tells them "Tonight is a special night! God has a plan for all of us; we are all in His plans because He knew us before we were born." She emphasizes that because God gave everyone free will, it is not always easy to follow God's plans. The emphasis this evening is on each person being part of God's plan and working to combat Satan in the world. The highlight of this fourth evening is a play called the "divine plan of salvation," enacted outside on the shrine stage. After dinner, the candidates take a seat in the back yard, and on their way there each is given an apple slice to eat. Little

Rey comes out and paraphrasing Genesis, says, "The day you eat the fruit is the DAY YOU DIE." Everyone is told that they have "sinned" and have disobeyed "God's law," because "the law is the law." Members of the crowd of about one hundred are asked to repeat "THE LAW IS THE LAW!" several times. The play is a humorous rendition of the story of the Fall. Adam and Eve sport oversized wigs, and Satan is a long puppet snake that provocatively dances with Eve after she has had a taste of the big red apple.

After the booming voice of "God" banishes them from the Garden, Adam and Eve are told by God that they cannot go back to his original covenant of grace, by which they had only to enjoy the beautiful garden around them and each other. Adam and Eve sadly leave the garden, and members of the audience are told to follow. "Satan" (John dressed up in a Devil's costume) tempts everyone by telling them that if they follow him, he will give them anything they need. Candidates, along with family and friends who have come to see the play, physically and vehemently push Satan away. Audience members make their way to the other side of the yard and watch a mock domestic violence scene in which Satan "tempts" a woman, who is being abused by her drunk husband, to "divorce him and take the children." As he taunts the woman, Satan tells her husband to "hit her, go ahead, it's OK."

In the next scene, cholos—Mexican American male gang members—deal drugs. One of the young men's mothers approaches the group and is told that her son is "one of them." She denies it and as she voices her disbelief, her son is shot dead by one of the cholos, who is being egged on by Satan. Satan then tells the young man to "go ahead and shoot her, no one is looking." The boy shoots the woman, who slumps to the ground, dead. Both scenes are a little too real and familiar to many members of the audience, who have experienced and/or witnessed domestic violence and have had sons and daughters involved in gang activity. Several women whisper that they are disturbed by the skits because they "are for real." Nervous laughter and gasps of not altogether mock horror accompany the whispers. Meanwhile, "Satan" revels in the violence.

Suddenly, "Jesus," played by Joe, another faith-course servant for the week, announces himself to Satan as God's son and "the light." "Follow the light," he tells the candidates and the rest of the audience, who follow him. Running off, Satan shouts, "I'll be back, just wait." Jesus stands on the stage, surrounded by audience members; he asks everyone to follow him. "Mother Teresa" (Terésa), dressed in a white and blue sari, walks over, carrying a handful of plastic rosaries. She hands them out, asking "who will take over my work now that I am gone?" Enthusiastic outpourings of "I will" answer her question. Rey then puts an optimistic spin on the Fall, exclaiming "thank goodness for Adam and Eve's sin because without it, we wouldn't know JESUS!" After a very quick transition to the Adoration of the Eucharist by Deacon George, Little Rey reminds everyone to "wear their grubbies" the next evening, which occasions some suspense, as the candidates have no idea what is going to occur.

Healing, Initiation, and a New Beginning

Reyes Sr. opens the next evening, night five of the course, with a forty-five-minute talk on Mary as the "star of evangelization." He begins by telling the candidates that he is "totally, totally in love with the Blessed Mother" and has been since he was a young boy working in the New Mexican farm fields. He emphasizes Mary's role as everyone's mother and her great love for her son Jesus. "She loves us even though we are so flawed." The Virgin is a great healer, Reyes continues, telling his own story of healing. When he was a young boy, he says, his father was run over by a truck as he was crossing the road and was killed instantly. "I was very angry with God for letting my father die, and my heart was hardened." But his mother's inner strength and her devotion to the Virgin of Guadalupe showed him how the Virgin could heal the pain. Because of the Virgin's love for him, Reyes tells the group, he "let go" of his anger at God.

The Virgin, Reyes says, gets involved in her children's lives as a loving mother: "she begs God to let her go and help her children when She sees they're in trouble." The Virgin of Guadalupe is one manifestation of Mary, a Mexican manifestation, Reyes stresses, who sought to save her children from themselves when they were performing human sacrifices and did not have God in their lives. Moreover, he continues, the Spanish *conquistadores* were enacting their own brutality on the Indians because "as human beings, we either want to destroy or convert." Reyes's version of the story of Guadalupe is that she appealed to Juan Diego, an Indian peasant, and once he accepted her, her evangelization in the Americas had begun. Millions converted, Reyes asserts, as they were "dazzled by the Virgin's power."

Reyes interweaves the story of Guadalupe, the story of Mary as mother to Jesus, and the story of Mary as the first evangelizer, creating a seamless, reconstructive historical narrative of motherhood, passion, and commitment. He emphasizes that Guadalupe came *especially* for Mexicans, "*una raza preciosa.*" Reyes points to his dark skin and tells the candidates that he, who had been teased at school as a child for his color, has "found a woman darker than myself." "We're all *mestizos,*" Reyes asserts, and Mary represents "all of us," but people of Mexican descent will relate to the dark-skinned Virgin on levels that Anglos cannot experience. According to Reyes, Guadalupe is the "star of evangelization" because she is the "great mother of the great sacrifice": she stopped both the *conquistadores'* slaughter and the Aztec sacrifices. After this impassioned speech on racial identity, fifteenth-century Mexican history, and Marian theology, Reyes implores the candidates to love Mary: "open your hearts, love Her, make Her your friend, because you will be able to go to Her for everything." A song to honor the Virgin, "I'm Your Mother," written by the popular Italian American Catholic singer, composer, and friend of the Ruiz family, Marty Rotelle, is sung by Marty's sister; when it has ended, there is scarcely a dry eye in the crowd. Marty, an Italian American and native New Yorker, has been a member of Mary's Ministries since the early 1990s and has been a featured speaker and musical performer at several of the December retreats to honor the Virgin of the Americas. He is currently making plans to move to South Phoenix to become a more integral member of Mary's Ministries, and perhaps to teach music at the charter school.

Reyes Sr.'s talk points to the Virgin of the Americas' centrality for Mary's Ministries: she is a *mestiza,* as well as a trans-bordered and evangelical Virgin who tells her "children" to evangelize in her name and Jesus' name. She is also a symbol for the barrio—members of this South Phoenix community interpret her messages as calling them to influence not only Mexican American and Hispanic communities throughout the Americas, but the Catholic Church itself.

When the tears have abated, the real "work for the Holy Spirit" begins as candidates are prepared for what is to be the climactic going "under the rope." Tonight's theme is "Tears of Joy," and the intent is to bring each candidate closer to the Holy Spirit. The days leading up to this have been preparing the candidates for an intimate experience with the Holy Spirit. Mary, as Mother, and God, as Father, are the twin themes that run throughout this night's session; the candidates are their "children" who are on the verge of showing their commitment to their "parents." An air of secrecy surrounds the evening, as everyone is dressed in old clothes, nervous and unsure of what exactly is going to happen. Around seven o'clock, after a light supper in the school cafeteria, the candidates are taken to a schoolroom for what is to be the beginning of a "beautiful night." It is dark inside and difficult to see, and nervous whispers dart across the room. Norma places a large pot of multicolored petunias in the middle of the floor inside the circle, and Reyes Sr. tells the candidates to pick a flower they identify with in terms of its color or size, and to focus on the single flower amidst the various flowers, imagining themselves "growing as it grows." God's understanding, compassion, and love are emphasized, as is God's capacity for forgiveness. On this note, each candidate is told to close his/her eyes and to allow himself/herself to be led into the next phase of the evening. Each candidate is taken by the hand to a dark and windowless room in the back yard and is told to stay in there until approached by a graduate who will lead him/her out of the room. This room is meant to symbolize both human sinfulness and hell. Crammed into this small, hot room, "hell on earth," the candidates listen to the "bad news, *malas noticias,*" that is read by "God" over an intercom (Ricky in a booming voice)— news of gang warfare, drugs, violence—juxtaposed with the "good news" of Jesus Christ. After ten minutes or so of this, the candidates are told over the loudspeaker that they are about to enter into the next phase of the initiation. Olga, a candidate who has become faint, is the first one out; she is led to a chair at the far right of the back yard. One by one, each candidate, led by a graduate, joins her.

Red lights have been strung to form a hanging pathway to the next scene, a "salvation experience." Johnny S. tells the candidates that he wants them to contemplate the picture he is about to unveil. He pulls the cloth away from an image of Jesus holding a man, slumped in his arms, who is wearing jeans and a T-shirt and limply holding onto a mallet. "I have felt as this man is feeling, I was broken and Jesus lifted me up," Johnny S. tells the crowd. The picture is framed by fifteen or so red lights, which are said to symbolize Christ's blood; potted lilies on either side of the painting symbolize Christ's resurrection and the candidates' chance at new life.

After five minutes or so of contemplation, each candidate is led by the hand to the front and center of the back yard and is placed before a graduate, who stands in a line with the others. Estela informs the group that the candidates are about to take the final step in joining the Holy Spirit. Thirty or so lit candles in paper cups have been placed on the shrine's altar. A freshly painted white plaster bird, representing the Holy Spirit, hangs from the shrine's roof. A rope has been stretched across the yard, directly in front of the shrine and altar, and wrapped around two trees. Estela says that everyone must "go *past* the rope to the Holy Spirit"—but not *over* it, as that would be too easy. Candidates have to crawl *under* the rope,

placed mere inches from the ground. This movement symbolizes acceptance of the Holy Spirit and stepping "into the light," as each candidate,
once past the rope, takes a candle and joins a semicircle of the newly initiated. The women go first: one by one, each woman crawls the hundred
yards or so on her stomach, like a worm, to the rope. Everyone now knows
why they were told to wear "grubbies." Several women cry as they slowly
make their way toward and then under the rope, reaching the shrine—and
the Holy Spirit. Cathie, one of the candidates, sobs uncontrollably; this has
been, she cries, "the most significant night of her life" because she now has
a family that accepts and understands her.

Next the female graduates "make the journey," and then the male candidates and graduates follow suit. The entire process takes about an hour.
The new initiates hold hands and sing to the modern Christian tune,
played many times during the course, "We Are One Body, One Body in
Christ," and then they walk over to the fountain to place their candles
around Christ's feet. Reyes Sr. then leads the group in singing several re-
frains of a "spiritual communion" song that he wrote, in Spanish and in
English:

> Padre Ñuestro
> Espiritu Santo,
> Canta con mi
> Á Santa Eucaristía.
> Our Father,
> Holy Spirit,
> Come Sing with Me
> To the Holy Eucharist.

Reyes says he wrote the song several years ago because he wanted to take
Communion, the Holy Eucharist, "more often than it is possible," and was
told by his spiritual advisor at the time that he could have a *spiritual communion* each day. The short song is sung at the end of the biweekly
rosaries at the shrine, as well as at all Ruiz family gatherings.

The next day, Saturday, is "hands-on training" day for the new initiates,
who will soon be evangelizing for Mary's Ministries. Fresh from their experiences of the previous evening, the thirteen women and ten men learn
about how to be effective evangelizers; they polish their techniques and
perform skits and presentations. The concept of "three persons of evangelization" is introduced: the Holy Spirit, the evangelizer, and the evange-

lized are part of an interconnected process. The evangelizer can only evangelize if the Holy Spirit is truly present, and an effective evangelization may take place only when the evangelizer is "open" to the Holy Spirit's power: Rosa María exclaims, "we don't do it, God does!" Johnny, who at the time hoped to enter a seminary on the West Coast but did not qualify academically, explained the "ABCs": **A**lways be joyful, **B**rief, and **C**entered in Christ. Rosa María emphasizes that the point is not to defend God—"to argue is the *worst* thing that we can do!" Instead, evangelizers are told not to engage in apologetics for the Church but to identify their home parish and to announce to people, "God loves you." "Most of the time we just plant the seed, we don't get to stick around to see the fruit, but that's okay," Rosa María says. "We are Jesus' hands, feet, and heart, and we need to love others as Jesus and the Blessed Mother love us." It is also necessary to listen to the evangelized, she says, because Jesus "was a great listener."

The candidates then make their way to Reconciliation at St. Catherine of Siena parish, which is just a mile and a half up the street from the Ruizes' home, underscoring the support the Ruizes have received from their priest and parish. The candidates are expected to confess their sins in order to prepare themselves for the tasks ahead. Father Ernesto, at this time a recently ordained young Mexican priest, listens to all of the twenty-three initiates in an open style, face-to-face reconciliation format, which lasts for two hours. After everyone has returned to the Ruizes' back yard, Reyes Sr. takes the opportunity to talk about the difference between "praying with" and "praying over" people, and emphasizes that Mary's Ministries advocates the former, as people are sensitive to other people touching them. "It is just as effective to lift our hands *above* the person, over his head and his shoulders. We don't need to touch them because the Holy Spirit doesn't need *our* help!"

The candidates are able to practice their new work that evening, as it is the "first Saturday" of the month, the day the Blessed Mother is said to appear to Estela with a message. As two hundred or so men and women sit in chairs and on blankets, awaiting the start of the rosary at 7 P.M., the candidates are all invited inside Reyes's and Estela's home for a private rosary. This is considered an honor, because no more than thirty people can cram into the living room where Estela sits and communicates with Mary. Estela says she always received the monthly message from Mary in the morning, although Mary oftentimes appeared to her with a short message in the evening for the public. Before the rosary begins, Reyes tells everyone that "many, many people" have seen the Blessed Mother smile and wink at them from the painting, but also reassures those who will not see anything that it is "okay . . . it does not mean that the Blessed Mother does not love you or that you do not have faith in Her."

After the rosary, Estela turns and faces the small crowd of kneeling men and women and, holding hands with Reyes, announces that the Blessed Mother gave her a special message. "She told me that you are Her children and that God loves you very much. She welcomes you all to Mary's Ministries and thanks you for your commitment to Her and to Her son, Jesus." Reyes then turns to her and says, "tell me if I'm wrong, Stella, but I do believe that the Blessed Mother appeared to you during the first decet and stayed the entire time." Estela responds with a barely audible "yes." The initiates form a line to hug Estela and Reyes, sharing their experiences with one another. Many claim to have received a "candy kiss" from the Virgin, a term devotees use to describe Mary's "gift" of making herself known to them by winking, blinking, and smiling.

After this intimate encounter with the Virgin Mary, with their spiritual "parents" Estela and Reyes, and with each other as "brothers and sisters," the candidates walk outside to hear Estela read the Virgin's message. In addition to the new initiates and graduates, there are close to 150 people in the back yard who have journeyed to hear the Virgin's message to Estela. After her tearful reading and the announcement that there will be only two more messages for the public, Reyes takes the microphone and tells the crowd that he is happy to introduce the newest Mary's Ministries evangelizers. As a result of the "Holy Spirit," several people lie on the ground and a few receive the "gift of tongues."

Evangelizing in El Barrio

After breakfast the next morning, the Ruizes hold a "sending forth" ceremony for the candidates presided over by Deacon George. He points to a large cross on the ground, on top of which lie twenty-three small wooden cross necklaces, one for each evangelizer, and small pins of the pope. Deacon George instructs the initiates to carry "His cross" that day as they go forth. Deacon George reads from a Roman Catholic pre–Vatican II blessing ceremony booklet, a translated *Manuale Curatorum;* he says he uses this book "to drive out evil" because the post–Vatican II book, the *Rituale,* "doesn't do it sufficiently."[4] The use of this text is a provocative window into Mary's Ministries' relationship with the post–Vatican II Catholic

Church; it has embraced many of Vatican II's reforms, including the emphasis on evangelization and ecumenicism, but it also looks to the preconciliar church for some of its rituals. Many in the Ministries feel that the current Church has abandoned many of the meaningful rituals that were part of the pre–Vatican II church. Although they are supportive of many of the Church's reforms since Vatican II and embrace ecumenicism (dialogue with other faiths), Mary's Ministries is also loyal to pre–Vatican II rituals and Catholic triumphalism.

The deacon proceeds to bless two small bowls, one filled with salt, the other with water; he does this "to trap any evil spirits" that may attempt to impede the evangelizing work the candidates will be doing. Each candidate is purified by the water, which is shaken onto his/her head with a red rose Deacon George dips into it; by the salt, gently rubbed onto their lips by Norma, "to purify all the words that come out of your mouth"; and by holy oil, which John places on each forehead in the sign of the cross. Each candidate is then presented with a Mary's Ministries T-shirt imprinted with the Virgin of the Americas' image, several scapulars and colored plastic rosaries, and small rosary prayer cards. Estela and Reyes hug and bless each candidate. Estela then forms the evangelizing "teams" by pairing men with women, making a total of eleven teams. Each pair is told that for the day, it is "wedded in a union for Christ."

Thus armed, the initiates drive over to St. Catherine of Siena church for 11 A.M. mass, and enter the church two by two. Walking behind a large banner that reads "Mary's Ministries," the group makes its way to the front two rows of pews, which have been reserved for them. They are a sizable and impressive cohort, more than fifty new and past initiates combined, and they walk down the aisle with a divinely inspired purpose. After mass, teams are driven to South Phoenix neighborhoods, where they walk door to door, evangelizing. It is a typical Arizona day, hot and dry, over ninety degrees, and the evangelizers, after they have worked their way through a street, are picked up by Little Rey and Armando in the vans and given water and snacks. When the teams have covered several neighborhoods, they are driven to Brighton Place Apartments, known in South Phoenix as dangerous and disreputable for the gangs, drugs, and shootings that have taken place there. None of the new evangelizers have ever been in this complex before, and many are nervous. Going door to door, they talk about the Holy Spirit, the Virgin of Guadalupe, and Jesus with those willing to listen. Two heroin-addled *cholos* with deep reddish-brown lines running up and down their arms are joined by a small group of evangelizers who hold the junkies' swollen hands and pray that they might be able to give up their life of drugs. Plastic rosaries, scapulars, and prayer cards are distributed freely by the fired-up evangelizers. A group of young men, sitting in the back of an old Ford truck drinking *cervezas* and listening to Mexican radio, are approached by the entire group of evangelizers, who pray with the young men, telling them that there is a "better way and a better life" for them.

After this excursion into designated profane territory, everyone—exhausted and famished, yet exhilarated by their afternoon evangelizing and the "fruits" they witnessed—walks the short distance from Brighton Place to Estela's and Reyes's home, where they are greeted by about sixty members of Mary's Ministries waving white handkerchiefs and dancing to the rhythm of the loud *fiesta* music. Reyes announces to the crowd that the white handkerchiefs are an Aztec Indian symbol of welcome. Weaving their way through the lines of fluttering white cloth, the candidates are each given a cloth which they raise triumphantly at the shrine. The back yard is decorated for a Mexican *fiesta,* with papier mâché streamers, balloons, and *piñatas,* and freshly picked pink bougainvillea flowers are everywhere in vases. The initiates are told that they can help themselves to the barbecued meat, salads, and *menudo* on platters, and to the blue-and-white-frosted graduation cake that reads, "Congratulations Faith Course #46 Graduates!"

The teams are eventually asked to go up to the shrine's stage, one by one, to discuss what has taken place during their evangelization and to reflect on their experiences in the course. Many speak of their initial nervousness and describe warming up as the Holy Spirit moved them. Initiates mention encountering mostly Catholics and Protestants, and a few Jews and Muslims; they say the majority of evangelized were receptive. Frances, a course graduate and active Mary's Ministries member who accompanied the groups, describes a woman with terrible back trouble: "When I prayed with her, she cried out and said that she had felt a movement in her back. I said 'PRAISE JESUS!' and the woman could clearly walk better. The Holy Spirit was working today, let me tell you!" Tony talks about a "tough looking *cholo,* covered in scars and tattoos," who listened to him celebrate Jesus' love. "I felt that this dude, tough as he was, was really receptive and I think that he might try going to mass again! Praise be to Mary and Jesus!"

After sharing their stories, each initiate receives a Mary's Ministries graduation diploma and a big hug from Little Rey and Norma; each is told "the work has only just begun, we have to continue to evangelize in the name of the Holy Spirit!" Little Rey passes around a sign-up sheet, informing the new graduates that there will be a three-evening follow-up course, the "Paul course," in two weeks. This is the next step in the evangelizing journey, in which Mary's ministers are trained to conduct faith courses. The third and final course offered by Mary's Ministries is the "Defense of the Faith" course, where evangelizers are trained in the ecclesiastical structure of the Church.

"New" Women and Men

When we take a step back and further analyze a typical Mary's Ministries faith course, we see that the week-long event reflects broader themes, primarily the heavy borrowing from Protestant evangelicalism and the overlapping nature of popular and official Catholic piety.[5] The faith courses that have been established or planned in the United States and more recently in Latin America emphasize, as we have seen, a personal encounter with Jesus Christ, receiving the Holy Spirit, receiving "gifts" of speaking in tongues, and healing through a version of laying-on of hands (praying "with" instead of "over"). A specific language of conversion is used; being "saved" and becoming a "new man/woman" is an integral part of the discursive world of the faith courses. The courses also emphasize the classic evangelical battle between good and evil/God and Satan, at the same time that they invoke the Catholic Virgin of the Americas' invitation to her children to be her "warriors" in the "fight against Satan."

The courses' skits, singing and dancing, and other "dynamics" provide the space for creative evangelical worship and involve the participants on physical and material levels: candidates get "worked up" for the Holy Spirit and prepare their bodies as well as their souls for its arrival. Biblical references and teachings complement the experiential component of these exercises with an emphasis on knowledge and information; faith course candidates and graduates are encouraged to prepare themselves for the "battles against Satan" the Virgin of the Americas refers to in her messages to Estela.

We are also able to see how the courses link a grassroots piety with the Catholicism of the Church. At this particular course in Estela's and Reyes's back yard, Deacon George plays an integral role, and Catholic rituals and beliefs pervade the week-long event. Reconciliation is a capstone experience; the candidates are not able to move to the next level without meeting with a priest to confess their sins. In recent years, priests have come to play even more important and public roles at the courses; they now give inspirational talks, administer the Eucharist, and are present for the sacrament of Reconciliation. When faith courses are held at Estela's and Reyes's house today, the sacrament takes place in a designated room next to the shrine, used as living quarters for visiting priests. What the faith courses display is a working arrangement between laity who are trying to reform the Church from the outside, to make it more relevant to Hispanics, and priests who are supportive of their endeavors.

The intent of the faith course is to show candidates that in order to be effective evangelizers for Mary, they must shed their old selves for new selves. As we have seen in the many skits and dynamics, they are told they must leave Satan behind and embrace Jesus and Mary. Once they have embraced this idea and have humbled themselves before God (getting dirty, going under the rope), they become one with the Holy Spirit and are part of a new, sanctified community. Evangelical language is used during the week to instill in candidates the necessity of experiencing a death of the old self and a birth of a new self. These "new" men and women then turn their lives over to Jesus and Mary and commit themselves to evangelizing in their names.

When we step back and look at how the faith courses are gendered, we see that it is within the communal, familial setting of the faith courses that Mexican American men and women are able to form relationships with others and craft meaningful roles for themselves. Spiritually energized by the Holy Spirit, they seek to help others to know Christ as intimately as they do. Faith courses provide opportunities for Mexican American men and women by offering them a performative space through which they can explore gendered codes and different options for themselves.[6]

Men and women are taught that heterosexual relationships are to be based on a marriage of mutual submission. Mary's Ministries' version of mutual submission, as we saw earlier, is practiced by candidates when they are "joined in a union with Christ" for the day of evangelization—a man is paired with a woman and the two are told they are "wedded" for the day in a "holy marriage." Throughout the day of evangelizing, the two are supposed to demonstrate submission to one another as they go door to door. Some couples even have children added to their "family"; I was paired with Tony and his young niece and nephew for the day, and several other couples also had children as part of their family. We were told that we were "married couples" for the day and that these were our "children." We were instructed to "show our children" what it means to be "married in Christ" that day. The shocked expression on my face when I was given an instant family belied my discomfort, and Estela laughed; looking right at me she told us it was "only for today." In addition to demonstrating Mary's Ministries' stance on marriage and the family, the teams reflect the profound familial hierarchy on which the organization is based: Estela and Reyes are seen as the group's parents, and their children, Little Rey, Armando, Fernando, and the others, are viewed as older and wiser siblings. Faith course candidates rank the lowest in terms of power in the family and are seen as "children" in need of guidance.

This exercise puts into practice the evangelical notion of mutual submission in Christ. Estela is a strong advocate for mutual submission and says that she counsels her daughters-in-law on how to be mutually submissive with their husbands. She tells them that they must trust their husbands enough to discuss their concerns openly with them, and that their husbands in turn should trust and confide in them. Estela interprets mutual submission as essential for strong relationships and marriages because "trust is the basis of a successful relationship."

A more troubling aspect of the Mary's Ministries version of mutual submission is that sometimes women are encouraged to stay with their spouses even during times of abuse. Recall the skit where "Satan" "tempts" a woman to divorce her abusive husband, and how Abel's wife's testimony focused on her supposedly selfish unwillingness to forgive his many transgressions. While there are women in Mary's Ministries who are divorced, and they are welcomed into the community, there is also an underlying message that one should preserve a marriage, even an abusive one, for the sake of the children. Here we see where the family trumps individual—specifically women's—needs and desires. Estela's own self was compromised for her family. Even though she arguably gained a more powerful and prestigious position as a result of her apparitions, she had to make concessions to her spouse and family, and to a certain degree she had to put her own needs last. Estela's gender ideology, reflected in Mary's Ministries rhetoric and in the dynamics and skits outlined earlier in this chapter, emphasize the need for men and women to be mutually respectful and are in line with other contemporary evangelical groups like Aglow, Global Ministries, and the Promise Keepers. For these groups, submission does not equal subjugation, and marriage is likened to a "loving teamwork" in which both members work for the collective good of the marriage and the family.

Like contemporary Protestant evangelical Aglow women, women in Mary's Ministries describe themselves as opposed to feminism per se, but their language incorporates traditional feminist concerns. As Marie Griffith notes, the interpretation of submission has changed within Aglow, and women are speaking more and more of "mutual submission" rather than women's "submission" to men.[7] Women in Mary's Ministries, like the women of Aglow, are encouraged to maintain their marriages, to make them work, and to "submit" to God's will (i.e., to stay married). Yet divorcees are not stigmatized in Aglow or Mary's Ministries.[8] Several of Mary's Ministries' leading women are divorced, but their status as divorcees (all were divorced prior to their participation in the organization) and as Catholics did not hinder their rise to the top of the organization; it is these same women who lead courses in the United States and in Mexico, Chile, Peru, and Guatemala.

Mary's Ministries' "feminist side" encourages women, many of whom have experienced trauma and abuse in their lives and who have never been in a position to delegate authority, to take leadership roles. Unlike women in the contemporary Mexican American evangelical organization Alcance Victoria, who are not allowed to be leaders in the movement, women in Mary's Ministries can and do lead faith courses in and outside the United States.[9] Mexican American women's involvement is crucial to the success of the faith courses, and they participate on many levels. It is Mexican American women who run the kitchen, cook the meals for the faith-course participants, give their testimonies, tend to the children of the participants during the course, and help to clean up after the course. Although both men's and women's work is important to the success of each faith course offered, women perform a wider variety of tasks, contributing their many skills and gifts. Apart from their involvement in the courses, the majority of these women hold down full-time jobs and several are pursuing college degrees.

Leticia Ruiz exemplifies Mary's Ministries' "ideal woman": she regularly gives her testimony at the courses, serves as head cook and organizer of the kitchen crew, helps to tend to the children who have accompanied their parents, and looks after her own children, ranging in age from two to eighteen years. Leticia demonstrates her ability to multitask when she gives her testimony; she manages to entertain youngest sons César and "Nando" (Fernando Jr.) as she speaks about her experiences with Christ and the Blessed Mother. Outside the course, she has a career that keeps her busy, as do most of the women who are involved in Mary's Ministries. A former vice principal at Carl Hayden High School before she was made junior high principal at NFL-YET Youth Academy, Leticia is currently working full-time on her doctorate in education at Arizona State University's main campus in Tempe.

During the faith courses held in Phoenix, Estela Ruiz serves as a role model for Mexican American women. Her intelligence, visionary status, motherhood, and outwardly professed humility are greatly admired by the many Mexican American and the fewer Anglo women who attend. Women are drawn to Estela and seek her company and advice on subjects ranging from marital to child-raising issues. Estela interweaves evangelicalism with liberating messages to the women who take the faith courses and who volunteer their efforts. She simultaneously emphasizes women's duties to their husbands as partners in marriage and the right of women to pursue an education and to succeed in their careers. Estela has been a major influence in Leticia's decision to pursue her doctorate. Yet she cautions women to be careful not to allow their careers to "take over" family and marital life, as hers once did. God, Estela emphasizes, must be foremost in women's minds as they succeed in their careers "in the world" and as mothers and wives—feminist leanings are tempered by evangelical Christian messages. So long as women realize that they must put God first in their lives, she says, everything else will "fall into place."

Even though these women believe the feminist movement hurt relations between men and women and refuse to be called feminists, their language and beliefs have been informed by a feminist-inspired gender ideology. The majority of the women who attend the faith courses have experienced hard times and seek the friendship and comfort of other women. They share similar life histories and are able to discuss the challenges of being a spouse and mother in a supportive environment where they will not be judged. Their problems are alleviated in the space of the faith courses, and while the problems may not simply disappear, these women gain a sense of empowerment through involvement in the courses and are equipped to re-enter family life armed with self-confidence.

Women in Mary's Ministries continue to deal with husbands who "don't do anything around the house" and who are not as dedicated to their spiritual lives as are their wives. But for the most part, the women in this organization do feel a sense of being empowered, and their friendships with men and women have given them a renewed confidence in their abilities. They keep praying for husbands and boyfriends who have not yet found God and are confident that the Holy Spirit will yet "touch their hearts." Most important for these women, they believe that they have an infallible safety net in Jesus and Mary—they are confident that Jesus and Mary will support them and "not give up" on them. When things go awry they do not blame Mary or Jesus; rather, they blame themselves for succumbing to the "Evil One." As the faith course skits demonstrate, the Devil's powers are seductive and wield considerable influence over men and women. Mary and Jesus remain these women's steadfast companions and confidants—they are more loyal than husbands, boyfriends, and friends and will not turn their backs on them.

María L., a divorced mother of three and a single parent, told me during our interview: "You are looking at a miracle. I am one of those conversions that Estela talks about." Describing her life as "a mess" before she became involved with Mary's Ministries, María says she was filled with anger and bitterness toward her alcoholic husband, who spent most of his paycheck on liquor and drugs and who was a "weekend dad," available and sober for his children only on weekends. María's conversion began after she divorced her husband and made her *Cursillo*. When she joined Mary's Ministries in 1992, attracted by the community of faithful believers, she felt as though her life was finally a good one.

The faith courses provide the physical and emotional space for women to heal from the suffering they have endured; they provide a setting where the pain of divorce, the anguish of having children imprisoned or children killed as a result of gang battles can be healed. Women are encouraged to take on a new and important task that will help to reduce their pain, maybe even overcome it, and they willingly dedicate themselves to doing God's and Mary's work. This is not to imply a functionalist argument that religion does "this or that" for women, or to come to easy conclusions and judgments about their faith. These women are doing the best they can to overcome the obstacles and complicated realities of their lives, and they are nourished by the community and fellowship offered them by members of Mary's Ministries. Above all, they learn to surrender their will to God and to place their hearts in Mary's "open arms." Like the evangelical Aglow women, the women of Mary's Ministries understand that inner healing begins with surrendering themselves to Jesus—and, in the case of the Catholic Mary's Ministries, to the Virgin Mary as well.[10] The faith courses allow the space and time for these women to vent their fears and frustrations and to "give it up" to Jesus and Mary.

Each of these women has a conversion story to tell, a story that acknowledges the suffering they have endured but also acknowledges the role they played in their dramas of suffering. These women take responsibility for their actions, and their personal resolve and strength is increased through their involvement in a supportive group. What we are able to see when we look at their narratives is that through their active participation, and in a particular kind of place, women are able to get beyond their pain and are even able to start to feel alive again. These women have all handed over their sin and suffering to Jesus and the Virgin and all say that they feel an incredible relief. As María S., a Mexican mother of four, said, "En este lugar estoy feliz y muy contente. Es possible sentir mejor sobre mis problemas. Gracias a Dios y a la Virgen! Gracias a la familia de Ruizes!" ("In this place, I am happy and very content. It is possible for me to feel better about my life here. Thank you God! Thank you Virgin [Mary]! Thanks to the Ruiz family!")[11] As María's comments indicate, the perceived presence of Jesus and Mary, the familial setting of the faith course, and the Ruiz family all help to create a geographic and spiritual zone in which spiritual healing can take place.

On the one hand, the organization supports "traditional family values," but on the other, it advocates leadership roles for women and men, as well as new outlets for men. Men are able to escape cultural prescriptions of masculinity, machismo, and they are able to play with boundaries—recall the "Two Timothies" skit that featured Johnny and Ricky in pink tutus. An argument can be made for an underlying homophobia, especially given the emphasis on marriage and traditional families, but I have never heard any anti-gay rhetoric used in my many years of fieldwork in South Phoenix. It is clear, however, that traditional, heterosexual marriages are normative in Mary's Ministries. Men are not paired with other men for the day of evangelization—they are always matched with women. What Mary's Ministries enables men to do is to explore various ways of being men, whether it be the embodiment of masculinity that Reyes Sr. upholds, or the "playfulness"—dancing, singing, dressing up—that his sons encourage.

While women's strength is nurtured in the faith course, men are challenged to be more sensitive and openly loving. "Mexican men are taught to be tough and not to show their emotions," Little Rey told me during one of our many conversations. Little Rey's comment contrasts with Jorgé Hernandez Valenzuela's observation that Latin men are inherently more sensitive. While Hernandez Valenzuela sees fewer cultural restrictions on men and, as a result, little or no machismo, Little Rey sees an abundance of machismo in his Mexican American culture. Most of the men I met in Mary's Ministries would agree with Little Rey that they felt bound by expectations—familial and culturally sanctioned—to be "tough" and to not show their emotions. As one male Mary's Ministries members told me, crying in front of your family would be tantamount to "saying that you're a sissy, that you are not a real man."

The faith courses provide men with a safe place where they will be admired, rather than ridiculed, for their honesty. During the week-long faith course, the majority of male participants can be seen crying openly, hugging each other and their "sisters." The Ruiz men set an example for this: Armando, Little Rey, Fernando, and Reyes Sr. can be seen expressing their emotion unabashedly. The various men who "witness" shed tears as well. Abel, who talked about cheating on his wife, had to pause for several moments to place his hand over his eyes and to wipe away the tears. Mañuel also shed some tears as he talked about the difficulties in life and the necessity of learning to depend on God.

This is not to say that publicly baring their souls is easy for the men who attend the course. On the contrary, it takes them a while to become comfortable with crying and hugging, which are usually thought to be "womanly" traits. The course instructs Mexican American men that being in touch with their emotional side is not weak but admirable. Spirituality is equated with the ability to bare one's pain and anguish, and crying is interpreted positively by observers. This message is in open contradiction to what is considered typical Mexican male attitudes and may be seen as a subtle (and at times not-so-subtle) message to men of Mexican heritage that they need to reform their ways. Those with "hard hearts" need to have them "melted" by the Virgin. The course dynamics, which have been designed to enable the participants to "let their guards down," help to facilitate the transition from macho manliness to a more sensitive image of manhood.

The rhetorics of submission we hear in a Mary's Ministries faith course underline what Judith Stacey calls the "curious amalgam" of evangelical Christian and postfeminist discourse. The messages Mary's Ministries men are taught parallel those heard at evangelical Promise Keeper (PK) rallies. Men in both organizations are instructed to "surrender their egos" to their wives and to be loving husbands and fathers; they are also told to reclaim, to "take back" their role as the head of the family. As is outlined in PK literature, men are encouraged to sit down with their wives, to apologize for giving the husband's role to them, and to take back the role. There is to be "no compromise": PK men are to be "sensitive" and "loving" toward their wives, but they are to take back the role as family patriarch.[12] Promise Keepers literature and rhetoric provides a complicated discourse on gender; men are to be sensitive and loving, and at the same time to be strong and uncompromising leaders of their family.[13] Like the PK rallies that, as the sociologist Michael Messner writes, give men "permission . . . to relax the masculine posturing with one's self and with other men," the faith courses offer a safe haven for emotional outpourings. Mary's Ministries faith courses are part of this larger "Christian masculinity therapy" emphasis in contemporary evangelical groups like PK and the larger, loosely aligned men's movement.[14]

Mary's Ministries faith courses also adhere to the "curious amalgam" of evangelical Christianity and postfeminist thought. As in PK, the dynamics, testimonies, and lessons provided encourage men to reclaim their roles as husbands and as fathers and to be more loving toward their wives and children.[15] While the two organizations share some basic evangelical and gendered concerns, Mary's Ministries infuses more "feminism" into its be- liefs and practices, the organization is co-ed, and it is headed by several prominent women who also have careers. In the way that his wife serves as an example of a strong, resourceful woman who is devoted to her husband and family, Reyes Ruiz Sr. represented, during his lifetime, the type of manhood that is encouraged in the faith course. Reyes stood for the move-ment's "ideal Mexican man." Even when he was sick with cancer, Reyes maintained an active, physical life and was the one responsible for main-taining the shrine and all of the backyard foliage, in addition to the physi-cal plant of the school. He talked openly of his former involvement with Arizona and southwestern farmworkers, the bricklaying business he started in the 1960s, and the many miles he traveled with his wife to spread the news of Mary and God. He was proud of his physical and spiritual ac-complishments, and he saw the two areas as complementary—he believed that strong bodies were ideally vessels for strong spirits. His skin bronzed to a dark brown from the many hours he had spent in the sun, Reyes was a masculine male yet a man who cried openly in his love for "*la mujer bonita*" and for Jesus.

Bobby also represents the masculine but sensitive manhood Mary's Ministries encourages. His muscular arms are exposed by the tight-fitting black T-shirts he wears, imprinted with sayings such as "The Lord's Gym: His Pain Your Gain." Bobby is active in the Ministries and gives his testi-mony without shame in his determination to show others that there is hope for everyone: if he, a man who was divorced from his first wife be-cause he cheated on her, can be converted, anyone can. Bobby says that he relates to the painting of Jesus holding the emotionally and physically bereft sinner, the one displayed to faith course candidates on the fifth evening, because he, too, was broken inside. This visual imagery encourages male faith course candidates especially to relate to Jesus. And Abel, a self-professed "macho" who never used to show his emotions, says he has undergone a "radical transformation." Whereas he was once a man "with a heart of stone," his heart has been "melted by Our Lady" and he can now cry openly for his love of God. Like the evangelical Protestant PKs, Reyes Sr. and Bobby combine earlier, turn-of-the-century muscular Christianity with a more feminized Christianity that lets them be men and cry at the same time.[16] Mary's Ministries men are "postmasculinist" in the way that the women are "postfeminist": they combine traditional gendered beliefs (men as heads of households) with more progressive beliefs, such as that their wives should have intellectually fulfilled lives. In yet another way, the organization confounds easy categorization as "conservative" or "liberal."

By participating in Mary' Ministries, Mexican American men can "reform" their machismo, to use the anthropologist Elizabeth Brusco's terminology; they can maintain their manhood, save their marriages, and live a life of Christ. There has been little written about the impact of culturally constructed machismo and Mexican American men, gender and emotions. Much of what has been written presents machismo as an almost essentialist, biologically derived trait—that Mexican men are a priori macho. Based on my own fieldwork in South Phoenix, it strikes me as more likely that machismo is a culturally derived concept that is as hotly contested by Mexican American men and women as it is accepted. Most men with whom I spoke talked openly about the desire to seem publicly "tough" and about the difficulty of maintaining the image of manliness. Most men, although they grew up seeing their mothers cry openly, rarely saw their fathers cry; and they were instilled with the idea that it is weak to show one's emotions as a man, that it is a feminine trait to cry to *la Virgen de Guadalupe*, for example. According to the historian George J. Sánchez, the positive side of machismo refers to physical courage, integrity, cleverness, wealth, health, land and cattle, and manliness. Yet, as he notes, there is a destructive side to machismo that is "a result of the breakdown of community control, a situation which better characterized the growing urban centers and the northern border communities."[17] It is this "destructive" aspect that most men and women I interviewed recognized and with which they identified.

Brusco's insights are useful for understanding the gender dynamics of the faith courses in relation to evangelicalism and the impact these courses have on men's and women's relationships. She argues that evangelicalism offers a means for women to reform their mens' behavior, that these women wield considerable influence on their marriage and home life by encouraging their husbands' participation in and eventual conversion to evangelical Christianity.[18] Her argument is seconded by Luís Léon, who writes that evangelicalism provides Hispanic women with the power to "manipulate the physical world through prayer."[19] As *evangelicos,* these women are given direct access to God, whom they implore to cure their husbands of alcoholism and abuse, and their prayers are said to receive responses.[20] Mary's Ministries women are strong-willed and consciously work on their husbands' macho ways. They will publicly tease their men when they think they are "acting up," and they do so in the company of other women. Men are also aware of their machismo; men like Abel openly admit that they were "typically macho" before their conversion experience and their involvement in Mary's Ministries as a way of keeping macho tendencies in check.

The male sensitivity displayed and encouraged throughout the faith courses is patterned after an image of a manly and gentle Jesus Christ. As the Virgin of Guadalupe and the Virgin of the Americas are on display as strong and loving women, Jesus is displayed as a compassionate and humble man who willingly embraces suffering. One of the backyard shrine's centerpieces is a twenty-foot-high wooden crucifix, carved by Reyes Sr., on which a bloodied Christ has his arms outstretched. A small sign attached to the crucifix reads "I love you this much." Christ's arms are stretched far, taut, and his kneecaps are bloody. The skin covering his ribs is stretched thin, and the crown of thorns atop his head cuts into the flesh and hair. Christ's body and his immense suffering are made real and are a palpable presence in the Ruizes' backyard. Men are asked to embrace suffering as Christ did, to combine his gentleness with his willingness to take on great burdens.[21] A "real man" suffers for his wife, family, Jesus, and Mary.

Yet the focus of Mary's Ministries is ultimately on redemption, not suffering, and on Mary's ability to heal her children's pain. The language, skits, and various other "dynamics" employed at the faith courses point to classic evangelicalism, yet we also see the overlap in Mary's Ministries of evangelical and Catholic identities. Mary's Ministries ultimately wants it both ways—it wants to remain faithful to the Catholic Church while it borrows from evangelicals' successes. It fashions a Catholic evangelicalism and claims that it is the Virgin Mary herself who demands this syncretism of faiths.

* 5 *

Catholic Evangelization
Fighting "Fire with Fire"

The faith courses, detailed in the previous chapter, have taken shape as a result of the Ruiz family's reactions to the major inroads of evangelical Protestantism in the past decade. The family acknowledges that the Church "does not always do enough" for Hispanics, and Mary's Ministries attempts to rectify these institutional oversights by redefining what it means to be Catholic and by staying connected with the specific needs of the Hispanic community. The religious historian Gastón Espinoza notes Hispanics' mass movement away from the Catholic church, calling it a "religious revolution" and a "seismic shift in Hispanic religiosity."[1] Mary's Ministries' leaders and members are aware of and are alarmed by this trend and hope to bridge the gap—linguistically, theologically, ethnically—between Catholic and Pentecostal/evangelical Protestant outreach at the same time that they strive to reclaim Catholics who have left to join Pentecostal churches.

The organization has recently turned to the rapid rate of Hispanic Catholic conversions to Pentecostalism (United States Southwest and the Americas more generally) and to the Church of Jesus Christ Latter Day Saints (primarily in Latin America). They "fight fire with fire," to use Armando Ruiz's language, by incorporating into their faith course and their everyday language elements of evangelical belief and fiery and passionate rhetoric. The organization's ambivalence—simultaneous admiration and loathing—toward evangelical Protestantism is apparent in Armando's statement: "I see the Mormons and the Pentecostals all throughout the Americas and I see how well they are evangelizing. I remember sitting on a bus in Lima, and seeing a group of Mormon missionaries get on; I asked myself, 'what are Catholics doing for young people?' My issue with Mormon and Pentecostal evangelizers is that they don't seek the truth."[2]

Armando clearly admires the success Mormons and Pentecostals have had, yet he says he is deeply disturbed by what both groups are saying in order to gain converts. He elaborated during one of my recent visits: "The evangelicals have a clear plan as to how they want to weaken the Catholic Church. They offer the people jobs, money, and a prosperity theology. But they also lie, they say 'here's what Catholics are doing wrong,' and they say that we Catholics put Mary on the same plane as Jesus and say that we *worship* Jesus and the saints. They have caused many, many ruptures in Latin American kinship . . . and we see it in the United States, too."

Armando here highlights the feeling among Mary's Ministries' members that they are under siege from Pentecostals and other evangelicals, whom they interpret as enticing Catholics away from the "true" religion, the Catholic Church. Fighting what Armando acknowledges is a "tough fight," Mary's Ministries members borrow heavily from Protestant Pentecostal language and dynamic style of worship and praise to keep Catholics within the fold of the "true Church." As we were able to hear in Abel's and Terésa's testimonies in chapter 4, the faith courses incorporate a Pentecostal focus on spiritual healing, conversion, testimony, and the Holy Spirit. Mary's Ministries simultaneously borrows and eschews Pentecostal and Protestant evangelizing methods and language.

What many South Phoenix Hispanics, as well as those in Latin America, believe is lacking in their Catholic Church, and what they desire, is a community that preaches and encourages a radical conversion experience, a personal relationship with Christ, and social reform. For its part, Mary's Ministries attempts to fulfill these demands for evangelicalism while maintaining its Catholic identity.[3] The Ruizes were well aware of Protestant denominations' successes with Mexicans when they contacted Jorge Arturo Hernandez Valenzuela in 1993 to ask him to help plan a faith course for their fledgling South Phoenix organization. They knew that Jorge was "their man" because of his success with the Vatican's evangelization efforts in Mexico—Hernandez Valenzuela has been the official liaison for the Vatican's evangelization programs in Guadalajara, Mexico, since 1990. By the time the Ruizes contacted him, he had proven himself a successful coordinator of evangelization programs in Mexico. He helped parishes throughout his country incorporate methods of their *evangelico* neighbors; parish priests worked with him to establish programs that would facilitate the kinds of personal encounters with Christ that they were having in Protestant faith settings. Hernandez Valenzuela accepted the Ruizes' offer and met with them October 1993 for an "intense" week-end in which the small group helped plan the seven-day faith course.

Like the Ruizes, Hernandez Valenzuela believes that the courses have a special appeal to Hispanics. This conviction is fueled by a belief in racially and ethnically based emotional "passions" that predispose Hispanics to intense religious experiences. He told me during one of our interviews that Hispanics are "just right" for the faith courses because "Latin cultures are more sensitive, they have more passion and are more open to expressing their feelings and showing love." He believes that South Phoenix, because it has a large Hispanic (Mexican American) population, is a "perfect" place to hold faith courses; and he has high hopes for the success of Mary's Ministries faith course communities in Latin America. Hernandez Valenzuela offers a racial essentialism that dovetails with Reyes Sr.'s belief, illustrated in chapter 4, that Mexicans and Mexican Americans are the race chosen by God.

Mary's Ministries is an example of what the religious historian James Davidson Hunter calls a "religiously based special agenda organization" that has clear denominational commitments. It is also part of the "small group movement" in the United States and what Robert Wuthnow calls Americans' "quest" for a meaningful community.[4] The Ruizes and Mary's Ministries members believe that they can make greater inroads, bring "more people to God," by maintaining their own group outside of, yet affiliated with the Catholic Church. By running their own organization, they can avoid having the Church "take it over," and, just as important, they can reach out to Hispanics. Little Rey has told me on several occasions that the Church tends to "take over" popular Catholic movements that prove successful with Hispanics. Yet he also acknowledges, as do family members, that institutional Catholic support is crucial for the ultimate success of Mary's Ministries.

The Ruizes and others in Mary's Ministries are aware that many in the Catholic Church are resistant to the more charismatic and evangelical forms of devotion and piety that are central to their organization and think it is not "Catholic." Yet the Ruizes are confident that it is the evangelicalism of their courses that attracts the Hispanic contingent they desire. Organizations like Mary's Ministries reflect the late-twentieth-century denominational move toward partisan organizations; it is broadly ecumenical, addressing issues that are of concern both to conservative Catholics and Protestant evangelicals. This organization strives to evangelize the Americas for the Virgin, and in order to do so successfully it incorporates those evangelical elements that have proven so effective in the Americas. Specifically, Mary's Ministries borrows heavily from the *Cursillo de Christianidad* movement and Charismatic Catholicism—it "fights" Protestant evangelizing by employing similar Catholic evangelization tactics to win souls for Jesus and Mary.

The Cursillo Influence

The popular *Cursillo* movement, lay-inspired and lay-originated, is focused on an intensive three-day course that provides an "in-depth discussion of the fundamentals of the Christian message and their relationship to the modern world."[5] Participants, called *cursillistas,* expect to have a conversion experience in which they are brought to a closer and deeper relationship with Jesus Christ and the Church. Although the Catholic Church now sponsors *Cursillos,* the movement, introduced in the United States in 1957 in Waco, Texas, was begun by laity. The goal of establishing a closer relationship with the Church is reinforced during and after completion of the course, and follow-up meetings, *Ultreyas,* help to sustain the conversion experience and to perpetuate the "extended family network" among the *cursillistas.*[6] Arguably more important than establishing a connection and commitment to the Church is renewing one's personal relationship with Christ. The primary significance of the *Cursillos* is that they enable Mexican American lay men and women to participate in the Catholic faith in a way that was not available to them before—enable them to "bare their souls to other men," making "the telling of sins in the confessional much easier."[7] The *Cursillo* is a spiritual retreat that takes place at an officially designated *Cursillo* center, at a church, or in a church-approved place such as *cursillistas'* homes.[8]

The confessional aspects of the *Cursillo* are clearly present in Mary's Ministries courses, where emotional testimonials are prominent and important components. And like the *Cursillo* movement, Mary's Ministries faith courses stress traditional Catholic instruction on morality and doctrine. Both courses offer Catholic teachings, but their primary emphasis is on encouraging direct and personal relationships with Jesus Christ. In *Cursillos,* Mexican American men are given the opportunity to experience faith in a new way; as the historian of Mexican American religions Gilberto Hinojosa emphasizes, they are able to overcome their unwillingness to share their inner thoughts and feelings and can express themselves in a safe and nurturing environment. And, according to the religious scholar George Kramer, one of the most significant aspects of *Cursillos* is that they allow for this "process of safe self-disclosure."[9] *Cursillos* were from the beginning a way Mexican American men could establish a relationship with Christ; by the mid-1960s, they were also a way of renewing relationships with the Church. The *Cursillo* movement began as a male-only movement, but when Mexican American men began to manifest changes in their lives, their wives wanted to have the same experience. As a result, *Cursillos* for women began to be offered in the 1960s.

All of the Ruiz family members, in addition to the majority of the faith-course graduate volunteers and candidates, have "made" their *Cursillo* and tell stories of religious renewal and spiritual awakening as a result of their experiences throughout the three days. Most of the Mexican American men and women I interviewed said that they had "made" a *Cursillo* and that the experience was the first step in their spiritual renewal. Many said it helped pave the way for the faith course they later took. These men and women remain involved in the greater Phoenix *Cursillo* network and both sponsor and lead *Cursillos*. Estela and Reyes were active *cursillistas* in the 1970s, and for most of his adult life Reyes helped lead Phoenix *Cursillos*. The faith course candidates/*cursillistas* with whom I spoke all told of reconnecting with the Catholic Church, strengthening their relationships with Christ, and seeing an improvement in their daily existence. Each cited "making" the *Cursillo* as a necessary step in renewing his/her faith and beginning a relationship with Christ. Making a *Cursillo* is seen as both a precursor to the conversion experience and the actual conversion experience itself. In either case, making a *Cursillo* was spoken of as a watershed in the course of spiritual preparation for accepting Christ into one's life.

Mary's Ministries faith courses draw on the larger *Cursillo* tradition and share its fundamental concerns. Both emphasize a personal relationship with Christ, living one's faith as an apostolic witness, and joining a community centered on serving and witnessing Christ. The role of the Virgin of Guadalupe also links *Cursillos* and Mary's Ministries faith courses and underlines their shared Hispanic identities. In the faith courses, Guadalupe plays a prominent role and is invoked (most clearly by Reyes Sr.) as the "evangelizer of the Americas"; she is the mother to the *mestizo* Mexican Americans. Guadalupe is also the acknowledged patron saint of *Cursillos* for Phoenix Mexican American *cursillistas,* and *cursillistas* can borrow a statue, which is available "*ofrecen palanca por el éxito de los próx-imos Cursillos, y por la perseverancia de todos los Cursillistas*" (to make an offering for the success of future *Cursillos,* for the perseverance of all *cursillistas* and for the blessing for their own families").[10] Guadalupe's role as the mother of Mexicans, protectress, facilitator to religious experience, and evangelizer is invoked in the language of faith courses and in *Cursillo* literature.

The two courses offer different gendered settings for seeking spiritual conversion and renewal: while *Cursillos* offer time and space for individuals at same-sex retreats, Mary's Ministries members who sponsor the courses encourage men, women, and families to attend together. Separate *Cursillos* are given for men and women, "to avoid the distraction of sex."[11] These gender codes support the belief that concerns of the world and of the body can impede an individual's spiritual union with Christ. Each man and woman has a "sponsor" who helps prepare him/her for the weekend experience and who celebrates with the new *cursillista* when the retreat ends; women are able to "bond" emotionally and spiritually with other women, and men with other men. The gendered realities of the courses carry over into the National Secretariat of the Cursillo Movement's recommendations to couples: although wives/girlfriends are not forbidden from making their *Cursillos* before their husbands/boyfriends, the men are encouraged to make theirs first and for wives to follow, as the man is to be the spiritual head of his family.

In contrast to the separation of the sexes at *Cursillo* retreats, the faith courses strongly encourage a commingling of the sexes and of families. Men and women, husbands and wives, children, and even grandparents are able—and heartily encouraged—to take the Mary's Ministries course together. Members of the Ministries prefer for the husband and wife, girlfriend and boyfriend to attend together to facilitate spiritual growth as an individual and as a couple. Little Rey, Norma, Reyes Sr., and other faith course organizers have all said that it is almost better not to attend the faith course than to attend without one's significant other, because, as Little Rey said, "one will be ahead of the other spiritually." Husbands and wives are encouraged to bring their children, as they are considered a vital part of the couple's spiritual life. Child care is available for young children at all of the faith courses, so that, as Little Rey says, "there are no excuses" for a couple not to come. Thus, while *Cursillos* focus on the individual's spirituality, the faith courses promote familial spirituality.

Charismatic and Catholic

Just as it is deeply influenced by the *Cursillo* Movement, Mary's Ministries is also directly informed by the Charismatic Catholic movement, which has its origins in the late 1960s. Mary's Ministries has had an important friend in the Ruizes' spiritual advisor, Father Charles "Charlie" Goraieb, priest of St. Catherine of Siena parish since 1998. A Charismatic Catholic since 1975 and a *cursillista*, Father Charlie was one of the first parish priests in Phoenix to offer a Mary's Ministries faith course, in St. Charles Borromeo parish in Glendale in 1994. Father Charlie sees evangelization as the key charismatic component of Mary's Ministries, and as offering the possibility of a "richer, deeper experience of Christ" that is a hallmark of Pentecostalism and the charismatic movement. He thinks the group's success is based on a combination of charismatic, Catholic, and Marian beliefs that all go back to the Second Vatican Council's openness to Catholics' "experiencing the Body of Christ in their daily lives." Father Charlie's observations point to the ways in which Mary's Ministries confounds a conservative-liberal dichotomy.

As the anthropologist Thomas Csordas notes, the 1960s Second Vatican Council's position on the "theoretical possibility of 'charisms' or 'spiritual gifts'" helped to pave the way for the adoption of Pentecostal phenomena in the Catholic Church.[12] Among its many reforms, the postconciliar, Vatican II Church opened the door to experiences that were akin to Protestant evangelicals' being overcome by the Holy Spirit. These new "Pentecostal Catholics," as they were called, promised "a dramatic renewal of Church life based on a born-again spirituality of 'personal relationship' with Jesus . . . and direct access to divine power and inspiration through a variety of 'spiritual gifts' or 'charisms.'"[13] Pentecostal and "neo-Pentecostal" emphases on healing, being "slain in the Spirit," and direct access to Christ are central to Mary's Ministries faith courses. The faith courses promote a central Catholic Charismatic belief that a "dramatic renewal" of Church life is possible if the individual forms a personal relationship with Christ as well as a "direct access to divine power and inspiration" through spiritual gifts.[14] What distinguishes Charismatics from other Christians, according to the sociologist of religions Mary Jo Neitz, is their "direct experience of God in their lives. . . . God, for them, is not the Prime Mover or the First Cause or even an old man with a beard rising on a cloud."[15]

For Mary's Ministries members, God intervenes in their daily lives and is perceived as always being "there for them," whenever they need him. Just as most members have made a *Cursillo,* many members have taken the Charismatic "Life in the Spirit" seminar, the seven-week, one-session-a-week Charismatic initiation rite that provides both "indoctrination and a controlled setting for the Baptism of the Holy Spirit."[16] Those who have not taken the seminar, as is often the case with younger members, are at least familiar with charismatic principles.

Mary's Ministries' seven-day faith courses are similar in design and intent to the "Life in the Spirit" seminars, which consist of four sessions that focus on the "basic Christian message of salvation" and the meaning of "baptism in the Holy Spirit." The fifth session is devoted to prayer, and newcomers have hands laid on them and are baptized in the Holy Spirit; the last two weeks of the seminar are "oriented toward further growth in the Life of the Spirit."[17] Aside from their structural similarities, both the Seminar and the courses involve worshippers' bodies. The dancing, singing, swaying, and clapping that are integral to faith course dynamics are important components of "Life in the Spirit" seminars. Call and response, a classic Pentecostal form of worship and praise, is incorporated in both faith courses and seminars: a leader praises Jesus and audience members respond in turn with a hearty "Praise Jesus" or "Thank you Jesus." [18] We are able to see this call and response pattern of praise most clearly in the faith courses. Recall Fernie, dressed as Jesus, and his initiation of call and response with the faith course candidates.

The faith courses also assert the Pentecostal/Charismatic emphasis on needing to be "born again": the candidates are asked to demonstrate their desire to be one with Christ when they crawl under the rope, for example. Candidates, as we saw in chapter 4, are likened to "babies" and "newborns," and after they go under the rope they are "new initiates" in Christ's family. The men and women who crawl under the rope get sweaty and muddy—they are experiencing the literal mess of birth and the wonder of new life when they join their brothers and sisters on the other side of the rope.

Almost all of the middle-aged members and leaders of Mary's Ministries were influenced by Charismatic Catholicism as adults and were initiated in its "Life in the Spirit" seminars. Faith-course candidates are taught how to "invite" the Holy Spirit when they pray with others, and they are told they can be graced with gifts as well if they surrender themselves to the Holy Spirit. The majority of Mary's Ministries members claim to have experienced the power of the Holy Spirit; they have been baptized through the gifts of tongues and tears and experience a new fullness of life in the Spirit. A "softening of the heart" is cited as necessary for the arrival of gifts to a person. Once the "intellectual barrier," as Estela calls it, that inhibits and prevents the acceptance of the Holy Spirit is dissolved, the person can begin to ready his or her heart for the arrival of the Holy Spirit. As with charismatic groups, a goal of the faith courses is to facilitate a connectedness between the "heart" and the "mind" so that the two are joined.

What connects Mary's Ministries faith courses to the Charismatic movement most strikingly is the emphasis placed on testimony in the courses, which the sociologist of religion Meredith McGuire observes is "the most fundamental aspect" of the initiation process into a new life with Christ.[19] Giving one's testimony during the faith course is tantamount to "arriving" at a new life with Christ and the Virgin Mary, as Rey Jr., Terésa, Abel, and Rosa María tell us through their testimonies. Testimonies, or "witnessing," almost always draw clear and sharp distinctions between the before/old life and the after/new life, and the men and women who give them speak freely of their sinful ways before they knew Christ. The process of giving a testimony invites not only the audience's attention but also its participation. The person giving the testimony has been taught how to do so at a Paul course, the follow-up to the faith courses that teaches graduates how to evangelize and how to lead their own faith courses. As we saw in chapter 4, the testimony-giver looks to the members of the audience for their response, hoping that they will relate to the story from their own experiences.

Mary's Ministries' incorporation of Charismatic elements into its faith courses is one way it attempts to appeal to people across racial, ethnic, and class boundaries. One of the appeals of Charismatic Protestantism in Latin America has been its leveling of social, economic, and racial determinants: Charismatic religion in Latin America appeals to the poor and the dispossessed who have been ignored or at the very least disappointed by the Catholic Church. Like these movements, Mary's Ministries appeals primarily to Catholic Hispanics but it focuses on the middle class—those Mexican Americans who are educated and, like the Ruiz family, are dealing with the very real tensions of living in-between Mexican and American realities. What Mary's Ministries hopes to accomplish is to motivate middle-class Mexican Americans and Hispanics who feel dispossessed to "go out and make a difference" in their communities.

Creating a Community

The men and women involved in Mary's Ministries have all undergone personal transformations and spiritual conversions, and they cite the community as a major reason for their continued involvement. As Abel's wife emphasized during her testimonial, being part of something "bigger than myself" gives her strength. The support she has received from her brothers and sisters in the organization has enabled her faith to flourish because she is surrounded by a new family who believes in the saving power of Jesus Christ, the love and compassion of the Virgin Mary, and the gifts of the Holy Spirit. Through the faith courses, men and women are able to find self-worth and a deep and meaningful connection with others that they have not experienced before. During the faith courses and through their interaction with each other, participants become a part of a new family, one with God as father and Mary as mother.

The vast majority of men and women involved in Mary's Ministries and the candidates who participate in the courses have experienced much suffering in their lives. They are the victims of abuse, the parents of gang members, and single parents who have struggled and are trying to raise their children on their own. They have caused pain and suffering; they have cheated on and abused their spouses; they have been addicted to drugs and alcohol. Many come to Mary's Ministries in despair, hoping for a radical personal transformation. In short, these men and women have all felt a profound detachment from their families, their culture, and their society; they are looking for healing, seeking a place where they can repent and have a fresh start. Mary's Ministries offers a spiritual and physical place where renewal can begin and where these men and women can return to a feeling of connectedness once again. In other words, Mary's Ministries helps to make suffering sufferable.

Men and women are able to openly discuss their problems and are encouraged to hand themselves over to Jesus and the Virgin Mary, who love them "no matter what." Along with the goal of helping participants establish closer relationships with Christ and Mary and with a new network of individuals comes another goal: to enable Mexican Americans and others to cope with the many challenges of urban living. Mary's Ministries faith courses in South Phoenix reflect the complexity of ethnicity, race, and religion, which converge most strikingly in the urban United States. Mexican Americans living in South Phoenix encounter the dominant Anglo culture on a daily basis and participate in this larger culture, of which they are a part, with varying degrees of success. The Ruiz family is well-educated and middle-class, and this status, which many Anglo Americans take for granted, has been hard-won. Estela and Reyes made sacrifices to educate their children at Catholic schools and to send them to universities. Their accomplishments make them stand out in their community in South Phoenix. Poverty, violence, broken families, and the schools' high dropout rate continue to affect Mexican American families in alarming propor-tions, and South Phoenix seems to be removed both geographically and socially from the wealthy, Anglo-dominated world of downtown Phoenix, just a few miles away.

Despite the fact that Anglos and Mexican Americans live in the same cities, social, economic, linguistic, religious, and racial barriers continue to divide the groups and to prevent meaningful interaction. The faith courses are set up to foster in Anglo participants an increased awareness and un-derstanding of Mexican American culture, and in Mexican American par-ticipants increased accessibility to Anglos. The majority of Mary's Min-istries members are Mexican American, and the majority of courses offered in the United States are sponsored by parishes with a predomi-nantly Mexican/Hispanic parishioners (South Phoenix, Safford, Chicago, San Antonio, Hawaii, Mexico, Central and South America). Yet courses have also been offered in "white" U.S. parishes in such communities as Madison, Wisconsin, and overseas in England and Ireland. By the end of the week, the once rigid boundaries between these two seemingly different cultures have become more permeable, and a connectedness to the "Other" is made real for both Mexican Americans and Anglos. The Anglo participants with whom I have spoken all cite "getting to know" Mexican American culture as one of the reasons for taking the courses; they were all sensitive to cultural diversity and recognized their own "whiteness," as many of them put it. The primary motivation for Anglos who take the courses, however, is to renew their relationships with Christ and the Catholic Church. They are attracted to the Charismatic, evangelical as-pects of the courses and see them as a way to reinvigorate their Catholic faith. In addition, most of the Anglo faith course participants, like the His-panic candidates, are Marianists and believe in the apparitions to Estela.

Faith course activities also introduce Mexican culture to Anglos in a safe environment, one in which personal and communal growth is en-couraged. The course dynamics work toward minimizing the many barri-ers that separate Mexicans and Anglos, and the walls are weakened little by little throughout the week. The various course activities address the universal concerns, desires, and hopes of the participants, creating an arena of equal opportunity for those involved. Even María S., a middle-aged Mexican woman who is shy around Anglos and self-conscious of her poverty and inability to speak English, said that she felt *"muy comodo,"* very comfortable, at the faith course and thought of her fellow candidates as *"familia."* Mary's Ministries members work hard to establish the family atmosphere that is so important to María; the goal is for members of Mary's Ministries in Phoenix to feel just as comfortable with their "brothers and sisters" in Hawaii, or in Chile, or in any of their locations.

Of course, during the process of building a community, problems do arise. Disagreements arise among some members, women get testy with one another in the kitchen, each used to running her own. Generally speaking, the fatigue Mary's Ministries members experience after an intense week of courses and evangelization can lead to short tempers. One woman in particular complained to me about her husband doing "nothing" around the house that week, even though they were both heavily involved in the faith course events. Others were irritated that they were doing "more work" than others at the course and were "tired of it." These tensions are normal; in a place so full of expectation, so replete with emotion, tempers will flare, spouses will disagree, and children will misbehave.

This barrio-based Hispanic Catholic evangelizing community signals a new direction in American Catholicism, one that reflects how laity are shaping twenty-first-century Catholicism. Mary's Ministries' faith courses combine Catholic rituals, beliefs, and symbols with Hispanic Catholics' needs and desires, blurring the boundaries between "official" and "popular" Catholicism. It is a lay-driven organization that incorporates Protestant evangelical enthusiasm, the desire for a personal relationship with Jesus, and language of conversion. As we saw with Abel's and Terésa's testimonies, the men and women involved in Mary's Ministries are *católicos* as well as *evangélicos*—they are both Catholic and evangelical. At a Mary's Ministries faith course, we are able to witness a Catholicism that blends evangelical Protestantism with both pre–and post–Vatican II Catholicism—classic Catholic devotionalism meets charismatic Catholicism. And, through their efforts, Mary's Ministries' leaders and members hope to bridge the gap, linguistically, theologically, and ethnically, between Catholic and Pentecostal/evangelical Protestant outreach as they strive to reclaim Catholics who have left for Pentecostal churches. Yet although it incorporates Protestant evangelical beliefs and language, Mary's Ministries ultimately views these evangelicals as competitors for lost souls.

In addition to its focus on men's and women's spirits, Mary's Ministries also addresses Mexican Americans' social, economic, and educational concerns. Through its sister organization, ESPIRITU Community Development, these needs are addressed and promoted—all the while with the acknowledgment that without"healthy spirits" no real gains can be made. ESPIRITU employees see themselves as warriors for Mary and are corporate evangelizers, spreading their faith in the "secular" realms of society.

* 6 *

Corporate Evangelizers
A Family's "Vision" for South Phoenix

Estela Ruiz's Marian piety and the messages she believes she receives from the Blessed Mother are the center around which the Ruiz family and their Catholic evangelizing group, Mary's Ministries, work, and this is unique among Marian visionaries and their families. Nowhere else do we find a grassroots Marian-inspired Catholic and evangelical organization that is based on a visionary's and her family's and community's interpretations. Estela and her family members all say that if the Blessed Mother had not appeared to Estela, Mary's Ministries and its offshoot, ESPIRITU Community Development Corporation (ESPIRITU, ECDC), would not exist, because it was she who was the "inspiration" for all of their religious and social endeavors. Although the Ruiz family is happy to speak of their individual conversions, they are even more eager to discuss the community-based initiatives they have launched, such as the charter school, the community homes, and the Catholic evangelizing community, Mary's Ministries. They take no personal credit for their many accomplishments and successes and cite the Virgin's appearances as their inspiration. According to Rey Ruiz Jr., "Little Rey," "The Virgin has taught us that we should never keep God to ourselves, we need to share the Blessed Mother and Her Father with others." And, according to Estela, "we just need to grab ahold to the Blessed Mother's mantle and she will show us what we need to do to make this world a better place."

Fueled by their evangelical and Catholic religious convictions, members of the Ruiz family, along with a group of South Phoenix community leaders, met in the early 1990s to address the neighborhood violence, high school dropout rates, and crime that was "killing the children's souls," as one of the participants put it. After a series of meetings held at a local diner, and after sketching their ideas out on paper napkins, they decided to form a community action branch of Mary's Ministries, a nonprofit group they named ESPIRITU. Specific concerns raised at the first meeting included the then-recent merging of several major banks, which was seen to have a potentially negative impact on community reinvestment issues, and the lack of strategy for community responses.[1]

The major catalyst to the formation of the nonprofit group, however, went deeper than economic concerns; it was a rash of gang-related deaths and violence that motivated residents to action in the Ruizes' South Phoenix neighborhood and others nearby. "We were sitting around one night," Armando Ruiz said, "and we counted the number of kids whose funeral we had attended lately . . . we counted 36."[2] Armando and the rest of ECDC's founders were deeply troubled by what they perceived as the "hopelessness" experienced by area children and residents, and by the escalating violence that reflected the overall stagnation and decline of their community. When Armando and Fernando Ruiz, Francis Castillo, Margaret Abril, Tommy Espinoza, and other local Mexican American businessmen and women met in 1993, the result was "Project Americas," an ECDC project so named because the group "felt this could be a model development plan for low-income urban and rural areas in all of North, South, and Central America."[3] ECDC was to be the vehicle through which the plan of enabling families to "better determine their own destiny" could be realized. At one meeting the group wrote ESPIRITU's mission statement, which encompasses developing "the human capital of a community by self-empowering our youth"; forming partnerships between private and government sectors and low-income communities; and "spiritually and economically empowering communities."[4] According to Armando, the group's primary goal is for communities to acquire a "value system that empowers them with the ability to determine and take control and ownership of their own destinies."[5]

A close examination of ESPIRITU shows how locally based Hispanic organizations can combine both local and global perspectives toward the goal of reforming neighborhoods, and how they consciously build on and perpetuate the rich history of Mexican American ethnic identity and activism in the United States. ESPIRITU's mission is to work toward community development and urban reform in South Phoenix. It is ultimately a business for God and the Virgin Mary, and the Ruizes and their associates are businessmen and women who infuse their work with a divine purpose. These men and women are corporate evangelizers who see themselves as "called" by the Virgin Mary. They are inspired by Mary's messages, which challenge them to undertake religious and social reform in their immediate community and throughout the rest of the Americas. Although their immediate goal is to purge South Phoenix of drugs, gangs, and violence, their long-term goal is to establish a "community of saints" of Catholic evangelicals who are committed to urban reform.

"Called" to Reform the City

Armando Ruiz has been ESPIRITU's president and incorporator from the beginning. His political background as an outspoken Democratic state legislator and aid to former governor Fife Symington, along with his numerous political contacts and his past directorship of the South Mountain YMCA and of YMCA-affiliated at-risk youth programs, made him the unanimous choice for president.[6] Though he is best known throughout the state for his political initiatives, Armando says that he learned his greatest lessons not from politicians but "from God," whom he felt was "calling him" to implement a profound change in his own life and in his community.

In the early 1990s, as director of the South Mountain YMCA in South Phoenix, Armando helped raise the funds for the completion of the new complex south of Baseline Avenue, as well as the restoration of the original Southern Avenue facility. He then went to work for Symington for a year and a half as coordinator of neighborhood revitalization in Phoenix.[7] It was during this time that Armando was undergoing what he describes as his "spiritual conversion." He was greatly influenced by his mother Estela's visions of the Virgin Mary, he says, which caused him "to change his ways." He began to see that "God works in significant ways," and he set out to dedicate his life to "doing good in the name of God."[8] By his own account he was divinely inspired to start thinking of the ways in which he could help form a kind of grassroots community organization rooted in the kind of spirituality he saw taking shape in his own family as a result of the Marian apparitions.

Although Armando had spent much of his adult life involved in community-related projects, he says that his motives were not "with God." He says he had an epiphany at this time that led him to realize that what he needed to do was to infuse his community-organizing skills with his newfound love for God and the Virgin Mary. "You know, during this time I was able to see lots of models, but what I learned was that not by power, not by might, but by the power of the Lord did work get accomplished. I saw that successful revitalization was spirit-based."[9] His new life vision culminated in his April 1992 announcement, much to the disappointment of area Hispanics and Arizona Democrats, that he would not seek reelection as a state representative.[10] Thirty-five years old at the time, Armando had already served nine years in the House of Representatives and a year in the state Senate, and had become widely known for his work with area at-risk youth. His decision came as a surprise to political analysts and Arizona politicians, but he "knew," he says, that he could be more effective as a community reformer by applying his newfound knowledge of "the need to incorporate God in our lives each and every day" with his commitment to neighborhood revitalization and to Mexican American families and youth.

Armando's self-described "conversion" paralleled the conversions that were occurring in his immediate family, as we saw in chapter 2, and among those men and women who became involved in both Mary's Ministries and ESPIRITU. The men and women involved are primarily Mexican American and middle-class, many have college degrees, and most hold down full-time jobs in addition to their involvement with ECDC. Most of the Hispanics involved in ESPIRITU choose to remain in the barrios of South Phoenix and feel a deep commitment to improving the communities in which they were raised. They see themselves as servants of God, "urban warriors" who are working toward being "saints" through their hands-on community service. Armando's descriptive term "martyrs by living" points to the goal of being "in the world" while living spiritual and exemplary lives for others to see. His integration of religious, social, political, and urban-related themes elucidates the group's urban religious identity.

Corporate Connections

ECDC operates under the same religious-reformist auspices as have other reformers—white, black, Hispanic—in Phoenix and other U.S. cities. Just as its sister organization, Mary's Ministries, has aligned itself with larger Protestant evangelical concerns, so too does ECDC share urban reformist impulses with Protestants. The main difference is that Mary's Ministries and ECDC are self-consciously ethnic organizations that work to improve the lives of Mexican Americans and Hispanics. The Ruizes, the primary catalysts behind ECDC, are not hindered politically and have used their many political connections to benefit the organization financially, and, consequently, to fund their urban programs. They have embraced the "team spirit" and public corporate organization mentality that the cultural historian Susan Curtis argues was a hallmark of the early twentieth-century Protestant Social Gospel urban reform and that helped make that movement so successful.[11] Like those earlier Protestant evangelical Social Gospelers, today's ESPIRITU members actively solicit funds from big business. The school is the most obvious beneficiary of these political and corporate connections; more than $1 million has been granted to the school from the NFL, and other monies have come from the city and state, as well as the National Council por la Raza (NCLR) in Washington, D.C.

Family members have tapped into their vast network of political contacts in order to facilitate the realization of their religiously inspired goals. Key supporters have included Lisa Graham Keegan, and Tom "Tommy" Espinoza, vice president of community development for National Council por La Raza (NCLR) in Washington, D.C. Graham Keegan, whose ex-husband was a Brophy Preparatory classmate of Armando and Fernando, was given strong support by Armando and Fernando Ruiz in her campaign for School Board Superintendent of Public Instruction in the early 1990s. Tommy Espinoza, a longtime political ally and friend of the Ruiz family and a member of Mary's Ministries and founder of ESPIRITU, helped secure a community development grant for ECDC. As a result of his efforts, ESPIRITU is part of NCLR's Strengthening Emerging Neighborhoods Development Program (SENDP), funded by the Charles Stewart Mott Foundation, which provides seed grants to emerging organizations involved in community advocacy, neighborhood development, and social services. ECDC is also part of NCLR's Southwest Initiative (SWIN), funded by the Ford Foundation and given assistance toward community development efforts.[12]

Of course, the Ruizes' political experience and contacts have directly contributed to their success, and for their part they see nothing wrong with the way they have proceeded and are grateful for their numerous connections for the extra edge they have afforded in the competitive world of grants. They invoke evangelical language to validate their ventures, asserting that their goals are not "of the world," but that in order to be successful they have to be "in the world." The Ruizes make no apologies for using their connections to further their community goals. In response to vocal critics like former Tempe Councilman Ben Arredondo who say that the Ruizes have succeeded because of their connections, Rey Jr. says, "Of course. You have to be politically smart to succeed in the world, but you don't have to be *of* the world. We know that we have to be a business to succeed. Without money, there is no school, and it would be impossible to realize our dreams in the community."[13] Brothers Armando and Fernando share this conviction, and they believe it is their duty to use whatever resources they have at their disposal, as their neighborhood reform is all for "the greater glory of God." The Ruiz philosophy is that it is necessary to work within the existing system in order to achieve the community reform they have planned—religious and community reform requires financial backing. Through their educational, community, and political ventures, the Ruizes "religionize secular things" and suffuse the focus of their reform efforts with religious meaning. For the Ruizes and ECDC, part of being in the world entails a level of political savvy, a willingness to take advantage of their contacts in city and local government in order to achieve their educational, religious, and community goals.[14]

Like other urban reformers who, since the first decade of the twentieth century, have combined religious and social action, ECDC has tried to reclaim South Phoenix in a grassroots effort to implement social, economic, and urban reform. These impulses constitute a distinctive urban religious response to crisis in South Phoenix. As an urban religion, ECDC, to use the language of Robert Orsi, comes from "the dynamic engagement of religious traditions with specific features of the industrial and post-industrial cityscapes and with the social conditions of city life. The results are distinctly and specifically urban forms of religious practice, experience, and understanding."[15] By many accounts, South Phoenix has not been the most ideal place to live for Mexican Americans. Aesthetically, it is not a pretty place; economically, it is poor; and socially, it is troubled. Large, empty lots of barren ground are littered with rusted-out cars and trash; the walls of buildings are boldly emblazoned with gang graffiti; and the streets are menacing places where men and women need to be always on their guard. These streets become more dangerous with nightfall, when the sounds of gunshots and squealing tires and the whir of police helicopters ("ghetto birds") fill the dark.[16] The high school dropout rate among South Phoenix youth is among the highest in the state, evidence of a pervasive sense of hopelessness among many local teens.[17] The bleak outlook for these Mexican American youth is projected throughout the state; cultural historian Mike Davis underscores this prediction, writing that throughout the United States, "young Hispanics . . . are massively fail-

A typical empty lot in South Phoenix. Photo by author.

ing to obtain the admission ticket to the virtual world of 21st century capitalism." Indicative of this trend, less than 5 percent of Arizona's 1 million Hispanic residents possess a college degree.[18]

The Ruizes and ESPIRITU are working to change what Arizona historian Pete Dimas calls white Americans' "hermetically sealed environment that has prevented or retarded contact with the poor."[19] Stories—some real, some invented—of danger and violence have contributed to a culture of fear regarding this place south of the central city, and because the primary goods and services available in South Phoenix can be obtained elsewhere, few nonresidents have a compelling need to visit. Gang violence has been habitually overemphasized in the news, despite the fact that gang shootings and violence are lower in South Phoenix today than they were a decade ago. In today's contemporary culture of fear, Davis writes that the contemporary "gang scare has become an imaginary class relationship, a terrain of pseudo-knowledge and fantasy projection."[20]

In addition to stories of violence that circulate, fears and resentments of the "other"—of the nonwhite, darker-skinned Hispanic—and of the Spanish language prevent other forms of social exchange. Arizona remains a racially and culturally divided state. Indicative of this fear and loathing is the English-only initiative Proposition 106, which was approved by voters in a 1988 referendum. This proposed amendment to Arizona's constitution, which declared English the official language of the state, was sweeping in its condemnation of the public use of any language other than English. The amendment required all official business to be conducted in English and made English the mandatory language on public school grounds—the same schools in which Hispanics make up a large percentage of the student body.

During this time an alternative movement, sponsored by then-state representative Armando Ruiz, dubbed the "Arizona English Movement," promoted English literacy while preserving the rights of Arizonans to use other languages. However, it was overlooked in favor of the "official English" initiative. The U.S. District Court in Phoenix struck down the Proposition 106 amendment in 1990, ruling that it "obstructs the free flow of information and adversely affects the rights of many private persons by requiring the incomprehensible to replace the intelligible."[21] Yet despite the court's decision, the English-only movement continues to be championed by Arizonans for Official English, the vociferous group that sponsored the referendum.[22] The campaign is and has been popular among white conservative Republicans, who resent the growing Hispanic population. In another display of the fear of the dark-skinned "other," Arizona was the last state to declare Martin Luther King Day a national paid holiday, holding out until 1995. It was estimated that refusal to recognize the holiday cost the state $47 million dollars when the NFL relocated the 1993 Super Bowl to protest this stance. Arizona's growing national reputation as a racist state ultimately convinced voters to vote against the initiative in a 1995 referendum.[23]

South Phoenix residents like the members of ECDC recognize the racism that affects their neighborhoods; they also emphasize that good things happen there as well. They complain that newspapers and broadcast news report only the violence that occurs in South Phoenix, neglecting the more positive aspects of the community, such as the connectedness to place many residents experience, the spirit of ethnic philanthropy, close familial and kinship ties, and a tradition of community activism. Mexican immigrants coexist with Mexican nationals, Mexican Americans, an ever-increasing Central American population, African Americans, and whites, contributing to the community's multicultural vibrancy. Moreover, new developments are springing up at the base of South Mountain, and according to Daniel Gonzalez, a reporter with the *Arizona Republic,* many middle-class Mexican American families who had moved away from the south side in the 1980s and 1990s are now buying these homes and re-claiming South Phoenix.[24] Yet these Hispanics are being met with some re-sistance by their neighborhood associations, which are run primarily by Anglos who view with suspicion such cultural differences as extended families residing together in one home.[25]

Building a Better Neighborhood

Since beginning operations in 1995, ECDC's community development branch, led by Fernando Ruiz, has worked to provide better homes, safer neighborhoods, and jobs for residents of South Phoenix. The community development is slated to encompass the neighborhoods that lie between 7th Avenue and 16th Street; the area will be zoned for retail, commercial, educational, multipurpose housing, and single-family housing. Fernando and Armando, along with representatives of the architectural firm ART in downtown Phoenix, have been planning this comprehensive development since 1993; the charter school was the first step in the process, which Ar-mando estimates will take about fifteen years to complete. The goal is to revitalize South Phoenix and to bring decent, affordable housing and jobs to residents who will be able to live, work, and invest time and effort in their community. "We want to create the ambiance of Mexico and San An-tonio's Riverwalk right here in South Phoenix," Armando says.

Fernando acknowledges that the plans are ambitious, but he says that "anything is possible" through God and the Blessed Mother. He is "amazed," he confesses, by everything that has been accomplished so far— what he and members of his family refer to as the "fruits." The initial plans for the project began to take shape in 1993, when Armando, Fer-nando, Tommy Espinoza, and some other business leaders were at break-fast and started "scribbling notes on paper napkins."[26] The new South Mountain YMCA had just recently been dedicated, and the positive re-sponse it elicited from the community, along with the knowledge that much more could be done to make South Phoenix a desirable place to live, inspired the brothers and their close friends and associates to begin planning on a larger scale. The opening of the Arizona Center and multi-plex theaters in downtown Phoenix angered them; they had been working on bringing a theater to South Phoenix for years, to no avail.[27] "Is that our future, our destiny . . . to always put the businesses on the fringe of our community but never in our community?" Armando asked.[28] There is no

ESPIRITU home. Photo by author.

movie theater in South Phoenix, no cultural arts center, no shopping mall—residents have to drive at least twenty minutes to the nearest entertainment district. The Ruizes and members of ESPIRITU decided to start working to change this. Says Reyes Ruiz Sr., "It's a change that has been long coming. We want to change South Phoenix. It's all about changing and helping communities. You know, where the school is now, it used to be a junkyard. We want to turn the junkyards into the kinds of places people dream of."

A comprehensive plan came out of the early paper-napkin drafts. It includes several development plans that are in various stages: Plaza de las Americas, "a place where regular folks can start their own businesses and a place where regular folks can go shop, kind of like a cross between the Arizona Center and a Mexican flea market"; mini-bus terminals at designated locations to make it easier for South Phoenix residents, many of whom do not own cars, to travel around the community. The present city bus system is inadequate for inner-city traveling; it has few stops in South Phoenix. The Ruizes also want to establish a center for Mexican American and Hispanic performing arts that will teach dance, theater, and voice. ESPIRITU also has plans to construct a cafeteria and auditorium on the school's campus.

The land on which the Ruizes would like to have the Plaza built is directly across the street from the homes of Estela and Reyes, Armando and Peggy and their six children, and Leticia and Fernando and their seven children. The lot comprises about ten acres bounded by Cody Street, Central Avenue, Roeser, and 2nd Street. The problem is that the land, a barren, glass-strewn empty lot, is owned by a prominent Phoenix family, the Baylesses, who have so far refused to sell. ECDC has been unsuccessful in its efforts to purchase the lot because, although it is trash-strewn and empty, it is a highly valuable piece of property; so far the Bayless family is asking for more than ECDC is offering. The Ruiz family says they have been praying for the past ten years that the land would be sold to them. As Reyes Sr. has said, "We all buried our scapulars there, and prayed for the consecration of the land." The lot is important to the Ruizes because it would be an ideal location for the Plaza, which they hope will be the center of the community. Across from the hoped-for Plaza location is Estela's

ESPIRITU advertisement for home. Photo by author.

and Reyes' shrine, which is not zoned for commercial use, so it will "always remain there," according to Armando. "What I imagine is for the Plaza de las Americas to be the commercial center of South Phoenix and the shrine as the spiritual center. We have the school behind the shrine which is the educational center. We see this as a cohesive development and not as a piecemeal, unrelated project."

As the historian Peter Baldwin notes, in any discussion of urban reform movements and politics it is "necessary to look beneath the rhetoric to discern how the proposed reforms might advance the reformers' selfish interests. . . . Campaigns to reform the use of public space were seldom examples of pure altruism."[29] Ostensibly, the successful purchase of the lot and the subsequent building of the Plaza would raise the value of the Ruizes' homes, which could then eventually be zoned for this purpose— with the exception of the backyard shrine. It would be surprising if the Ruiz siblings did indeed zone their homes for commercial use, given their longstanding efforts to maintain a familial unit on the same street and the opportunities they have passed up in order to stay in their modest South Phoenix homes. Their commitment to the barrio would seem to outweigh financial concerns, though they would indeed stand to benefit should the land offer be accepted. Based on my personal knowledge of the family, it seems doubtful that the siblings would attempt to zone their land for profit. The actions their children and grandchildren might choose to take is less clear, however.

Baldwin's thesis that reformists always have a personal stake in the reforms and stand to gain personally from their efforts is put to the test by the Ruizes, who have built more than a dozen single-family housing units under ECDC's comprehensive plan. According to Fernando, all the homes planned, like the ones already built, will be Salt River Project (SRP) energy-efficient and will be constructed from Tegra blocks, which are foam-filled for insulation and designed to keep the homes cooler in the summer and warmer in the winter.[30] The houses are built by "sweat equity," meaning that the future owner puts in a certain number of hours of work on the home to keep the cost down. The Ruizes have detailed plans for the community of homes, even down to the kind of paint, a type of low-sheen paint that gives the home "a nice, quality look that lasts," Fernando says. The Independence Park community on LaSalle and 37th Streets has served them as a model for their envisioned community of homes, as has the Habitat for Humanity development in South Phoenix. The Ruizes have worked to secure Local Initiative Support Corporation (LISC) money, part of the National Equity Fund, to help prospective buyers.

Prominent "Fruit": NFL-YET Youth Academy

ESPIRITU's charter school is the pride and joy of the Ruiz family, who see it as the most visible "sign" of the Virgin's presence and blessings on the family and community; they consider it one of the "fruits" of Mary's appearances to Estela. The NFL-YET (National Football League Youth Education Town) Academy is adjacent to Estela's and Reyes's home, tucked between busy Central Avenue and 2nd Street, right in the heart of South Phoenix. The school's architecture is modern, and bright primary colors adorn the main building, which houses a vast, open computer room, a television studio, an auditorium, and rooms where the high-school classes meet. Looking at the school from 2nd Street, one sees a regulation-sized football field with green grass—a rarity in this dry city—to the right. Ten air-conditioned modules, dispersed around the large main grey-colored building, serve as kindergarten through eighth-grade classrooms. A basketball court, a cafeteria, an outdoor kiva, and a recently built administrative office block constitute the remainder of the property. The Esperanza ("hope" in Spanish) Montessori preschool is located in the back of the campus; an outdoor playground, an ecology center with fish, and an organic garden are incorporated into the hands-on learning the teachers emphasize. There are approximately 660 students attending the school, which regularly has a waiting list of about 100.

The school, formerly called Esperanza Montessori Academy, today carries the National Football League's name and official logo, after receiving a $1 million grant from the league in January 1996, one of Super Bowl XXX's largest single charitable donations to date.[31] This large grant, in addition to $250,000 from the city of Phoenix and several million dollars from Maricopa County Community College District for computers and a television broadcasting studio, enabled the small Esperanza Academy to expand to its current size and operating budget.

NFL-YET is a charter school, a public school with a state contract to provide a public service. The school receives funds from the state to pay teachers' salaries and to cover annual per-pupil operating costs; the state does not provide funds for rental, mortgage, or other structural costs.

NFL-YET Academy, main building off 2nd Street, South Phoenix. Photo by author.

Organizations establishing charter schools are responsible for raising money through grants and other means for initial setup and maintenance costs, which is why such institutions are private businesses. Initial charters are granted for fifteen years, with review every five years by the school's sponsor. Students are admitted on a first-come, first-served basis because the school is public. Charter schools were written into Arizona law in 1994; there are currently more than 165 now operating in the state under the jurisdiction of the State Board of Charter Schools, and more than 351 total in the state.[32]

For parents and educators in the state who are dissatisfied with the public schools, charter schools seem to be a way to address more adequately the needs of minority students, poor students, and students who do not fit well within traditional schools' methods and structure. The schools, like magnet and private schools, are growing in popularity throughout the United States, especially among Hispanic and African American parents and educators who feel that inner-city public schools are failing to adequately educate and address their children's special concerns.[33] In Arizona, the spread of charter schools has been driven by demand among Hispanics and Native Americans, most strikingly in three cities—Tucson, Phoenix, and Flagstaff—where parents and educators felt the children were ill-served by their district's schools.[34] The schools have received bipartisan support from politicians; during his presidency, Bill Clinton publicly supported them, doubling charter school funding from $20 million in 1994 to $40 million in 1995.[35]

While they maintain their belief that charter schools can improve public education, many of these supporters also recognize flaws in the system and offer concrete suggestions for improving upon charter schools. Educational psychologists Thomas L. Good and Jennifer S. Braden note the major positive aspect of the schools (their popularity among the students, parents, and teachers) as well as the negative (there has been only a marginal return on public dollars spent on charter schools to date). Good and Braden spell out four concerns they have with charter schools: the overall failure of charter schools to serve as "locations for experimentation and innovation"; the spending ratio (more money is being spent on administration than on direct classroom instruction); the tendency of charter schools to "further segregate" students by ethnicity, income level, and special needs; and the run-down, poorly maintained physical environment of many charter schools.[36] In spite of their strong critique of charter schools, however, Good and Braden are ultimately optimistic about the charter schools' future and are supportive of the concept. They recommend

Esperanza Montessori Preschool. Photo by author.

greater competition for charters; a detailed financial plan that must be made available to the state's legislators by charter operators; assurance that charter operators understand and comply with special education laws; and detailed plans for state monitoring of charter schools' performance.[37]

Critics of charter schools charge that there is too much leniency, and they point to the relative lack of checks and balances in comparison to the public school system. The majority of these critics are affiliated with the National Education Association (NEA), and are administrators and unionized public school teachers threatened by charter schools' existence.[38] Some are concerned that charter schools may be able to blur and even violate federal boundaries between church and state.[39] Teachers in public schools, these critics also assert, must have a four-year degree (B.A.) and a teaching certificate, whereas charter school teachers, while they too must have a B.A., are not required to have a teaching certificate. This less stringent criterion makes opponents wary, and they question these teachers' ability to teach effectively. For their part, charter school advocates defend the schools and say that poorly performing schools are tracked through annual tests that gauge performance and can be used as a basis for revoking those schools' charters.[40]

The NFL-YET Academy was the fourth charter school to be established in the state of Arizona in 1995 by the Arizona State Board for Charter Schools. The state board is one of three bodies empowered to sponsor charter schools in the state, the other two being the State Board of Education and any local school district governing board. Prior to the granting of the charter, the Ruizes were already sponsoring Esperanza Montessori Preschool, which was privately funded. Unlike the preschool, which remains private, the Academy cannot teach religion and must abide by charter school bylaws and maintain nonsectarian policies and practices, because it is funded by state money. The Ruizes, all of whom are inspired by their Catholic faith and by the challenge of fulfilling the Virgin of the Americas' "call" to them, claim to have worked their way around the regulations by developing a "values-based" education in which strengthening the child's "spirit" is the focus. ESPIRITU members believe that one of the reasons the public schools are "failing" the kids of South Phoenix is that they do not attend to the sacred; the Ruizes feel strongly that schools must address children's "spirits" as well as their minds.

Because ECDC receives state funding for the charter school, the NFL-YET Academy is required to maintain a secular identity, to remain in compliance with the separation of church and state. The board members have solved this dilemma, Armando says, by placing religion with Mary's Ministries, and the rest, the "secular" concerns, with ECDC. The relationship between the two nonprofit organizations is a complex one that involves detailed financial arrangements intended to permit them to officially maintain separate identities. For example, Mary's Ministries owns the property on which the school was built and receives rent from ECDC in the amount of approximately $400,000 annually. This income represents a sizable portion of Mary's Ministries' annual operating budget, because the Catholic evangelizing organization does not rely on donations or tithes from its members. For its part, Mary's Ministries gives ESPIRITU $150,000 annually for the implementation of "spiritual development" programs at the school.[41] The major portion of the school's annual operating budget comes from the State Board for Charter Schools, which gives ECDC an average of $4,000 per child.

The Ruizes justify the combination of religious and secular at the charter school with carefully worded statements. According to Reyes Ruiz Jr., "You have to be a business to succeed and to spread God's word." Rey, who works at the school as coordinator of food services and as the main director of Mary's Ministries' evangelizing efforts, says that the official relationship the two groups maintain is to satisfy the state, but that "in reality, you can't separate the financial, spiritual, economic, and intellectual from each other. It's all one thing, inspired by the Virgin Mary."[42] For his part, Armando sees no problem with what critics see as teaching religion in the school. Armando has said, "We're going by President Clinton's latest executive order, stating that students can pray on campus if they don't compel other students to participate. We're not teaching religion . . . we're teaching students to respect each other. And, we're teaching an attitude of tolerance."[43] Armando sees the school as joining recent moves toward "civic" education. Although teachers are not allowed to talk about God in the classroom, he says, they can "teach by example." The Ruizes assert that "spirit," "values," and compassion for others are not necessarily religion, but simply a necessary component of education that must be taught alongside the more standard math, science, history, Spanish, and English courses. It is this focus on the child's "spirit" that the Ruizes feel gives their charter school an edge over others that focus exclusively on learning through more traditional ways.

The comments from Rey Jr. and Armando underline an observation made by Diane Winston, a historian of American religion: "the interplay between religion and society is not an either/or proposition . . . the sacred and the secular have been ceaselessly combined and recombined, and . . . these categories have regularly dissolved in lived experience."[44] That the sacred and the secular have historically been combined by American religious groups makes it necessary to address and analyze the complex issues that arise as a result of the Ruizes' and ECDC's beliefs. Like other urban and ethnic groups in America that have lobbied successfully for neighborhood change, religious convictions are major vehicles for the Ruizes' educational reform.

Architectonics and Mission

While the school's architecture, colors, and logo reflect its corporate ties to the NFL, the school mission is deeply informed by the religious convictions of Mary's Ministries. In reality, the school's architecture announces through a kind of sacred architecture—architectonics—Mary's Ministries' urban evangelical Catholic convictions. The Mark Ten administrative building, for example, is biblically inspired—"Ten" refers to the ten ECDC administrators, all core Mary's Ministries' members, who see themselves as Christ's disciples. According to Little Rey, the administrators are "servants" of the school and of the larger community of South Phoenix. The administrators I interviewed all conveyed a sense of divinely inspired purpose; they told me that they were "led" to the school by God. They all see themselves as "meant to be" at the school and believe that they are obeying God's will. These servants/administrators see their roles as school employees and as Mary's Ministries members as one and the same; they call themselves "servant leaders" in both the faith courses and the school. The major difference is that, under Arizona charter school law, they cannot evangelize at the school. Yet their Mary's Ministries convictions carry over to their jobs at the school. Just as they, as Mary's Ministries members, are told to "be like children" in their faith in Jesus, so too are they in their administrative roles—they strive to be like the children they serve and to simultaneously help the children in what they believe to be a divine mission from God.[45] Their enthusiasm, which is conveyed in the language they use and in the way they decorate their offices, underlines their Catholic and evangelical beliefs.

The problem, of course, is that they may very well be in violation of charter school invocations against incorporating religion into public schools. During my various visits, it was impossible not to notice crucifixes, prayers, and devotional cards and literature attached to walls and featured prominently on desks. Employees are clearly aware of the rules and regulations; however, they insist that they are doing nothing wrong by displaying religious icons and sayings in their offices. NFL-YET's staff reflects the integrated relationship between Mary's Ministries and ECDC and the insistence on carrying forth their "mission" from Mary to evangelize. The most prominent members of Mary's Ministries all hold positions at the school. Most administrative members were first active in Mary's Ministries and were later hired on as teachers or in other capacities such as secretaries or accountants. These men and women carry their strong religious convictions with them to their jobs and blur the lines between "secular" and "nonsecular" in their work. Although they cannot, by law, teach religion at the school, employees live their religious beliefs each day at work. They consciously try to promote what they refer to as spiritual leadership, good morals, and love of God. Upon walking into the Mark Ten building, where pictures of Jesus, St. Teresa the "Little Flower," the Virgin of Guadalupe, and other saints are displayed on office walls and desks, one cannot help but observe the relationship between work and faith.

ESPIRITU employees are like those early twentieth-century Protestant Social Gospel reformers in that they work to solve the "very real problems on earth." As reformers, they are convinced that using one's religious convictions for the benefit of others is the only way to do reform.[46] Yet these beliefs have gotten them all into some trouble. The display of religious icons on school walls was interpreted by a charter school board official in 1997 as violating the separation of church and state. At this time the administration was asked to remove a prayer and picture of the Virgin of the Americas from the wall, which it promptly did.[47] However, religious icons and artwork continue to remain in conspicuous places.

The teachers and NFL-YET school employees are motivated by what they believe to be an innovative approach to state-sponsored education. All of the teachers, from kindergarten through twelfth grade, are broadly trained in Montessori techniques of hands-on learning and combine them with founder Maria Montessori's "spirit-based" approach to teaching children.[48] The school hosts workshops and training sessions each year before the start of school, and midway, during the year, to train and refresh teachers in the basics of the method. Estela Ruiz, the school's elementary education administrator, says that she likes the Montessori method because it focuses on children actively engaging in their education, rather than relying too heavily on book learning. "Of course," she says, "reading is extremely important, but it is the way in which learning is traditionally taught, that students are taught to think in a boxed-in way."[49] Encouraging students to engage in their education, Estela asserts, is the most effective way for them to learn. Preschool and elementary school children, for example, learn biology in hands-on ways by gardening and hatching chickens in an incubator and in the school fish hatchery. Middle- and high-school students also extend their biology and chemistry lessons outside the classroom, and there are school "spirit sessions" at the end of each Friday to teach "civic values." These methods are meant to provide what is seen as lacking in traditional public school teaching methods.

Fernando has formed a leadership group at the school, from which he hopes a cadre of exuberant young men and women will emerge to lead their peers at the Academy. The group, formed in 1998, meets each week to discuss strategies for how they can contribute to their school's productivity. The leadership students have to maintain a minimum GPA of 3.0, and they have to participate in all the meetings. Fernando periodically schedules excursions to challenge the students and sharpen their critical thinking skills.[50] The school also hosts an annual "HOPE" course for the leadership students. This two-day workshop, run by Fernando and Armando, is designed to motivate the students to become better leaders, to get them to think about how they can contribute to their communities. "Leadership students" from NFL-YET as well as those from the satellite NFL-YET charter school in Safford, "Los Milagros," participate.

Safford is a small town about three hours south of Phoenix. In comparison with the NFL school's 660-plus student body, the student population at the Safford school is about 110, kindergarten through twelfth grade. It was chartered in 1996, a year after ECDC was given the charter for what is now the NFL-YET Academy, and was started largely by the efforts of Rosa, a Safford resident and Mary's Ministries member. Rosa told me during an interview, "I was visiting the NFL school and I saw the kids eating their lunches quietly in their uniforms and I knew that I wanted that kind of place in my town." Rosa cites the difficulties of operating a charter school—funds are scarce, the immediate community is not very supportive of the school, the school does not have a lot of things public schools have, like organized sports and music. But she says that Los Milagros ("miracles") is teaching the students things they cannot learn at other schools, like discipline, values, and hope. Rosa says that she and the others at the school work hard and do many things themselves to save money. Her daughter, Lucita, does the cooking and cleaning for the school, and

Rosa regularly stays after hours to help the small office staff finish their work for the day. But all of the work "is worth it," according to Rosa, when she is able to see the contentment of the students, and the progress they are making in class. Rosa draws on her own life experiences as a cotton picker in the southern Arizona fields and tells the students that they have to work in order to succeed. Rosa worries that "today's kids think that they can get things without working hard for them. I tell them that work is a reality, and that being lazy won't get them to where they want to be in life." She says she tries to set a "good example" as the school's administrator and that the Blessed Mother helps her to stay calm and be a good leader. Like her compatriots in South Phoenix, Rosa says "all of what you see . . . the school, the happy kids . . . is the work of our Blessed Mother. The school's name, *milagros,* means miracles, and you see them happening each day here."

Rosa says that she sees miracles happen when she attends the HOPE courses. The young men and women who participate in these sessions are put into "teams" to work collaboratively on projects assigned to them; for example, they are given materials (popsicle sticks, glue, cardboard, paint) to construct what they would consider a positive addition to the school and/or the community.

The students tend to support the statistics that show high student satisfaction in charter schools. All but one of the twenty-five students I interviewed were pleased with their experiences at the school and say they would recommend the school to others. Rosa, a junior who moved from Mexico to Arizona in 1996, says that the teachers pay a lot of attention to the students. "Mis experiencias son bonitas, por que esta una escuela diferente. Hay mucho atención de las maestrias" (My experiences have been good here, because it is a school that's different. A lot of attention is paid to the students by the teachers). She is sometimes bothered by the school's strictness, but says that it is good because the students need it.

Linda, a senior at the time of our conversation, was preparing to graduate. She thinks that the school has prepared her for her future career as a photographer or a cosmetologist and that her self-confidence has grown during her years at the school. Linda says she likes the school because she feels "safe and loved." "I especially like the leadership group because we all communicate real well, and Mr. Ruiz [Fernando] is really great." Lola also says she liked the school because she feels "safe." Her mother transferred her from a nearby high school where it was "kinda dangerous and had way too many people." The small number of teachers and students is good, she says. The sentiments expressed by these three students are echoed by their classmate Mariel, who arrived from Mexico in the fall of 1998 and who spoke only Spanish. Mariel was very enthusiastic about the school, and was relieved to be able to speak her native language at NFL-YET. The young men I interviewed were also positive about their experiences at the school. Daniel, a sophomore, said that he liked the "closeness" of the students and faculty, and that the school was more like a "caring family." The students' overall assessment of their school is that they are happy to be there and feel fortunate; they find the school a much better alternative than the local public schools, they feel the Ruizes and school administrators really care about them, and they believe the school has a positive effect on their performance.[51] Most students look forward to coming to school, as they know they are welcome there.

Members of the administration, like the students with whom I spoke, say that they are a family at the school. In addition to their co-commitments to ECDC's endeavors and to Mary's Ministries, these men and women are bound by a Mexican American kinship that spans generations. They demonstrate how *la familia* is integral to the decisions they make each day, and to those they will make in the future.[52] The younger members' parents know each other; their parents and grandparents made their *cursillos* together, binding several generations religiously and culturally. Deidre, Fernando's assistant at the school, emphasized the importance of family and said that the school provides both familial and spiritual guidance for her. After her father died, she turned to Reyes Sr. as a father figure, telling him of the struggles she had in her marriage and family. She says that she and her five sisters are all "very spiritual," but the problem, she says, is that their husbands are not. When she turned to Reyes for advice, he told *her,* she said, to be the spiritual head of her family. Deidre put in her application to be Fernando's assistant at the urging of her mother, who was already working as the school nurse. Deidre was drawn to working at the school, she says, because the staff resembled a family, and she knew that just being around her coworkers would cause her to grow spiritually. Deidre's commitment to the school translates into trust in the system it generates; she has enrolled her youngest child, Aurora, in the preschool.

Armando J., the school's Student Advocate, parent-teacher liaison, and student conflict mediator, also emphasizes the family networks that brought him to the school. He grew up in Phoenix's Golden Gate barrio, and his grandfather, Abraham Arvizu, helped build the historic Mexican American Sacred Heart parish.[53] Arvizu knew Reyes Sr. through Phoenix-area *cursillos,* and Armando and Fernando helped get his grandson accepted into the elite Jesuit Brophy prep school. Armando J. credits "someone watching out for me" for not getting arrested during his teens, when he engaged in what he referred to as "crazy stuff." He is now in his late twenties, married, and the father of three young children, two of whom attend NFL-YET. He says he tries to teach kids to respect others and to take responsibility for their actions, something he admits he did not always do. He believes that parents should be involved in their children's education, and he says he gets frustrated with parents who don't seem to value education. Yet it is the challenges his job poses that make him want to continue devoting his efforts to the school. He sees his coworkers and students as a family to which he has made a commitment. "We're more than just any school here, we're a family—a community school. At the graduation ceremony, we tell the kids that we are walking with them to a new part of life, and we have the parents give their kids their diplomas." Armando J.'s commitment mirrors the organization's motto, that a faith kept to oneself is "selfish," for it has to be shared with others: "You show your faith through what you do—you have to live it."

Not everyone at the school embraces the evangelical language of faith and obligation that Armando J. and others use. Cory, a young African American male and the school's physical education teacher—one of the few non–Mexican American instructors at the school—is not part of Mary's Ministries but says that he enjoys his job because he "sees results" in the students. In his fourth year at NFL-YET, Cory says that "fate" brought him to the school and to a position that "perfectly fit" his ten years' training with the city's Parks and Recreation Department. Working at the school has been a challenging experience, Cory says, because the school does not have amenities such as a swimming pool, a volleyball court, or a track as do other schools. But despite these challenges, which are often overcome by renting time in the facilities of nearby schools, Cory says he is "happy" to be at a school like NFL-YET, where he is able to feel like he is making a difference in the children's lives: "You know, some of these kids will complain about the strict rules—about not chewing gum and about having to tuck in their shirts. But I can tell you that they really feel like they are important here—that the teachers really care about them."

Deidre, Armando J., and Cory all focus on the importance of a supportive, family-like setting in educating children and are themselves drawn to the close kinship networks at the school. Diedre's example of having family members from three generations of women at the school as student, administrator, and nurse is not uncommon, and points to the tightly woven connections between family, education, and ethnic identity. Even Cory, who is not Mexican American, says he feels drawn to the family-like atmosphere he experiences at the school. And Armando J., whose own children attend the school, has long-standing bonds with the Ruiz family, and feels an obligation to serve as a role model for the school's students, as he was once helped and mentored by the Ruiz twins.

The school's geographic space, the symbolism incorporated in its physical appearance, and the language used all support the nurturing of students' dual worlds—Mexican and American. Walking around campus is much like visiting a school south of the United States–Mexico border. Although fluency in Spanish is not a requirement for teachers at the school, roughly 90 percent do speak Spanish. The majority of students with whom I spoke preferred to speak Spanish over English. Students are encouraged to speak Spanish at the school and they tend to speak Spanish rather than English during lunch and between classes. Raúl, for example, a middle school Spanish teacher, tapped into Latin American cultural and linguistic pride when he established a chapter of MEChA (Movimiento Estudiantil Chicano de Azlán), the Chicano Student Activist Movement, in 1996; about thirty students are now involved. Mexican art is taught by Debbie, the fine arts teacher, who introduces her students to Mexican pottery, painting, rugs, and masks.

Jeremy, another of the few non–Mexican American teachers at the school, recognized another side of being a part of two cultures—the painful in-betweenness that students can experience. He decided to bring someone who could address the complexities of being Mexican and American to his fourth-grade class, and he sought out and invited the prominent Hispanic American poet Sandra Cisneros.[54] Her readings let the students know that she understood what it was like to grow up without a lot of money and in a big city and what it was like to be a Hispanic American. Her talk had a profound effect on the students; one student interviewed by the *Arizona Republic,* Arizona's largest newspaper, which ran a front-page story on the school and the author's visit, felt as though she had known Cisneros her whole life. "It's like me, she's like me. . . . I felt like the way she was talking."

Cisneros's talk focused on the cultural richness of two traditions as well as the challenges that accompany growing up Mexican and American. While growing up *mestizo/a* is portrayed in a positive way at the school, administrators and teachers acknowledge the difficulty of growing up in between worlds and recognize the contested nature of identities.[55] For its part, the school's administration promotes bilingual literacy as a way of ameliorating the tensions between the identities. As we have seen, the Ruizes have a strong background in bilingual education, especially Estela, who was the bilingual education superintendent of the Murphy School District. She was motivated by seeing what she felt was the failure of Arizona's educational policy of immersion, "a philosophy that plunked [students] into English-speaking classrooms and expected them to learn the language through their skins."[56] Her experiences and successes within the district helped form the basis for NFL-YET's bilingual philosophy. The school administrators and teachers alike strongly believe that through a focus on bilingual education they will make inroads in a city polarized in terms of wealth, race, ethnicity, and class.

"A Gang . . . that Prays You In"

Despite the positive assessments by students, administrators, and teachers, not everyone is happy with the way the school is run; there are vocal critics. Conchita, who was in her fourth year at the school in the fall of 1998, says that she sees problems with the school. She is especially disappointed that the administration did not build "a real cafeteria" and that she has to eat her lunches in the trailer that serves as the cafeteria. Conchita admits that she "isn't the best student," but she says that if she were, and if she were thinking about going to college, she would be going to a more rigorous school. Another sore point with Conchita is the number of teachers who have quit. "It seems like one day they're here and the next, they're gone. . . . I don't understand what's going on." Conchita's comments point to one of the problems the school has had in the last several years: teacher retention. The pay is lower than at the public schools and the work load is just as intense, if not more so. There have been arguments between teachers and administrators over what is best for the students; some teachers think that administrators should be paid less and that the money should be going toward school supplies, which some teachers say they pay for themselves. Many of these complaints, primarily the one about more money going to administration than to students, dovetail with the major concerns identified in studies on charter schools, listed in Good and Braden's comprehensive study.

Mary Hartley, state representative for Arizona's 20th legislative district (representing parts of Phoenix, Glendale, El Mirage, and Surprise), has been one of the most outspoken opponents of Arizona's charter schools. She refers specifically to NFL-YET and writes that there are "loopholes the size of the Grand Canyon" in charter school laws, as evidenced in the violation of the separation of church and state, "rampant nepotism," and discrimination against special needs students, all of which has been documented by charter school officials.[57] Hartley goes on to cite the religious paraphernalia on office walls and the Ruizes' nepotism, as well as other questionable practices in other Arizona charter schools, as evidence that the state's charter laws are in need of reform. She writes, "The Arizona charter school movement is heading for a train wreck, and the legislature is asleep at the wheel."[58]

In addition to Hartley's sharp critiques, a thick file of parent complaints against the school is available to the public at the Arizona State Board of Charter schools. I had the opportunity to speak with one of the state's top charter school administrators while I was researching NFL-YET's file. This official, who preferred to remain anonymous, acknowledged that NFL-YET has more complaints on file than any other charter school in the state, but that it also has the highest enrollment in the state, which accounts for the higher volume. The files document parents' formal complaints, which range from the school not being in compliance in special education matters to anger over the firing of teachers popular with students, mismanagement of funds, "dishonesty" on the part of administration, and administrative insensitivity to parents' concerns.[59] The 1997–1998 school year was especially tumultuous: a dozen or so parents withdrew their children from the school after four teachers, popular with students and parents, were fired by ECDC for "abandoning their classrooms." An anonymous phone call from a "concerned parent" to the NFL headquarters accused the Ruizes of "stealing money" from the school and added to the escalating tension between the school's Concerned Parent Board and the administration.[60]

José, a high school math teacher who submitted his resignation after just one year, has been the most outspoken former "insider" critic of the school. He is critical of the administration, and says there are high numbers of unqualified teachers and apathetic students who are "bored and disruptive" in class. His criticisms mesh with broader critiques of charter schools; he says that the administrators, whose salaries in the late 1990s were in the high-$90,000 range, are paid "way too much," that the so-called experimentation in pedagogy is failing, and that the school structure will not last because of the cheap materials, mainly the module units. José calls NFL-YET a "dumping ground for kids who can't function anywhere else" and stresses that the school's claim that it is "college prep" is far from reality. He complains that the teachers are not paid enough for the amount of work required of them and that the administration does not like to have teachers' input on the way the school is being run. Teachers' morale is low, he says, because of an absence of open communication between administration and teachers.

José, who has his teaching certification, also disagrees with the policy of not requiring charter school teachers to be certified, only that they have a college degree. He also cites the Ruizes' religious beliefs as "inappropriate" at the school, "They pray you in and they pray you out here, it's like a gang that jumps you in and out."[61] He thinks that art classes, leadership meetings, and computer classes all add to the quality of education, but that these activities need to be scheduled for later in the day, after school, so that the more difficult subjects are taught in the morning and early afternoon when the students are at their peak. Overall, José thinks that the school has the potential to be "the Brophy of South Phoenix" but says that a lot of work needs to be done before this goal is realized.[62]

The Ruizes and ECDC say that they are aware of the complaints and are making attempts to rectify the problems. During the spring 1997 controversy over the teacher firings, Fernando, then the school principal, wrote a letter of resignation to parents. In the letter he announced that his sister Becky, who had more than fifteen years of experience as a school administrator, would be the new principal. Fernando wrote about the origins of ESPIRITU and why his family and dedicated community members decided to open the school. In the letter, he made clear references to the mission he sees himself and his family working to fulfill and wrote that it was for the "greater glory of God." Fernando made his family out to be contemporary Christian martyrs—making sacrifices for the greater good of the community. He also wrote about the financial sacrifices and commitment to the school his family had made. His letter can be read as making the attempt to connect the Ruizes to the saints they strive to emulate:

> my wife, she has been the guiding light of my life. She has put up with the other woman in my life, "Esperanza Academy." She has given more than anyone for the school. She took our children out of a good school and put them into "Esperanza," knowing that we would struggle for two years . . .

my parents, brothers, and sisters all left better paying jobs and careers to take a chance in shaping the future of "ESPIRITU." My mother came out of retirement to work behind the scene and work long hours for very little money. My father continues to work like a twenty-year-old though he has cancer. My brother Armando took a huge pay cut in order to run ESPIRITU and bring structure to our organization, he cannot even afford to fix his own house. . . .[63]

Fernando stressed his family's sacrifices and added that his "only regret" was that he had not communicated better with parents. He emphasized that he had worked "sixteen hours a day for months on end, to 'never say never,' and to have faith that God would allow me to move the mountain." He admitted that the school was "not where it needs to be" and that "things could have been different," but he said the mistakes that were made were unintentional and that he, his family, and school administrators always tried to work in the best interest of the students. Fernando offered a positive interpretation of his family's nepotism; he stressed that his brothers, sister, and mother all work for the school because they are deeply committed to South Phoenix youth.

Like Fernando, Estela acknowledges that there have been major problems with the school, but she argues that it was a combination of factors that resulted in the events that occurred in the first three years of operation, 1995–1997. "The problem is that our main focus was forgotten, which is that we are here to nourish the kids' minds and spirits. There was a lot of fighting and not enough educating going on." The problems with the school are due to the fact that it is a new school, going through growing pains and being "susceptible to human errors." Estela realizes that the teachers work extremely hard, and that the typical work day for NFL-YET teachers is more than the typical 8 A.M. to 4 P.M. day. "Our teachers usually stay until five or six o'clock as there is so much work to be done. The ones who can give the time stay and the ones who just can't give this much leave. I understand because this is an incredibly demanding place to work. Our kids need so much." Many of the school's problems hinged on what Estela called the school's "dual identity" as a place for at-risk kids as well as a college preparatory school. The administration made the decision before the 1998–1999 school year to make the school a preparatory academy and to focus on educating the students so that they would be able to succeed in universities. It was a difficult decision, but a necessary one, Estela says, because "we had to realize that we could only do so much for the child—we are only human and we can't do everything. I pray for these kids every day but had to realize that there's only so much I can do . . . the rest is up to God." In response to these contentious years, ESPIRITU's board, teachers, and staff sat down in a series of meetings and discussed how they could improve their school. The administration then printed copies of what is referred to as the "brown book," school improvement plans for 1998 and 1999.[64] Armando and Estela both say that the school is showing improvement; in a 1997 parent survey conducted by the Hudson Institute, an independent conservative think tank, parents of NFL-YET students overall were pleased with the school's performance.[65]

Yet a well-documented list that detailed "questionable expenditures" on the part of ECDC was submitted to the Arizona State Board of Charter Schools in September 1996 by a former ECDC employee. This letter detailed fourteen separate concerns, including accusations that the Ruizes engaged in "moral, ethical and possibly criminal actions which constitute misappropriation of state funds." The letter's author alleged that school money had been used to pay for employee meals, various Mary's Ministries expenditures, and the employment of undocumented workers for school contract work. The letter also charged that personnel was overbudgeted and certain school programs underbudgeted, echoing a critique commonly made of charter schools in general. If substantiated, these complaints could implicate the school in a variety of offenses.[66]

I have asked many questions of the Ruizes regarding how money is allocated for Mary's Ministries and ECDC, and family members have explained to me on several occasions that the accounts are set up specifically to prevent school money from being used for Mary's Ministries events and purposes. One thing that I have observed in my years of fieldwork is that Mary's Ministries regularly makes use of NFL-YET school property for its faith courses. Faith course "dynamics" have been held in classrooms, candidates are fed in the school lunchroom, and seminars have been held in the computer room. Moreover, school vans are used to transport faith course candidates and visiting priests to the school and to Estela's and Reyes's home. While this usage may or may not be in violation of Arizona's charter school rules and regulations, what is clear is that for all of the efforts to keep Mary's Ministries and ESPIRITU separate, in reality there is much overlap. The evangelical fervor behind Mary's Ministries fuels ESPIRITU's enterprises at the school.

When we look critically at the Ruiz enterprise, the truth seems to lie somewhere in between scathing criticism and hagiography. The Ruizes are neither charlatans nor saints, but a well-educated, middle-class Hispanic family that is trying to run a major operation with the accompanying large operating budget. In addition, charter schools in general are hotly contested; they are passionately defended and derided by educators and parents, and given their relatively recent origin, their effectiveness is as yet largely unproven. Despite the acumen of various family members—Fernando's and Armando's business and political skills, and Estela's strong background in education administration—the family lacks the necessary background to run such an enterprise. Hartley has noted problems with nepotism at the school: the Ruizes have worked hard to keep the power within their own family and the Mary's Ministries family; the majority of family members are employed by the school; and key Mary's Ministries members have administrative positions at the school. The problem is that the family does not want to relinquish any power, a reluctance that could threaten the continued existence of the school. That the family members are employed by the school is not the main problem; the problem is that they have a difficult time sharing the burdens of their enterprise with anyone outside of the family and Mary's Ministries.

As self-proclaimed evangelizers, the Ruizes see themselves as working toward sanctification and see the physical exhaustion from working too many hours, the accusations and infighting at the school as inevitable, since the path to sainthood is perceived as being necessarily difficult and arduous. Fernando's letter demonstrates this view most clearly. The Ruizes and those they have allowed into their inner circle of power are determined, even if it means spending less time with their own families and risking their health due to lack of sleep and poor eating habits, to see the family's vision come to fruition. They see their vision for an improved South Phoenix as directly inspired by the Virgin of the Americas' messages, and they are unstinting in their efforts to see it happen. Although it is Estela who is the Marian visionary, the family considers itself a family of visionaries, and they are all determined to bring about religious and social reform in South Phoenix.

The Ruizes and Mary's Ministries tread a fine line between church and state in some of their affairs at the charter school, and they refuse to back down, believing that the Virgin Mary herself has called them to reform their community. They see themselves as working for God and Mary, and they refuse to allow their critics to distract them from what they see as their "mission," to reform their barrio. Through ECDC's programs they inject their religious beliefs into comprehensive educational and social plans for South Phoenix and strive to "spiritually uplift" their community. They acknowledge that their efforts are yielding "fruits," yet they refuse to "stop working" until South Phoenix has shown dramatic improvement in the educational and social realms. And, for the most part, ECDC members neither rest on their laurels nor take credit for the successes they have had. They all cite a woman who has inspired them to take the risks they have taken and to maintain their hope when their plans and projects are threatened—the Virgin of the Americas. The Ruizes and members of Mary's Ministries and ESPIRITU are working to counter South Phoenix's negative reputation and to demonstrate how ethnicity and religion can be used as vehicles toward reform. Their goal is to combine the concept and reality of an extended family network with religious and ethnic values to transform their neighborhoods. Placing the Mexican American family and their evangelical Mexican American Catholicism at the center of their work, they "do religion" in their neighborhood and attempt to chart a new future for South Phoenix that differs from its past in that members of the community are the ones determining the economic and social direction it takes.

"Doing" religion in their neighborhood and abroad takes a lot of strength and effort, and family members say that it is the backyard shrine to the Virgin of the Americas that offers them a special kind of strength. The shrine renews them so that they can continue their evangelization efforts in Mary's Ministries and through urban reform. The shrine is the capstone of ECDC's Project Americas, the "spiritual force," according to the Ruizes, that is the "center" of the Virgin's vision for them. It is the shrine that spiritually refreshes them and the hundreds of others who journey seeking spiritual, physical, and emotional healing.

* 7 *

Hope and Healing
The Dialectics of Faith and Place

Late one recent December evening, a small group of Peruvian, Colombian, Guatemalan, Mexican, Brazilian, and Mexican American Catholics gathered inside Estela and Reyes Ruiz's backyard shrine to pray for a young girl's healing. The group of thirty or so men and women included twelve Matachina dancers, who were still wearing the sequined and embroidered outfits they had worn earlier to dance for *la Virgen,* the Virgin of Guadalupe.[1] At the front of the circle stood a man, his wife, and their four-year old daughter; facing them as the young girl shyly approached were Estela, Reyes, and Padre Alejandro from Colombia. As the somber young padre placed his hand on the girl's shoulder, Reyes gently lifted the hat off of her head, exposing the downy hair underneath. Reyes softly announced that the young girl had cancer and that her parents were asking for prayers of healing. As the girl bent her head down, the tight circle of people all raised their hands over her as Padre Alejandro placed his hand on her head. The prayers, whispered in Spanish, went on for approximately a half hour inside the small barrio chapel, and when the prayers were through Reyes gave the child a ride on his electric wheelchair, much to her delight, as her parents received warm embraces from those who had prayed fervently for their daughter.

These prayers of hope and healing that took place at a recent Mary's Ministries annual retreat/*retiro* to celebrate the apparitions of the Virgin Mary to Estela Ruiz are an auspicious entryway into a religious world that is rooted in a South Phoenix barrio. Since 1990, the first weekend of December has been set aside by the Ruizes and Mary's Ministries to commemorate the nine years of public apparitions from the Virgin of the Americas to Estela. A close look at the annual retreats that honor the apparitions of the Virgin of the Americas to Estela affords us a greater understanding of the power of place, the process of pilgrimage, and how personal transformations are named by the devout. It is in the context of the annual celebration of the Virgin that pilgrims establish and reestablish special relationships with Mary, Jesus, and saints; the space of the shrine affords them the opportunity to forge lasting bonds with their heavenly intercessors.

Individual pilgrims' enthusiasm for the Virgin is reflected by priests who claim to make the space sacred by their presence. In previous chapters we have seen the ways in which official and popular Catholicism overlap during the faith courses; the retreats are another medium for the coming together of popular and official Catholicism. Yet, as we will see, the original shrine dynamics are shifting, demonstrating the malleability of faith and place. The shrine today is very different from the shrine of the early 1990s. A close look at the annual *retiros*/retreats to honor the Virgin enables us to view the ongoing dialectics of popular and official piety and how ordinary places are made sacred by pilgrims. And a look at the shrine's two Virgin Marys, Guadalupe and the Virgin of the Americas, shows how ethnic identity is constructed and contested at the shrine and how physical, ethnic, and spiritual healing are brought about by devotion to the Virgins. This shrine is a place where *mestizos/as* can find healing from the cultural and ethnic in-betweenness they experience.

The Annual Retreat

The Ruiz family and their organization have hosted these weekend December retreats since 1990 to celebrate the Virgin's appearances, and, increasingly, Mary's Ministries' evangelization. Marian devout work diligently to make Estela's and Reyes's home, back yard, and shrine resplendent for the weekend retreat. Every year up to his death in 2003, Reyes Sr. and several hired assistants would spend the two weeks prior to the weekend applying white paint to the exterior of the Ruiz house and to the stucco fence surrounding the yard. And, until the shrine was enclosed in 2000 to make it a chapel, Reyes, Armando, and Fernando painted white the wooden frame of the Virgin's outdoor altar; they continue to paint white the surrounding trees' trunks, to ward off the sun and to freshen the yard's appearance. Shrubs are trimmed, plastic lawn chairs are set out in rows, and statues are cleaned and carefully placed on the altar. The shrine to the Virgin on the first morning of the retreat is decorated with baskets

Mary's Ministries December *Retiro*/Retreat sign.
Photo by author.

and vases of fresh multicolored roses, poinsettias, and chrysanthemums, a framed portrait of the Virgin of Lourdes, the baby Jesus in a wicker basket, and the plaster statue of the Sacred Heart of Jesus dressed in a crimson velvet robe that matches the altar's velvet background. All of these images and items stand below the framed painting of the Virgin of the Americas that is hung in the altar's center. A white plaster dove, the "Holy Spirit," is hung to the left of the Virgin of the Americas and a large framed image of the Virgin of Guadalupe stands directly to the right. And in keeping with the Christmas season, red velvet and gold lamé fabric are strung across the top of the altar, over the two Virgins and the Holy Spirit.

The shrine's material culture is very much in the Mexican folk art tradition; the colors are vivid and Jesus and Mary as Guadalupe look like the men and women who revere them. They are approachable and they are meant to be touched. Reyes Ruiz Sr., a self-trained artist, made all of the statues that fill the backyard space, and painted the numerous oil paintings and watercolors that hang inside the small chapel. The statues include: a five-foot-tall statue of the Virgin of Guadalupe which stands against cacti and a stucco wall; a bloodied and life-sized crucified Christ; and the three-member "holy family"—Jesus, Mary, and Joseph—which was added in 2000 on top of the enclosed chapel's roof. Reyes had a story behind each of the statues and he was especially proud of the crucified Christ because "He shows how much He suffered for us." Reyes's depiction of Christ has real human hair, donated "by a young woman who went through chemotherapy and sent it to me," he told me. The crown of thorns on Christ's head is made of orange tree wood from migrant farmworker fields, the fields in which Reyes ministered to farmworkers for many years for the Diocese of Phoenix. And the cross is made of "old prison wood" from a former Phoenix prison where Reyes used to minister to prisoners.

Estela's and Reyes's backyard shrine altar decorated for Christmas. Photo by author.

Reyes Ruiz's backyard shrine statue of the Virgin of Guadalupe. Photo by author.

All of these statues, paintings, and flowers personalize the outdoor shrine space and provide a link to the larger home shrine culture of Mexican American Catholics. As the folklorist Kay Turner writes, "In purely visible terms, the Mexican American home altar draws a relationship between the human and the divine worlds; the maker creates an assembly of religious and personal images composing a sacred site. Mexican American home altars shed light on how the shrine to the Virgin of the Americas reinforces pilgrims' relationships with the divine."[2] The outdoor shrine to the Virgin of the Americas is complemented by the Ruizes' indoor home altar, where the original acrylic painting of the Virgin of the Americas is normally kept to protect it from the intense Arizona heat. This indoor home shrine is less elaborate than the one outdoors, but the basic components are there—images of the Sacred Heart of Christ, Mary, Santo Niño, and porcelain angels. Pictures of loved ones (granddaughters, grandsons, great-granddaughter) grace the wooden altar mounted on the wall; they are the "visible presence of the sacred power" of Jesus, Mary, and the saints.[3] A wooden crucifix hangs above the indoor altar, and a smaller one hangs to the upper left. The outdoor shrine is a public declaration of the Ruiz family's faith and the faith of those who visit the shrine; these visitors claim it for themselves and add to the layers of meaning.

The outdoor shrine was a focal point during the 1990s weekend retreats and the backdrop for the numerous testimonies and religious perfor-mances that took place, such as the Ruiz family testimonies of the "mirac-ulous changes" that occurred in their lives. The retreats incorporate these religious performances; Reyes and Estela, Fernando and Leticia, Peggy and Armando, Little Rey and Norma, and Rosie and Ronnie all took the stage at different points to talk about their spiritual growth and how the Virgin contributed to strengthening their marriages. Prominent Mary's Min-istries members Rosa María, María, and Teresa also took the stage, and, holding hands, described the radical changes that took place in their lives, much as they do during the faith courses. These personal narratives were interspersed with Christian music provided by Catholic performers such as Donna Lee of San Diego, Marty Rotelle from New York, James Milanesa from California, Scottsdale-based Michael John Poirier, and twelve-year-old local devotee Danny, who sang "Ave Maria" *a cappella* to the crowd's delight. Before beginning their performance, each singer provides the crowd with a brief testimony. James and Marty focused on the "holiness"

The newly enclosed backyard shrine chapel. Photo by author.

The crucified Christ in the backyard shrine.
Photo by author.

of the shrine's grounds; Donna talked about how she was able to get out of an abusive relationship with Jesus's help: "it is only because of Jesus that I am here before you all today." Donna's gripping story of abuse and of her "salvation through Christ" was followed by former Lutheran and practicing Catholic Tom Collins's narrative of his conversion to Catholicism. While Donna focused on Jesus' "loving grace," Tom emphasized how the Virgin Mary had been "missing" in his Lutheran faith and was what ultimately prompted him to officially convert to Catholicism. The two testimonies emphasized the tenderness of Jesus and Mary and that the retreat is a time to "give thanks to Mary and Her Son."

Each year's retreat to the Virgin of the Americas has a theme that is in accordance with the Vatican calendar. At each annual retreat, priests attend the events, give their testimonies, and recognize the visions and organization of Mary's Ministries—further evidence of Mary's Ministries' ties to the Catholic Church hierarchy and the way it blends popular and offi-cial piety. Although the visions have not been approved by the Catholic Diocese of Phoenix, area priests give the apparitions their blessing and proclaim their belief in them. Father Jack Spaulding of Scottsdale, Father Charlie Goraieb of South Phoenix, and Padre Chelelo of Namikipa, Mex-ico, have all given talks on the importance of living one's faith, of attend-ing mass, and of taking the Eucharist. They have declared their devotion to the Virgin and their belief in the validity of the apparitions of the Vir-gin of the Americas. They have also described their involvement with Mary's Ministries and praised the evangelizing group as furthering the Catholic faith and devotion to Mary. As further outreach to those Catholics who may not have been to church in a while, Padre Chelelo, at the end of his presentation, offered to hear confessions; minutes after his talk, a line of close to fifty Mexican American men and women (mostly women) had formed outside the small backyard guest house where Chelelo was to hear them. Padre Chelelo's popularity extended beyond his duties as a priest; his youth and good looks drew giggles and whispers from several of the women who stood in line.

In addition to the featured and keynote speeches, many other stories of Marian devotion, love for Jesus, and the Catholic faith are shared by pil-grims in more intimate conversations throughout the retreat, over lunches and dinners at picnic tables and on blankets. I have had the opportunity to talk with several pilgrims who invited me over to take part in their discus-sions. They shared stories of their encounters with Mary, their healings, and the specialness of the retreat for them. Although roughly one-fourth of the men and women with whom I have spoken at the shrine are from the Phoenix metroplex, many pilgrims, both Anglo American and Mexi-can American, journey from other states, such as Texas and California, and book rooms in Phoenix motels in advance. Others who are close to the Ruiz family stay with family members, and still others who journey from Mexico, cross the border in the morning and return home in the evening, or camp out in their cars and vans. Several busloads of pilgrims drive in from Los Angeles for the weekend; these are the same men and women who attended the first-of-the month rosaries and reading of the Virgin's message from 1990 to 1998. Though the Virgin has stopped giving Estela messages for the public, these pilgrims still travel to the shrine, by way of their chartered bus, each December.

Pilgrimage implies making a sacred journey to a specific place, often-times in a hard-to-reach location, yet this place need not be far away—

indeed, it can be down the street, as is the shrine to Our Lady of the Americas for several devotees. Going to the shrine never loses its excitement for these pilgrims, even if they go there every day. This place is out of the ordinary and is distinguished by the sacredness that the pilgrims give it and that they encounter there. As the anthropologist Jill Dubisch observes, the distance traveled to a pilgrimage site is irrelevant; pilgrims from both near and far experience the site as "a place where the everyday world comes close to, even touches, the spiritual world, and where the (everyday) world is altered by such an encounter."[4]

The heavenly and earthly worlds are understood by pilgrims as converging at this South Phoenix shrine, and the sacred journey of pilgrimage is undertaken for the annual retreat for the Virgin of the Americas. Pilgrims' comments and stories at this shrine have shown that a common denominator of their pilgrimage experience is the combination of familiarity and newness. There is a sense of anticipation, both among the more regular pilgrims, who go to the shrine on a weekly basis, and among those who go to the shrine less frequently, that some new miracle could occur. These pilgrims both hope and expect to detect shrine phenomena—to have their rosaries turn gold, or to experience the scent of roses permeating the air; both phenomena are referred to at this shrine as Mary's "candy kisses." These "kisses from heaven" are an integral part of the shrine healing discourses. The miraculous, or the hope of it, attracts pilgrims to Marian shrines around the world, including the shrine to the Virgin of the Americas. The historian James Preston refers to the powerful pull pilgrimage sites have for pilgrims as "spiritual magnetism," which "derives from human concepts and values, via historical, geographical, social, and other forces that coalesce in a sacred center."[5] What Preston is emphasizing here is that shrines and other places considered holy are not *a priori* sacred but are made sacred through the social process of pilgrimage.

Yet while it is clear that it is the pilgrims who make the place sacred through their stories and journeys, Mary's appearances *are* interpreted by devotees as making the place sacred *a priori*. It is the Virgin's rendering Estela's home and back yard sacred that attracts pilgrims there in the first place—they interpret Estela's and Reyes' backyard shrine as sacred because they believe it is a place visited by the Virgin Mary herself. It is a sacred place that they make even more sacred through their prayers and devotions. Shrines, including the one devoted to the Virgin of the Americas, are Mary's chosen places, what William Christian Jr. calls "critical points in the ecosystem—contact points with other worlds," and what Dubisch refers to as "a bridge between worlds." Thus, the heavenly and earthly worlds are linked both by Mary's appearances and by pilgrims' journeys to the shrine.[6] These Virgins resonate with Hispanics who journey to the shrine.

A New Mestiza

The Virgin of the Americas who appeared to Estela was not technically the Virgin of Guadalupe, the Mexican Virgin who is believed by Mexican devotees and, more recently, by the Vatican, which canonized the apparitions, to have appeared to Juan Diego in 1531. But the Virgin who *did* appear to her is a composite of the Virgin of Guadalupe and the Euro-American Sacred Heart of Mary. As we saw in chapter 1, Estela claimed that the Virgin of Guadalupe spoke to her on several occasions from a painting of her image in Estela's living room. Guadalupe appeared to her in dreams months before her first apparition. Estela says that in her first vision, the Virgin of the Americas arose, quite literally, out of a portrait of the Sacred Heart of Mary that hung on her bedroom wall. The Virgin of the Americas was, from the start, a combination of dreams and voices of Guadalupe and the image of the Sacred Heart of Mary.

For Estela and Hispanic women and men who revere her, the Virgin of Guadalupe has a specific ethnic and racial appeal. She is an ultimate mother figure, a "master symbol."[7] Like this Virgin of Guadalupe, who is believed to have appeared to Juan Diego at the exact location of Aztec Goddess Tonantsi(n)'s temple, the Virgin who came to Estela also has a syncretic Marian and Catholic heritage. Moreover, the Virgin of the Americas' messages resonate with the kind of religious rhetoric that has been associated with the Indian-Mexican Virgin of Guadalupe; her language links her to her *mestiza* counterpart. It is Guadalupe who has been invoked as a warrior, protectress, and guardian of morality, as well as the patron Virgin for Mexicans and Mexican Americans. She is continually being reinterpreted by contemporary Hispanos and Hispanas who see her as a liberating symbol for brown-skinned women and men.

Guadalupe is also an urban Virgin of the streets; in South Phoenix, her image can be seen in numerous murals, and on Chicano gang members, *cholos,* who have her image tattooed on their backs as a form of divine protection. Yet another local constituency that visits the shrine and pays homage to Guadalupe, these *cholos* come to the shrine to venerate *la Virgen de Guadalupe.* They wear her on their bodies in large, colorful

South Phoenix wall mural of the Virgin of
Guadalupe. Photo by author.

tattoos on their backs, arms, chests, and shoulder blades as a form of protection. They see her as their protectress and as a warrior like them. Arturo, a Mexican American "O.G." (original gangster) of South Phoenix,
says that gang members "cover their backs" with Guadalupe to protect
themselves from rival gang members' bullets. Ruben and Mark, two South
Phoenix gang members who frequent the shrine, say that Guadalupe is the
mother to Mexican gang members and that wearing her on T-shirts and
tattoos honors her. These same gang members also visit the shrine, asking
Guadalupe to protect them and their families. Although class and racial
boundaries are for the most part maintained at the shrine, one boundary
is blurred; members of rival gangs can visit the shrine at the same time
without fighting. The shrine is considered to be one of the few neutral
zones in South Phoenix for the gang members.

Devotion to the Virgin of Guadalupe is intimate and racially charged.
Just about every Mexican American woman and man with whom I have
spoken in this South Phoenix barrio claims a special devotion to *la
Morena* and *la Morencita*. Moreover, the Mexican American pilgrims who
visit Estela's backyard shrine to the Virgin of the Americas and Guadalupe
say that they have a special devotion to Guadalupe. María L. acknowledges

her preference for Guadalupe and says that she feels "badly" for not having stronger feelings for the Virgin of the Americas: "I pray to Our Lady of the Americas but it just comes so naturally to me to pray to *la Virgen de Guadalupe*. I don't know, I just relate to her more." She says she felt her anger and frustration with her life gradually "melt away" in the presence of *la Virgen,* and that she relates to the Virgin of the Americas because the Virgin too is a mother and a woman who understands her (María's) sufferings. María says she feels profoundly connected to the darker-skinner Mexican Virgin of Guadalupe but that she also prays to the lighter-skinned Virgin of the Americas, because, as she says, she "came here, to South Phoenix, for us." María was surprised when she saw the picture of the Virgin of the Americas for the first time—she thought she'd be "darker." She says that she is also able to relate to other Mexican American women at the shrine who are going through what she has gone through— many are single mothers, have children involved in gangs, and have alcoholic husbands—and that it is these women, like her, who pray to *la Virgen.* Bernadette, a Mexican American woman in her thirties who is not a member of Mary's Ministries but who goes to the shrine, also says that Guadalupe is her "favorite Virgin" and that she relates to her because "she has skin coloring that is similar to mine. She is dark, like me, and I feel extra comfortable praying to her."[8] These women relate to *la Virgen* best because she is dark and because she is Mexican. They renewed their devotion to Guadalupe at the Basilica in Mexico City and each made a *promesa* to her, a promise that if the Virgin would help them, they would be forever indebted to her. Guadalupe is considered to be the "Virgin Mary," but more than just the Catholic Church Mary—she appeared especially for Mexicans and is considered to favor "her children."

The Virgin of the Americas who appeared to Estela with messages for the public from 1988 to 1998 *is* and *is not* the Virgin of Guadalupe. In one sense, she is Guadalupe's newest incarnation, a new *mestiza,* a Hispanic Virgin who appeared, according to Estela, for "all of Her children of the Americas." The Virgin of the Americas is bilingual and bicultural, blue-eyed, dark-haired, and with a light olive complexion, a border-crosser like the women and men who live in the barrio in which she is believed to have appeared for more than ten years. She is like Guadalupe in that she appeared to *mestizos,* but she appears primarily for late twentieth- and twenty-first-century *mestizos* and their particular struggles.

Like Guadalupe, the Virgin of the Americas appears in a particular time and place. The woman to whom she appears is a middle-class, light-skinned

Mexican American who lives in a barrio along with other middle-class Mexican Americans, recent Mexican migrants, and undocumented workers. The shrine offers two Virgins for two distinct communities. While the Virgin of Guadalupe is a national Virgin, the Virgin of the Americas is nationless and borderless. Her nationality is amorphous, and she is said to represent "all of her children in the Americas." Because of her "American" identity, her light skin, and her broadly worded messages of "loving God," Anglo Catholics who frequented the shrine from 1989 to 1998 could relate to what she was saying. And the Latin American members of Mary's Ministries who attend the December retreats can relate to her because her nationality is "American." Through the Virgin of the Americas, the Ruiz family reaches out to middle-class Mexican Americans like themselves who are devoted to Guadalupe but who are searching for a more contemporary American Virgin who understands and addresses their particular needs and struggles.

Mary in the Streets

When pilgrims take the Virgin of the Americas to the streets during the retreat's evening candlelight procession, there is a heightened sense of both ethnic awareness and religious intimacy. The procession, begun in 1990, has grown into one of the most important components of the annual retreats and is a lens through which we can understand better both the relationships people form with saints and the Mexican American Catholicism that is on display. The historian Jeffrey Burns refers to processions like this as "an important public aspect of Mexican American spirituality."[9] The significance of public processions in Mexican American culture is enacted at each retreat as songs are sung in Spanish and images of the Virgin Mary, Jesus, and various saints are carried. The processions display religious and ethnic identities and enable people to claim the streets, and the pilgrims in South Phoenix make themselves seen and heard in the barrios of South Phoenix, chanting phrases like "*Viva la Virgen de Guadalupe!*" and "Hail Mary, full of grace" at the top of their lungs. Cars slow down on busy Central Avenue and residents open their doors to watch as the hundreds of devotees chant that Mary will clean up the neighborhoods and get rid of gang violence. A religious performance, the parade winds through the trash-strewn streets of South Phoenix as pilgrims claim the dangerous spaces and make them sacred through their songs and by sprinkling the streets with holy water from the fountain of the Virgin of the Americas. Pilgrims take over and mark the profane streets with their bodies and voices, sacralizing place. The water they sprinkle on the streets, the songs they sing, and the candles they burn are meant to purify the mean streets of South Phoenix and to purge the area of drugs, gangs, and violence. The procession shows how the pilgrims intend an "alternative vision for the neighborhood," one that posits prayer as the destroyer of social ills.[10] And even though most of the pilgrims in the procession live outside of South Phoenix, they believe in the "power of prayer," as one woman told me that night, to "work miracles in communities." These out-of-town pilgrims offer up their prayers for the "healing" of South Phoenix as well as for personal petitions. Throughout the procession, Catholic material culture is used as protection: several Mexican American pilgrims with whom I have spoken talked about how they carried their rosaries throughout the parade to protect them. Despite the late hour of the procession and the barrio neighborhoods through which it winds, none of the men and women seemed to be afraid. As one woman told me, "*La Virgen* will watch over us."

Depending on the number of pilgrims who participate, the parade can last anywhere from one to two hours. The candlelight procession at the 1998 retreat, where Mary's final public message was read, included about a thousand participants and lasted for almost two hours. The numbers were especially large that year, because it was the weekend of the Virgin's last public message. In earlier years, the numbers of participants ranged from a couple of hundred to close to a thousand. Leading every procession are the Mexican American Matachina dancers from Flagstaff, flanked by Mary's Ministries volunteers with flashlights. These dancers, *danzantes*, have driven to the retreat since its first year and they dance their sacred dance to the Virgin of Guadalupe. They keep time to the steady beat of the drum, and the bells on their ankles make a loud jingling sound. This Matachina community is tightly knit, and the thirty or so dancers comprise four generations of women, men, and children who put in weeks of practice for the retreat.

The second row is led by a small group of men, women, and children who have been invited by members of the Ruiz family and Mary's Ministries to carry statues of saints, the large banner of the Lady of the Americas, the large multicolored felt banner representing the Mary's Ministries faith course communities, and the infant-sized plastic baby Jesus in the basket. Two women carry the large framed portrait of the Sacred Heart of

Matachina *danzantes* at the December retreat.
Photo by author.

Mary, the one out of which the Virgin of the Americas originally appeared
to Estela. One woman carries the framed portrait of the Virgin of the
Americas Reyes Sr. painted; to her right, another carries a framed portrait
of the suffering Christ. Certain pilgrims are asked to carry the paintings,
statues, and other religious items, and most of those chosen are Mary's
Ministries members. All procession participants carry candles that are
loosely secured inside plastic cups perched on top of cardboard disks and
wooden sticks. In the procession these candle holders prove a bit dangerous, however; several of them catch fire during the procession and have to
be extinguished, prompting some excitement and laughter among the participants. The mile-and-a-half-long procession route, roughly square in
shape, traveled four main streets in South Phoenix—Roeser, 2nd Street,
Central, and Broadway—and ended back at the Ruizes' home on Cody
Street.

A personal experience during this evening offers some insight into the powerful relationships people form with saints. Armando Ruiz asked me to carry the statue of Santo Niño, and I agreed. As soon as I stepped down from the altar, a small group of Mexican women surrounded me, effectively preventing me from walking any further. As I held the plaster statue, which was clad in a golden cloak and a blue velvet dress, these five women bent down and kissed the saint, stroked it lovingly, and murmured "*Santito!*" and "*Santo Niño, que precioso!*"[11] After addressing the little saint, the women made the sign of the cross and bowed their heads, showing respect for him; familiarity did not offset their respect for Santo Niño. In maintaining relationships they had forged with the saint, these women were demonstrating what Kay Turner calls the "aesthetic of connectedness."[12] Since I was expected shortly at the head of the procession, I had to extricate myself from their devotions, which I did with a murmured apology— "lo siento señoras"—for taking El Santito. I left and made my way quickly to the procession line where I was expected to take my place. I found it uncomfortable that I, rather than one of them, had been asked to carry the statue; I realized that I, too, was part of the shrine hierarchy by virtue of my position as an anthropologist and a friend of the family. I was so bothered by this realization that I almost handed the saint over to one of the women to carry, but I was pushed along and into my place in line.

Especially intriguing to me was that no one seemed certain of the saint's formal title. A few of the women thought it was the Infant of Prague, and others believed it to be Santo Niño de Atocha. When I asked my friend Terésa afterward what the exact name of the saint was, she too was uncertain. This confusion about the saint's origin is akin to the merging of Saint Xavier and Saint Francis at shrines on the Mexico-Arizona border.[13] In South Phoenix, the saint's identity was a composite of two saints and the "real" name was not important, as the saint *was* the one and only Santo Niño to these women. What is especially significant is how these women demonstrate how pilgrims actively forge relationships with saints. Their prayer involves an intense exchange and interaction with the saints. They kiss them, pray to them, stroke their images, and ask for their help. These women show how pilgrims engage in making a shrine and its saints sacred. While the shrine may be sacred because it was chosen by the Virgin, pilgrims show how they too define the place's sacredness. Through their own words, in their prayers and in the stories they tell, and through their actions, these men and women sacralize place and time and reaffirm the ties between saints and humans. These *Mexicanas,* invoking Robert

Orsi's language, "express what is needed from the saint, even when the object of their prayers is someone else." In addition, they "undertake the necessary devotions" to the saint, in the process "making and keeping bargains that bind heaven and earth together."[14] The women in this small group prayed for husbands, sons, and daughters, and for their continued health. They saw the *Santito* not as an unapproachable force but as an entity with whom they were intimately familiar, one who had gotten them through earlier struggles, and one they could continually count on. They had forged a relationship with him and continued to cement their devotion through their actions at the shrine.

As these women's devotions demonstrate, heaven and earth are acknowledged to be tightly bound at the shrine, and the language used by pilgrims, such as "a slice of heaven," reinforces the tie. Heaven is spoken of as a reward for devotion to Jesus and Mary in the earthly world, as Estela's comments to the crowd after the procession indicate:

> She [the Virgin] is the most precious gift ever given to me, and I will continue to work for Our Lady and Our Lord for the rest of my life. I expect to be taken to heaven to be with my Father and my Mother one day, as I know that my reward is in heaven.

After she said this, Estela began to cry, for she was "so sad" that this was the Virgin's last message for the public. As she sobbed, her son Rey Jr. played Canadian singer Celine Dion's "Because You Loved Me" over the loudspeakers to set the stage for the rosary and reading of the message. When the recitation of the rosary began that evening, Estela remained seated outside. Normally during a first Saturday she prayed to the Virgin in the living room, the "apparition room," but as this evening was the final public message, Estela said that she wanted to experience the rosary with all of the pilgrims. She then read the final public message, in which the Virgin emphasized (as discussed earlier) her role as healer. In the message she implored her "warriors" to "never put down your weapons" and to "pray for peace, God's love and joy, to reign in the world." Her language draws on Mary's Ministries' use of war metaphors along with messages of peace—the war that the Virgin implores her "children" to engage in and to do battle in is considered a just war by these Catholic evangelicals. Fighting Satan to bring about good and the millennium is considered a worthy and divinely sanctioned cause.

Mary as "Ultimate Doctor"

Following the reading of the Virgin's message, six Eucharistic ministers distributed the sacrament to the approximately fifteen hundred Catholic pilgrims present. The back yard was packed with people, many sitting on each other's laps; the overflow crowd spilled out into the street and the parking lot across from Estela's front yard. More pilgrims sat behind the shrine, on the sidewalks leading to the charter school. In this final message the Virgin implored her children to partake of the Eucharist as one "weapon" against Satan, as her son, Jesus, was "truly present to physically give Himself to you." Father Jack of South Phoenix, Fathers Charlie and Ernesto of St. Catherine's, Father Chelelo of Mexico, and Father Dennis of West Phoenix led the small group of Eucharistic servers out into the crowd and had pilgrims form lines to receive the sacrament. Despite the large numbers of men, women, and children packed into the small space of the back yard, the lines moved quickly and the distribution took only about forty-five minutes.

The distribution of the Eucharist reasserted the interdependence of spiritual and physical healing described in the Virgin's final message. As the "affliction that the world had been suffering was the separation of man from God," what better way to ameliorate the suffering than through partaking of spiritual food? This food would give Mary's warriors "the strength and courage to help Me fight the battle against evil." The Virgin's final message implores her children to stop starving and to nourish themselves, for the sacraments "let that faith grow stronger each day by nourishing your soul with God's holy words." In closing Mary urged her children to feed their souls, because, she asserted, bodies cannot be healed when the soul is in need of nourishment. In this final public message, the Virgin declared herself to be a healer and the shrine to be an oasis of hope and healing.

> For those of you who have received healing of the spirit or the body here at My chosen site, I remind you to give thanks to your God. I have chosen this place as a place to dwell and I say to those who suffer, that I will continue to be here for those who hurt, that I may bring comfort to your hearts and to your suffering. This place I have chosen will be a place where anyone may come to receive healing of the body and the soul.

The Virgin's powers are believed to surpass those of physicians. Leticia Ruiz, during her faith course testimony, told the crowd,

> If you are hurt and are suffering, all you need is Mary. You can spend lots of money on going to psychiatrists, psychologists, and doctors; but you will not be truly healed until you ask Her to help you. She is the One who will heal you, the only one who can, and you need to accept her candy kisses, for She is right here, waiting to answer your prayers. Just grab a hold of her mantle, and She will take you into her arms.

The pilgrims with whom I spoke all acknowledged that Mary was behind their healings, whether they have been healed at the shrine to the Virgin of the Americas or elsewhere. They journey to the Virgin of the Americas' shrine to ask for healings and to give thanks for healings that have occurred in the past.

Robert, a Mexican American man in his mid-fifties, told me that he came to the shrine of Our Lady of the Americas to give thanks to the Virgin of Guadalupe, whom he credits for saving his legs from amputation after a terrible accident. A former electrician, Robert had been working on a telephone pole in the mid-1970s when some wires caught fire and he fell the fifty feet or so to the ground. He recalled sitting in his hospital bed, unsure whether he would lose his leg, when he saw the Virgin of Guadalupe. Robert says that she did not say anything, just smiled at him, telling him "that everything would be okay." After she departed, Robert says that an image of a dove and the Virgin's silhouette appeared on the back of his wheelchair. "It was a miracle, and to thank *la Virgen de Guadalupe,* I built a small shrine in my back yard with the money I won in the lawsuit." The shrine, he said, attracts dozens of pilgrims each month who go to hear his story of healing. Although he journeyed to the shrine of the Virgin of the Americas, Robert laid his flowers and candle in front of the statue of Guadalupe and not in front of the shrine to the Virgin of the Americas. Robert considers the South Phoenix shrine to be sacred because of the apparitions to Estela, but his devotion is to the Virgin of Guadalupe. Robert's story is paralleled by the other Mexican American men and women I interviewed and spoke with at the shrine—they came to the shrine because it is a site of apparitions, but they feel no particular devotion to the Virgin of the Americas. By contrast, the Mexican American women and men I interviewed over a ten-year span at the shrine all claimed a devotion to the Virgin of Guadalupe.

In addition to elucidating the variances in Marian devotion at the shrine—not all Marys are the same—Robert's narrative concerning his healing in a hospital setting points to the divine powers that are believed to be behind doctors' abilities to heal. It was not the doctor's treatment of Robert's legs that saved them from amputation but the Virgin's consoling appearance and smile. Robert's crediting the healing to the Virgin counters what he had been told by the hospital doctors—what Orsi refers to as the "constricted space and time of sickness" of the medicalized twentieth century.[15]

Like Robert, Deidre says Mary interceded for her when she was in the hospital. Although she did not see the Virgin as Robert did, Deidre said that she is convinced that if it were not for Mary's intercessory healing powers, she would have bled to death.

> I was in the hospital and was bleeding internally but the doctors could not figure out where I was bleeding from, so they gave me transfusions. I remember lying there, thinking that I might die and worrying about my husband and kids. Soon after, I felt warm—it was the Holy Spirit healing me, entering me. I knew that Mary interceded for me that day in the hospital and because of it, I am alive.[16]

Deidre says that Mary had a history of coming to family members' aid when they were sick; she had interceded on Deidre's sister's behalf when she was going through a difficult pregnancy. Despite toxemia, Mary enabled Deidre's sister to give birth to a healthy baby, Deidre said. It is Mary, not the doctors, who is given credit for the many healings that have taken place in her family.

Reyes Sr.'s story of his operation to remove prostate cancer is another example of how the devout take control of the spaces and time of sickness that have been claimed by doctors. When he was diagnosed with cancer, Reyes was told he needed to have an operation immediately to prevent the cancer from spreading. He said he prepared for his surgery by telling his friends and family to pray for him. When he talked about his hospital experience, it was clear how painful it was for him.

> I was at the hospital with my family and friends when I was told to go to a room where nurses were waiting for me. I did, and I mean, as soon as I walked into this little room, I was asked by a doctor and a female nurse to remove my clothes. I was so embarrassed and ashamed. Here I was

supposed to take off my clothes in front of people I did not know! I *never* take off my clothes in front of other people, not even my wife, and here were these *strangers,* telling me to get naked and expose my flesh! I was *so* uncomfortable![17]

Reyes obeyed the orders and when Estela was able to go into the room, he asked her to hold his hand and to sing a "spiritual communion," a song he wrote that is now sung at Mary's Ministries retreats (see chapter 4). As he was wheeled down the hospital corridor to the operating room, Reyes said that he and Estela continued to sing the song. When he was in the operating room, Reyes made three requests of the physicians. He asked that they not remove his plastic rosary from his hand, that they allow him to keep wearing the scapular around his neck, and that they allow him to sing before being anesthetized.

The doctors made a fuss when I asked them not to remove the Rosary, they tried to tell me that they *had* to take it off! I told them then I would not have the surgery. So they agreed, and wrapped surgical tape around and around the rosary on my hand. They also let me wear my scapular . . . and I got to sing too.[18]

Reyes said that he knew the Blessed Mother was "watching over" him during his operation and that she would not let the "Evil One" interrupt the surgery. Reyes was able to successfully transform the frightening and embarrassing situation in the hospital—a place that was alien to him—into a place where the Blessed Mother was in control, not the doctors, who were at best instruments of the Virgin's healing powers.[19]

While not all stories of physical healing are as dramatic as is Robert's, Deidre's, and Reyes's, all attest to pilgrims' deep faith in the ability of Mary and Jesus to heal and to ward off Satan. The story shared with me by Doreen, a lifelong resident of South Phoenix and a member of Mary's Ministries, shows the interrelation between physical healing and inner spiritual struggles. Doreen said she was both physically and spiritually healed at the shrine—"cured" of her depression and diabetes. She was in a "cloud of darkness" after her brother's death, and she felt Satan's continual attacks, which she said "knocked me down." "I felt like I was going to die. I was continually attacked and the Evil One would make my blood sugar levels low." She told me that when she went to the shrine, she felt better and the Evil One stopped attacking her. "Estela told me that I was going to be healed at the first Saturday—and I was! I was tested at the doctor's and had no more diabetes! Jesus and Mary healed me! I also had no more depression. We pray to Her and feel the love of her Son." Doreen's advice to others is for them to "hang on to Her mantle. She is so smart; when we are in chaos she puts us on the right track."

A common thread in Doreen's and Reyes's testimonies is that the Evil One is behind sickness. The Virgin of the Americas' final public message on December 5, 1998 reinforces and perpetuates this belief:

> Yet Satan, the great deceiver, became powerful only because men and women allowed him to work in their lives. He is like a deadly disease, that once one person receives it, it can spread easily to others. That is what was going on—evil was having his way with the children of God. . . . The affliction that the world had been suffering was the separation of man from God. Man began to believe that he did not need God anymore and because of that grave mistake Satan and his evil were able to penetrate the hearts of men and women and hatred, anger, and greed became the demons that have overpowered those who have allowed it.

Reyes was afraid to be anesthetized because he was convinced he would be unable to maintain his vigilance against Satan, and Doreen believes that her depression caused an opening for Satan to enter her body and to manipulate her blood sugar levels. Both believe in the power of Satan to enter bodies like a disease. In contrast to Satan as disease-bringer is Mary, the healing counterpart. Mary—Guadalupe—was the only one who could have cured Robert's legs in the hospital; and Mary's mantle protected Doreen when Satan had covered her with his "dark cloud." What may seem to be radical, outlandish claims by nonbelievers make perfect sense to those who believe in the curative abilities of the Virgin, who for them is the antidote for the sickness and doubt that Satan spreads.

While I was conducting fieldwork, my own medical history became entwined with the men and women with whom I talked and lived, allowing me entry into their healing discourses, for I too was a pilgrim.[20] I experienced illness, accompanied by physical pain and suffering, during my fieldwork, and it was this pain and my search for answers that linked me to the men and women who pray to the Virgin at the shrine for intercession. Thus, an inauspicious pain led to an auspicious connection with my interlocutors. Suffering from a sharp pain on my right side, I went to see a doctor. The doctor ordered a CT scan, the results of which indicated to the surgeon that I had a tumor about the size of a small orange on my right ovary. When an ultrasound proved inconclusive, an exploratory laparoscopy was scheduled at St. Joseph's Hospital to determine the cause of the pain. My pain was immediately embraced by Mary's Ministries members, who prayed for me and over me. The "ovarian tumor" was the topic of prayer meetings at the shrine, and I received prayer cards, rosaries, and medals from friends and acquaintances in the organization. I was given items of Catholic material culture, including a coconut-shell-and-turquoise rosary from Hawaii by Norma Ruiz and a Padre Pío medal from Jeannie (a Mary's Ministries member and friend), to protect me during my surgery and to guide the physicians' hands. What began as an unwelcome intrusion in my fieldwork turned into an auspicious way to relate on a personal level to healing discourses among the devout.

When it was found that I had no tumor and that the source of the pain was an inflamed appendix, which was promptly removed, the community rejoiced; everyone was convinced that the prayers offered had caused my "tumor" to disappear. The rosary and the medal were said to have aided in the healing process, and two friends from the faith course, who attended a healing mass in my honor, said that they had specifically asked the priest to pray for my health. The Virgin was credited by all with destroying the "tumor" that had shown up on the CT scan. While the surgeon had told me that the "tumor" was really a shadow of my uterus, which was found to be slightly tipped to the right, the Marian devout's explanation was that I had indeed had a tumor and that it was eradicated by the Virgin. This belief is yet another example of how the devout are able to claim the spaces of sickness for themselves and to show how the Virgin is believed to intercede on the faithful's behalf. She is believed to have dominion over doctors, and it is she who is responsible for healings.

"Candy Kisses"

A regular feature of the first-Saturday-of-the month Rosaries and annual retreats at the shrine is the laying-on of hands for any pilgrim who desires to be healed. As discussed more comprehensively in chapter 4, pilgrims talk about being "slain in the Spirit" here, and general rejoicing occurs when a pilgrim has this experience. Although it is the individual pilgrim who is healed, the healing group also benefits, as it has successfully channeled powers from God. Yet while the laying-on of hands that takes place at the Ruizes' shrine helps to bring about healing, this is not typical of Marian shrines, where other methods of healing take place. The most common medium through which physical cures are said to occur at shrines is through healing waters, like those of Lourdes, France.[21] As the historian of American religions Colleen McDannell writes, it was the waters of Lourdes that gained fame for their healing capacity and not the local herb that Mary is said to have told Bernadette to eat, because, she writes, water as a symbol of "sustenance and regeneration" has a long history in Western religious tradition.[22] The waters of the fountain "blessed" by the Virgin of the Americas are said to have healing powers, and pilgrims faithfully fill gallon-sized containers to take the water back for themselves and their loved ones to use. The water from the Virgin of the Americas' fountain can carry the same healing potential back to families and friends who did not make the pilgrimage, and can be saved for the pilgrim to use at home. As the archeologist Sabine MacCormack writes, it is the appropriation of the water's holy qualities through souvenirs and other magical tokens that pilgrimage sites are distinguished from "neutral" places.[23]

While hands that heal and Mary's waters are said to help bring about physical healings, personal prayer can also invoke healing at the shrine. Like Doreen, who says she was cured of her physical sickness by praying at the shrine, Jim, a young man in his twenties, claims to have been cured of his terminal brain cancer after praying in front of the Virgin of the Americas' portrait. His tumor, which his doctor had told him was too large to be operated on safely, was reduced and rendered operable, he says, by the Virgin's intervention. Like Doreen and Jim, other pilgrims pray for physical cures and sometimes inflict pain on themselves as part of the petitionary process. Some pilgrims kneel for long periods of time, testing the limits of their bodies, and stay in that position despite pain in their knees and aches in their backs. The physical discomfort they may experience is considered insignificant in comparison to Jesus' suffering; as one pilgrim told me when I asked her how she was able to kneel on arthritic knees for so long, "it is the least I can do." Reyes Sr. was known to encourage pilgrims at the weekly Rosaries to kneel for the entire prayer if at all possible: "I know it is uncomfortable, but I ask you to offer your pain up," he would say. Even though many pilgrims go to the shrine for relief of their pain, Reyes's comments show that the belief that *some* suffering is necessary for graces to be offered is very much present at the shrine. The bodily pain that is experienced is believed to enhance the possibility for spiritual graces as well as physical cures.[24]

Spiritual and physical healing is facilitated by a visual and sensory engagement with the religious images that are displayed in the indoor and outdoor shrine and altar to the Virgin of the Americas. The study of pilgrimage is also a study of religious performance, as several scholars have noted. The anthropologist of religion David Haberman has written about pilgrimage as a bodily performance in which pilgrims' bodies are intimately connected with the quest for something that promises "to fill the painful holes in their lives."[25] Through pilgrimage, people's performances take place on a more public, open stage at this shrine site and they ask Mary and Jesus for healing—emotional, physical, and spiritual. The images the pilgrims pray to represent something larger than themselves and act as conduits for divine powers. What David Morgan, an art historian, calls "visual piety" is directed toward the objects and constitutes a dialogue with Jesus, Mary, and the saints. Morgan calls visual piety "the art of looking itself" that "contributes to religious formation and, indeed, constitutes a powerful practice of belief."[26] Orsi calls the devout's seeking a saint's gaze "a kind of divination." This divination is enacted by the pilgrims who kneel, stand, and sit before images of Mary and Christ at the Ruizes' backyard shrine and who invoke the powers of the saints. These devout show how piety is an active engagement with the saints—eyes, bodies, and lips interact with Mary and Jesus, who stand before pilgrims in the visible forms of plaster statues and paintings.

Oftentimes, this looking discerns divine light and colors and gives the objects a certain three-dimensionality, as though the paintings and statues are talking back to them. Jenny, a middle-aged Mexican American woman from California, said that her blind father had seen light form around the framed portrait of the Virgin of the Americas several years earlier in Estela's apparition room. Marty, a featured singer at the 1998 retreat, said he had seen St. Joseph in the clouds that very afternoon. "The pink and red rays were the blood of Divine mercy. The blue was the blue of Our Lady." Another spectacular sighting was claimed by close to twenty pilgrims during the 1998 retreat. During the Saturday morning Mañanitas, the traditional Mexican morning greeting songs for the Virgin, the sun began to rise and when it was visible from the altar, several women gasped aloud that they saw the sun pulsate. The men and women who sat nearest to the center altar all claimed to have seen the sun "dance," which was said to be a "kiss" and a "gift from Mary."

The pilgrims who told me that they had seen the sun dance and shine brightly pointedly asked me if I had seen it too. I recall being flustered, not wanting to lie and say that I had, but not wanting to seem as though I had not seen *anything,* which I feared would make it appear that I did not believe what they told me when in fact I was very much interested in hearing what they had perceived in the morning sky. Questions and challenges like these force the researcher to engage in reflexivity, what anthropologists Barbara Myerhoff and Jay Ruby call "consciousness about consciousness; thinking about thinking." This kind of reflection is unavoidable in the fieldwork context, and the researcher in the postmodern world in which we live must expect to be questioned and challenged by his or her informants. As the boundaries between the scholar/researcher and informant are blurred, questions like these must be expected and taken seriously.[27]

During my years of fieldwork in South Phoenix, I had the opportunity to get to know a number of the "regulars" at the shrine, many of whom are members of Mary's Ministries. These men and women are pilgrims, too; they just don't have to travel very far to get to the shrine. All have told me that they have experienced Mary's "candy kisses" and "slices of heaven" at the shrine, smelling fresh roses, having their rosaries turn to gold, and seeing Mary's image smile and wink at them. I have been given detailed and rich sensorial descriptions of encounters with Mary. Dominic, a young man I know from the Mary's Ministries faith course described in chapter 4, told me that he saw deep colors of blue and purple swirl around the Virgin's head. He went on to say that Mary first touched his life when she saved his dog, who had contracted parvo as a puppy. "Barclay, see, he's my friend, and I was afraid that he was going to die. So I prayed to Mary to watch over him. He lived, and I know that Mary helped save him."[28] Dominic's story points out that Mary's powers of intercession are not exclusively for humans; Mary's touch is for "everyone."

Another pilgrim described Mary's heart pulsating on fire: "it was like Her heart was going to burst from the heat and flames." What pilgrims refer to as Mary's "candy kisses" are part of the larger healing discourse of the shrine: Mary lets them know that she cares about them and that she is "there" for them. Pilgrims do not have to suffer alone; Mary offers her companionship and comradery through her winks and smiles.

Catholics like those who go to the shrine of the Virgin of the Americas have a history of creating the space and time in which the saints are able to mediate pain and suffering. The "telic decentralization" of pain that cuts the sufferer and her suffering off from the rest of society is penetrated and reversed at the shrine by the pilgrims who are searching for an amelioration of and eventual end to their physical and spiritual suffering.[29] At the shrine, pain is discussed and ultimately transcended. It is by touching and looking at religious objects, praying to the Virgin and Jesus, and talking with each other that they take an active part in the healing process. As Orsi writes, "Any notion that the Christian response to pain and suffering is one of passive acceptance clearly must be revised. . . . The sick resist the constriction that can characterize the space and time of sickness, and they can struggle against the threat of meaninglessness."[30] We are able to see through the narratives presented by Robert, Doreen, and Rey Sr. that these believers create meaning out of their pain and suffering, and that they are active interpreters in the direction it takes.

While the sickness Orsi describes primarily refers to physical ailments, his interpretation can be expanded to include spiritual suffering. Although the shrine to the Virgin of the Americas is known as a place where physical healings occur, it is better known as a place where ailing spirits can be doctored by Mary. Most of the pilgrims who go to this shrine can be considered "healthy"—that is, they do not manifest outward signs of illness. However, inwardly they describe themselves as having lost hope, and many say they are "lost." Some say that they have brought this sickness on themselves by their distance from God, by their spiritual laxity, and by Satan's grip over their souls. Their involvement with "the world," they say, has caused them to lose sight of what is important, and they seek to rearrange their priorities. Mary reaches out to those who are suffering on many levels and offers her help. All of the Marian devout with whom I have spoken—male and female, young and old, Anglo and Mexican—have had a powerful encounter with Mary at least once in their lives, and most have experienced many such encounters. These devotees say that they have been healed by Mary and touched by her, and their responses point to Mary's healing capabilities.

Damian, a young Mexican American man in his early twenties, told me that Mary helped him "set his priorities straight." Before he became involved in Mary's Ministries and started going to the shrine, he was easily influenced by his group of friends, who were into the "ways of the world . . . you know, like partying, wearing the latest fashions, driving cool cars." Damian said he started to get too attached to things and lost sight of "what's important" in his life. Since becoming involved with Mary's Ministries and starting to attend the rosaries, he said, he feels more "spiritually alive"; and although he still hangs out with some of his friends, he understands that they are "not everything." He said he was "touched" by the Blessed Mother and that she has helped guide him to a better way of living.

Sightings of the Virgin, conversations with her, and "just knowing She's there," as Damian experienced, all have healing components; the individual feels better, more connected to a higher power after the experience. These stories focus on meaningful contact with the Virgin that is remembered as having a profound impact: Mary is said to "touch" hearts and lives, interceding "when I needed Her," "just in time." The "kisses" from the Virgin were described to me as having occurred at the shrine to the Virgin of the Americas, in bedrooms, in cars, and in dreams. But wherever they occurred, Mary touched each of these devout, who in turn remembered the moment and considered it among the most important in their lives.

Pilgrims visit the Lady of the Americas' shrine because it is, as Mike, a pilgrim from Texas put it, "the real thing." Mike, a brewer for a major domestic beer company who drove "all day and night" from Houston to make it to the 1998 retreat, said that he enjoys going to the shrine to the Virgin of the Americas because "the Virgin is here!" Pilgrimage is his way of continuing his relationship with Mary, who first touched him in 1988 in Lubbock, Texas, where he claimed the sun pulsated for one and a half hours. Mike talked about his encounter with Mary as the most profound moment in his life.

> Nothing has equaled this day, it was like being on a beach; the sun warmed you but you didn't sweat, it wasn't too hot. Everywhere rosaries turned to gold, and everyone got a great tan, *everyone* was the same color! I think it was a little bit of heaven and showed that the earth will be like Eden once again.[31]

There are many pilgrims like Mike who, in the mid-1990s, traveled a Marian apparitions circuit that included South Phoenix; Lubbock, Texas; Conyers, Georgia; Medjugorje, in the former Yugoslavia; Lourdes, France; and Fatima, Portugal. Since most of these apparitions and sightings of Marian "miracles" died down by the year 2000, it would be interesting to see if these particular pilgrims have continued their rounds of the shrines. Based on my ten years of fieldwork at the South Phoenix shrine, I believe there has been a tremendous drop-off in the number of pilgrims who journey to the retreats each December; since the final public message of 1998, fewer and fewer pilgrims go to the shrine. Today most of the pilgrims are Mary's Ministries members from South Phoenix and Latin America, and the once well-attended retreats now host, at most, fifty non–Mary's Ministries members from the community.

Institutionalization of the Shrine

This shrine to the Virgin of the Americas in Estela's and Reyes's back yard was an established pilgrimage site from 1989 to 1998; pilgrims journeyed not only from the Southwest, but from all over the United States as word spread that this was an authentic apparition of the Virgin, even though the former Bishop of Phoenix did not validate it as such.[32] This shrine became one of the most frequented apparition sites in the United States in the late 1990s. Pilgrims usually found out about the apparitions through word of mouth, through Marian conferences and conventions, and through the Internet: the Ruizes began to advertise the messages on Marian apparitions websites in 1989.

In the early 1990s, the shrine to the Virgin of the Americas became part of the apparition circuit mentioned above. Pilgrims' demarcation of the Virgin of the Americas' shrine as sacred and as the site of a Marian manifestation points to what they call the "fruits" of the visions: the Ruiz family's collective "conversions," the "miracles" that were said to take place at the shrine, such as rosaries turning gold, the smell of Mary's perfumed roses, and clouds that appeared as Mary and Jesus; and the evangelizing and community organizing that resulted. Moreover, the shrine became a strong link in what Orsi calls the "chain of concern and consolation" that is nurtured and perpetuated at Catholic shrines around the world.[33]

The Ruiz family began to make plans to enclose the open-air wooden shrine soon after the Virgin's final public message in 1998. Family members told me that it was "Mary's will" that her shrine be enclosed and made into a chapel. Reyes Sr. informed me that the new chapel was to be a "place where people can come and pray at any time and they can stay comfortable and cool." By the fall of 2000, the original structure had been dismantled and a glass-enclosed, air-conditioned chapel had been built. The recently enclosed architectonics and material Catholicism of the shrine dovetail with the increased institutionalization of Mary's Ministries—greater clerical involvement, and a much stronger emphasis on the Church's teachings on Mary's role as mediatrix to Jesus.[34] And, whereas the early 1990s retreats focused on the Virgin Mary and her mes-

The newly enclosed backyard shrine. Photo by author.

sages of redemption for individuals, there is now a much greater effort to connect the Virgin and her messages both to Jesus (and his body and blood through the Eucharist) and to the language and rituals of the Church.

Priests' involvement has grown significantly in the last ten years. In the early 1990s, diocesan priests in South Phoenix and surrounding towns showed their support for the fledgling group by sponsoring faith courses in their parishes and by giving inspirational talks at the annual December retreats. In 1993, for example, Father Doug Nohava of South Phoenix and Father Mark Posada of St. Louis offered confession in a small space next to the life-sized statue of the Virgin of Guadalupe; they acknowledged the yard as an ethnic and Catholic space and gave the grassy area next to *la Virgen* a church-sanctioned sacredness. About twenty Mexican American women from South Phoenix lined up to talk to the two priests; while they waited they placed petitions in front of *la Virgen* and prayed their rosaries. At this time the Eucharist was not displayed by priests; their presence was noted and appreciated but not integral to the workings of the retreats. The focus of the early retreats was on Marian devotion and the Virgin's relationship to Estela Ruiz and her family. Estela, Reyes, and their grown children and their spouses would offer their testimonies and

Priest's vestments hanging inside the backyard chapel. Photo by author.

discuss how their relations as husband and wife had grown as a result of their Marian devotions.

At these early to mid-1990s retreats, the Eucharist was displayed by Deacon George of St. Catherine of Siena Church in South Phoenix; mass was not held and communion was not offered until 1998, the year in which priests became much more actively involved and began to help shape (and change) the language and direction of the retreats. The Eucharist has become a central part of the annual December retreats, and priests are highly visible and integrated into the weekend celebrations of Mary's arrival and messages of and for evangelization. The shrine dynamics have changed as well; from 1989 to 1998 pilgrims to the shrine included community members as well as those who had traveled from elsewhere in the United States to hear Mary's messages to Estela. Since the Virgin stopped appearing to Estela with messages for the public in 1998, the number of pilgrims has shrunk dramatically and those who attend the annual retreats today are primarily Mary's Ministries members from Latin America. The shift in the pilgrims' demographics parallels Mary's Ministries' new focus on the Americas and on evangelization rather than on the messages themselves.

What was especially intriguing to me when I attended the December 2002 retreat/*retiro* was that the shrine itself, and its material culture, is now much more enclosed and even closed-off than before. Compared with the early 1990s outdoor altar and open/unlocked shrine policy, the shrine is now, depending on how you look at it, more secure or less accessible—it is encircled by a gate that is locked up at night. The new chapel, which seats fifty, is now the most prominent feature of the backyard shrine, and one needs a security code to open it. In the early 1990s one could pray inside the shrine space at any time; there was no gate barring entrance, and a wooden sign at the front announced the times of the biweekly rosaries. From 1992 to 1998, almost every time I stopped by Estela's and Reyes's house there was someone praying in front of the Virgin of the Americas' altar or the statue of the Virgin of Guadalupe. Today the sign announcing the rosaries is gone, the main entrance to the back yard is usually blocked off by a metal gate, and the majority of the statues and paintings are inside the chapel. The life-sized statues of the crucified Christ and the Virgin of Guadalupe are the only two statues that remain outside. The shrine is now open only at specified times; as a result, far fewer people visit the shrine on a regular basis.

The December retreats are an exception to the new closed-off rule, but even then, fewer community members attend. Since the organization went global in 1999, retreat attendance has consistently been 90 to 95 percent Mary's Ministries members; in the early 1990s, retreat attendance reflected a more Southwestern United States demographic (Texas, California, Arizona). As Mary's Ministries has become more institutionalized and Latin American in its focus, its membership has become more exclusive, and non–Mary's Ministries member, Phoenix-area residents are not nearly as involved as they were in the organization's earlier years. Mañuel, a long-time South Phoenix resident and Mary's Ministries member, shared his skepticism at the 2002 December retreat, wondering whether what Mary's Ministries members call the "new evangelization" has been good for South Phoenix: "We're spreading Mary's messages all over which is good, but I think that this community is being neglected as a result of the new focus. Mary came to us in South Phoenix and I think we should be focusing more on this area."

The shrine dynamics have changed and what was a "new" phenomenon in the early 1990s gave way to a more institutionalized shrine that tied its success more self-consciously to the Church. While the Ruizes have always courted the support of local priests, today there is more of a dependence on clerical support. Successful evangelization is intricately connected with the good will of local bishops and priests, and the Ruizes and their organization are well aware of this. Because of the shift in focus, today the retreats are small and less than one hundred women and men participate, most of them Mary's Ministries members. What has happened is that Mary's Ministries has eclipsed the Virgin's messages—new members of Mary's Ministries are not as familiar with the family's story or with the Virgin's messages. Most are aware of the apparitions, but in nowhere near the detail and depth—a sharp contrast with earlier pilgrims to the shrine. These new "pilgrims" go to the shrine to receive strength for their evangelization—they still seek healing, but they are more focused and know what they want to accomplish. Their journey to the shrine is tied to the organization's plans for them, and as a result, the spontaneity of the earlier pilgrims is largely gone and the shrine has become, in a very real sense, corporate. Their visits are paid for by Mary's Ministries, so they are there as invited guests. The organization also pays for the airfare, food, and lodging of the visiting priests from Latin America, Africa, and Europe. Now pilgrimage takes on something other than a voluntary characteristic; one must have the desire to go, but one also has obligations.

Yet there is still a spark of the kind of community that we saw in the early to late 1990s retreats. The young Matachina dancer whose parents and community implored Padre Alejandro and Mary's Ministries members at the 2002 retreat and sought healing from her cancer provided an incredibly moving, emotional moment for everyone who was present. This tiny girl's suffering made her the focus of a group that fervently prayed for her, laying on their hands for close to half an hour. It was a respite in the retreat, a break in the talk of evangelization methods and goals; and it was more like the retreats of the past in which individuals communed with Mary and the saints and sought healing. As we have seen, Padre Alejandro was an important link between the girl's family, Mary's Ministries, and the Virgin, to whom the family's prayers were directed. As this encounter illustrates, the shrine can still be a place where people go to pray for miracles. It has changed in many ways, but it is still a place of hope and healing. The question that remains is what will happen with this shrine. Will it cease to be a place where pilgrims go to pray? Will it become a place for just the Ruiz family and their close friends? Based on my years of observations and research, I believe the shrine will continue to exist but will become even less open to the public, as the Virgin has ceased to bring messages to Estela for her "children." Right now, the future of the retreats is bound with the future of Mary's Ministries—and inextricably with ESPIRITU, which funds Mary's Ministries' evangelization with the rent it pays for the land on which the school stands.

What keeps pilgrims coming at all seems to be Mary's Ministries retreats, especially the December retreat. As long as Mary's Ministries continues to exist, there will be a steady flow of pilgrims at this shrine, though the reasons they come have changed over time. But despite the obstacles, the shrine remains a special place where one can still go to pray to *la Virgen* and to Jesus, and where one can enter into another world. It may be harder to get to that world today, it may take extra effort, but the possibility is still there and the backyard shrine retains much of the wonder it had when it first opened to the public in 1989. For now, the shrine remains a place of hope and healing in the religious imagination of the pilgrims who go there.

Conclusion
Grassroots Catholicism

On one level, this book is a study of a typical middle-class Mexican American woman and her family who have seen their share of struggles and challenges. From drug abuse to marital difficulties, the Ruiz family's experiences are shared by many families. Yet what sets this family apart from the norm is that it claims to have a special relationship with the Virgin Mary. An anthropological exploration of Estela's and her *familia's* dealings with the Virgin enables us to understand the psychological, sociological, and cultural basis for apparitions. Because Estela's experiences are complex and are informed by multiple sites—her childhood history, her family, her Mexican American culture, her Catholic faith, and her community—an interdisciplinary approach to understanding the apparitions is the only way to do justice to her rich experiences.

Estela was a woman torn between the individualism she enjoyed in the "Anglo world" and her familial commitments in her Mexican American home. The apparitions were a way for her to bridge the two worlds she found herself caught between; she went on to become a highly visible and sought-after visionary and she made concessions to accommodate familial expectations. Although she may have left her career as a public school administrator, she gained even greater power and prestige in her capacity as a Marian visionary. For Estela and her family, as well as for those who go to her shrine, the Virgin is a source of empowerment, one that enables them to transcend their daily struggles and to work constructively toward what they consider a more fulfilling life. Like Estela, many of them are torn between being "in the world" and "of the world," and they turn to Mary to help keep them grounded in their daily lives.

What connects Estela with other Marian visionaries is that her apparitions are inextricably connected with her social milieu; what sets her experiences apart is that her interpretation of the visions and their meaning are taken on by, and in some sense overtaken by, her family. That her husband, sons, daughters, and future daughters-in-law had their own powerful visual, locutionary, and sensorial experiences with Mary is unusual in the history of Marian apparitions and shows just how intense familial ties are in Mexican American culture. If Estela had been the only one to experience the Virgin, Mary's Ministries would not have been formed and the messages would leave no lasting legacy. Her family's claims of Marian phenomena are what validated her own experiences and catapulted their collective conversations into the public realm. As a result of familial justification and validation, the messages to Estela were interpreted as a call for religious and social reform—in their immediate neighborhoods and beyond. And the postmillennial thrust of both the messages themselves and the organization that arose distinguish them from other modern Marian apparitions, around which no similar grassroots religious movements have arisen.

On another level, this has been a study of *communidad*—a community of faithful Mexican American Catholics who find deep meaning at the shrine of the Virgin of the Americas. Some of these pilgrims commit themselves to the Virgin's call, and as her "soldiers" they become evangelists in her name. *Communidad* is, of course, connected to and informed by *familia*—pilgrims see themselves as members of a family and a larger community of pious Catholics, and Mary's Ministries members see themselves as a big, loving family. The Ruizes have worked the family metaphor to their advantage. They maintain control of the organization and draw others into their embrace. The "new" family is extended; Mary's Ministries members and pilgrims to the shrine form a kinship network.

What is particularly interesting from a sociocultural viewpoint is that the organization and its members have, in the eleven years of Mary's Ministries existence, crafted what historian David Gutiérrez calls a "third space" of Catholicism, one informed by a mixture of popular and official Catholic faith and doctrine but also by Protestant evangelical theology and language.[1] Most importantly, this Catholicism is created by Mexican Americans, historically a group neglected by the Church, but one that is now defining its future. A case study of Mary's Ministries illuminates the negotiation and contestation of identities—religious, ethnic, and gendered. The Ruizes and their organization, Mary's Ministries, have crafted a Catholicism that courts institutional support even as it maintains a separate, popular identity. As is described in chapter 7, in the last four years there has been a shift from a grassroots back-yard–based phenomenon to a more institutionalized group that has become much more dependent on diocesan support and approval for its enterprises. As it attempts to balance its popular and official Catholic identities, Mary's Ministries engages in a balancing act of evangelicalism and Catholicism. Not quite rejecting their evangelical Protestant competitors, Mary's Ministries instead borrows heavily from Pentecostal methods of evangelizing and prayer. The faith course dynamics and skits fit squarely within evangelical Protestant traditions and evangelizing modes. Indeed, what this organization represents is a complex Catholicism—one that blends independent, institutional forms of worship and prayer. These Catholic evangelicals confound categories as they experiment with and borrow from each of them. Yet the challenge for this organization is to maintain its original enthusiasm and excitement; recent institutionalization threatens to undermine the grassroots elements.

Ethnic and racial identity is also continually negotiated within this organization. The Virgin of the Americas crosses borders and boundaries and is comfortable with her middle-class, light-skinned Hispanic "children" because she looks like them, talks like them, identifies with them. This in-betweenness, or *nepantla,* "a continuous encounter of two or more divergent worldviews," is on display at the shrine and reflects the transculturation of Mexican Americans in the Southwest.[2] *Nepantla* is not syncretism or even *mestizaje*—it is the acknowledgment of different perspectives meeting—as the two Virgins meet in the back yard. Sometimes the worldviews have commonalities and will show overlap, what the sociologist of religion Fenggang Yang calls the process of constructing "adhesive identities."[3] The two *mestiza* Virgins—the one Spanish and Mexican the other Mexican and American—coexist at the shrine and are reinforced by the pilgrims who journey there. We see overlap with the Virgins but we also see a distinctiveness that shows that they are indeed two different manifestations of Mary. The Virgin of the Americas is a symbol for the barrio; members of this South Phoenix community where Mary first appeared interpret and manipulate this symbol to suit their needs, and they interpret Mary's messages as calling them to influence not only Hispanic and Latino communities throughout the Americas, but the Catholic Church itself.

Women play prominent roles within Mary's Ministries, and in our examination of Mary's Ministries we are able to see how gender is negotiated, especially among women. Taking their cue from Estela, who has an expanded power base since the onset of her apparitions in 1988, Hispanic women find opportunities to flourish in Mary's Ministries, which gives them chances to serve their community. All of the women I interviewed for this project say they have been empowered through their relationship with the Virgin—they feel a new sense of worth, a "calling" as many of them put it, and they find ultimate satisfaction in the work they do for evangelization, for the school, or for community development. These women are careful not to take the credit for their renewed confidence, new sense of self, and ability to make a difference in their communities; they make clear that it is based on the courage and strength they have received from the Blessed Mother and Jesus Christ. They have been empowered by their Catholic faith to transform their own lives as well as the social and economic realities of South Phoenix. Empowerment for these women means being able to take the lessons they have learned from their relationship with Mary and Jesus and to use them to accomplish social, educational, and economic reform—personal transformations become the political and social.[4]

What Mary's Ministries represents is the new face and new direction of American Catholicism: a face that combines Catholic rituals, beliefs, and symbols with Hispanic Catholics' needs and desires. The faith courses, with their blending of institutional and grassroots, backyard Catholicism, directly challenge the traditional dichotomies that scholars of Catholicism have set up between official and popular piety, and between Catholicism and evangelicalism, pointing to both overlap and contestation. Faith, family, and community are the overarching values of Mary's Ministries, a primarily lay-driven organization that incorporates evangelical enthusiasm, the desire for a personal relationship with Jesus, and language of conversion. At a Mary's Ministries annual retreat we are able to see a variety of Catholicisms: the Matachina dancers' sacred *indio* dance to *la Virgen de Guadalupe,* Roman Catholic devotionalism, Adoration of the Eucharist, and charismatic healing. Through their efforts, Mary's Ministries' leaders and members hope to bridge the gap, linguistically, theologically, and ethnically, between Catholic and Pentecostal/evangelical Protestant outreach, at the same time that they strive to reclaim Catholics who have left for Pentecostal churches.

Mary's Ministries, through its faith courses, South Phoenix charter school, and barrio community development, crosses boundaries and borders between the church hierarchy and laity. The ethno-religious identity Mary's Ministries promotes reflects the increasing collaboration between laity and clergy and the permeability of borders: ethnic, gendered, and geographic. Members cross religious borders by borrowing and experimenting with Protestant Pentecostal language. Exhibiting what Timothy Matovina calls the "blurring of national boundaries in the western hemisphere," the organization links U.S. and Latin American Hispanics' concerns and points to a new global American Catholicism.[5]

Like all organizations, Mary's Ministries struggles to make its mark on the religious landscapes of the Americas, and its members work to make their Catholic faith relevant and meaningful for Hispanic Americans in Phoenix and, more recently, Latin Americans as well. Members of this Marian-vision-inspired group are fashioning a Catholicism for the twenty-first century. These men and women are crafting a new community and a new version of Catholicism—one defined by the needs and issues of Mexican Americans. As cultural and religious *bricoleurs,* Mary's Ministries members aim to win souls for Jesus and Mary in the highly competitive American religious marketplace. They are crafting a new Catholic identity, a grassroots Catholicism—one that emphasizes the hopes, dreams, and desires of Catholic laity and builds a faith based upon them.

Notes

Notes to the Introduction

1. Throughout the book, I will use the terminology Hispanic, Hispano, Hispano–Mexican American, and Mexican American interchangeably. These are the ethnic identities my interlocutors use, and they also correspond with Hispanic academics' usage. I will avoid using the terms Chicano and Latino; the former refers to politicized Mexican Americans and is not used—in fact it is rejected—by the Ruiz family and those I interviewed; Latino is too broad a term and is also not used by my interlocutors in South Phoenix.

2. Peter Berger, *The Sacred Canopy: Elements of a Sociological Theory of Religion* (New York: Anchor Books, 1969), 19.

3. Robert A. Orsi, *Thank You, Saint Jude: Women's Devotion to the Patron Saint of Hopeless Causes* (New Haven, Conn.: Yale University Press, 1996), 150.

4. Estela Ruiz, interview with author, South Phoenix, Arizona, March 28, 2002.

5. For a comparative historical overview of Mexican American families in the Southwest, see Richard Griswold del Castillo, *La Familia: Chicano Families in the Urban Southwest 1848 to Present* (Notre Dame, Ind.: University of Notre Dame Press, 1984).

6. Robert A. Orsi, "The Religious Boundaries of an In-between People: Street Feste and the Problem of the Dark-Skinned Other in Italian Harlem, 1920–1990," in *Gods of the City*, ed. Robert Orsi (Bloomington: Indiana University Press, 1999), 257–288.

7. Richard Rodriguez, *Brown: The Last Discovery of America* (New York: Viking, 2002), xi.

8. For full accounts of *mestizaje*, see: Virgilio Elizondo, *Galilean Journey: The Mexican-American Promise* (New York: Orbis Books, 1983); and *The Future Is Mestizo: Life Is Where Cultures Meet* (Boulder: University Press of Colorado, 2000).

9. See *Mexican Americans and the Catholic Church, 1900–1965*, ed. Jay P. Dolan and Gilberto M. Hinojosa (Notre Dame, Ind.: University of Notre Dame Press, 1997) for a good overview of the Catholic Church's stance toward Mexican Americans.

10. C. Gilberto Romero has argued that Hispanic practitioners of popular piety have an "intuitive insight," and offers an apologetics of Hispanic popular piety in

Hispanic Devotional Piety: Tracing the Biblical Roots (New York: Orbis Books, 1991), 40, 41. Stephen Holler's work also privileges Hispanic popular piety. He has referred to Hispanics who attend Catholic mass regularly as "losing their identity." Holler, Latino Studies lecture, Indiana University, April 9, 1999. His published work does acknowledge that there is a relationship between U.S. Hispanic popular piety and the Church, but it does not explore the relationship in depth. Holler, "Exploring the Popular Religion of U.S. Hispanic/Latino Ethnic Groups," *Latino Studies Journal* 6, no. 3 (September 1995): 3–29.

11. Robert Orsi, *The Madonna of 115th Street: Faith and Community in Italian Harlem, 1880–1950*, second edition (New Haven, Conn.: Yale University Press, 2002), xvii.

12. Robert Wuthnow, *The Restructuring of American Religion: Society and Faith since World War II* (Princeton, N.J.: Princeton University Press, 1988).

13. See Ronald D. Cohen, *Children of the Mill: Schooling and Society in Gary, Indiana, 1906–1960* (Bloomington: Indiana University Press, 1990) for a good overview of Gary's history through the lens of mill-based society.

14. I taped many of the interviews with Ruiz family members, and did not tape many others. Those I taped were almost always prearranged interviews, while those I did not tape were usually spontaneous. This was also the case with my interviews with non–family members: Mary's Ministries members and pilgrims to the shrine, the two focus groups of the study after the Ruiz family. The interviews I conducted were both formal and informal. Formal interviews were prearranged, taped, and usually took place in a home or office; informal interviews were usually more spontaneous and happened when someone had some extra time and motioned me to sit down to talk. During the latter type of interview, I jotted down notes on my "field notepads" and returned as soon as possible afterward to my room at Norma's and Rey's or to a local taco shop, where I would write a more detailed account of the conversation in a separate notebook. I used a dual system of taking notes: separate notepads, small and easily portable, for my field notes, and larger notepads for the transcribed notes and reflections. This method of note-taking was important because the "field data" were kept separate from my reflections—a distinction I felt important and necessary to maintain.

15. Quoted in James Clifford, "Spatial Practices: Fieldwork, Travel, and the Disciplining of Anthropology," in *Anthropological Locations: Boundaries and Grounds of a Field Science*, ed. Akhil Gupta and James Ferguson (Berkeley: University of California Press, 1997), 188.

16. For provocative discussions of what it means to do ethnography today, see Renato Rosaldo, *When Natives Talk Back: Chicano Anthropology since the Late Sixties*, Renato Rosaldo Lecture Series Monograph, Vol. 2 (Tucson: University of Arizona Mexican American Studies and Research Center, 1986); Caroline B. Brettel, ed., *When They Read What We Write: The Politics of Ethnography* (Westport, Conn. and London: Bergin & Garvey, 1993); R. Marie Griffith, *God's Daughters: Evangeli-*

cal Women and the Power of Submission (Berkeley: University of California Press, 1997), Introduction.

17. Ruth Behar, *The Vulnerable Observer: Anthropology that Breaks Your Heart* (Boston: Beacon Press, 1996), 166–168.

18. Ibid., 161–176. Behar discusses the importance of making oneself vulnerable when researching and writing anthropology.

19. Swanson grapples with these issues of accountability and gives the following advice: "Imagine them (informants) as being in the audience. Imagine their jokes, their laughter, their anger. Then when we speak we are not talking about Indians (informants) in general but about these specific people to whom we hold ourselves accountable. Do they recognize themselves in our descriptions?" Tod Swanson, "Through Family Eyes: Towards a More Adequate Perspective for Viewing Native American Religious Life, " *American Indian Quarterly* 21 (winter 1997): 70. Swanson, who was the director of my master's thesis and my mentor, has also helped me think about how to approach these sensitive issues in personal conversations. I am grateful to him for sharing his insights with me when I was in Phoenix conducting my dissertation fieldwork and needed some scholarly advice and conversation.

20. Ibid., 71.

21. Karen McCarthy Brown, *Mama Lola: A Vodou Priestess in Brooklyn* (Berkeley and Los Angeles: University of California Press, 1991), 12.

22. Jay Ruby and Barbara Meyerhoff, eds., *A Crack in the Mirror: Reflexive Perspectives in Anthropology* (Philadelphia: University of Pennsylvania Press, 1982), 5.

23. Ibid.

Notes to Chapter 1

1.The Ruizes' eldest son, Inocensio, "Lolo, " was a practicing evangelical Protestant living in Los Angeles with his family, and Estela says she was not concerned about his faith.

2. Throughout the book, several titles will be used interchangeably to identify the Virgin Mary. These names include: Blessed Mother, Mary, Virgin, Virgin of the Americas, Our Lady of the Americas, Lady, *la Virgen,* and the Virgin of Guadalupe.

3. Estela Ruiz, interview with author, South Phoenix, Arizona, October 27, 1993.

4. "Apparition" refers to seeing/the visual component of the manifestation and is used as an umbrella term to describe the phenomenon of seeing the Virgin Mary, while locution refers to the hearing/aural aspect of the experience.

5. William Christian Jr., *Apparitions in Late Medieval and Renaissance Spain* (Princeton, N.J.: Princeton University Press, 1981), 4.

6. Michael Carroll's various works use psychoanalytic theory to argue that Marian visions are primarily caused by underlying sexual neuroses on the part of both the visionaries and those who believe in the visions. He forces an overarching thesis

onto all of the apparitions he studies and makes the apparitions and those who experience them seem mechanistic and virtually indistinguishable. This theory is the basis for his arguments in all of his works, including *Catholic Cults and Devotions: A Psychological Enquiry* (Montreal: McGill-Queen's University Press, 1989); *The Cult of the Virgin Mary: Psychological Origins* (Princeton, N.J.: Princeton University Press, 1986); *Madonnas that Maim: Popular Catholicism in Italy since the Fifteenth Century* (Baltimore, Md.: Johns Hopkins University Press, 1992); and *Veiled Threats: The Logic of Popular Catholicism in Italy* (Baltimore, Md.: Johns Hopkins University Press, 1996). Carroll also uses psychoanalytic theory to explain the visionary phenomena in "Visions of the Virgin Mary: The Effect of Family Structures on Marian Apparitions," *Journal for the Scientific Study of Religion* 22, no. 3 (1983): 205; and "The Virgin Mary at LaSalette and Lourdes: Whom Did the Children See?" *Journal for the Scientific Study of Religion* 24, no. 1 (1985): 56.

7. Estela Ruiz, interview with author, South Phoenix, Arizona, October 27, 1993.

8. Ottawa University is based in Ottawa, Kansas, and has branches in Phoenix and Tempe, Arizona, and Milwaukee, Wisconsin, as well as several international branches. The university's slogan is "Ottawa University: A University For Adults," and it advertises itself as a Christian-based school.

9. Estela Ruiz, breakfast conversation with author at Phoenix restaurant, September 20, 1998.

10. Estela Ruiz, interview with author, South Phoenix, Arizona, November 15, 1998.

11. Armando Ruiz, interview with author, South Phoenix, Arizona, April 4, 1993.

12. Estela Ruiz, interview with author, South Phoenix, Arizona, November 15, 1998.

13. Moises Sandoval, "The Organization of a Hispanic Church," in *Hispanic Catholic Culture in the U.S.: Issues and Concerns,* ed. Jay P. Dolan and Allan Figueroa Deck (Notre Dame, Ind.: University of Notre Dame Press, 1994), 141–146.

14. Reyes Ruiz, interview with author, South Phoenix, Arizona, September 27, 1998.

15. Richard Rodriguez writes about his own immersion in the predominantly Anglo academic world and his painful memories of being distanced from his parents and culture. In his moving autobiography, Rodriguez writes about the complex process of acculturation, the cost of social success, and the loss of culture that accompanies the process. See *Hunger of Memory: The Education of Richard Rodriguez* (New York: Bantam Books, 1982).

16. Estela Ruiz, interview with author, South Phoenix, Arizona, September 19, 1998.

17. See George J. Sánchez, *Becoming Mexican American* (Berkeley and Los Angeles: University of California Press, 1993); Vicki L. Ruiz, *From Out of the Shadows: Mexican Women in Twentieth-Century America* (New York: Oxford University Press, 1998).

18. *Las Mujeres: Conversations from a Hispanic Community,* ed. Nan Elsasser, Kyle MacKenzie, and Trixier y Vigil (New York: McGraw-Hill, 1979), 37–38.

19. Sarah Deutsch, *No Separate Refuge: Culture, Class, and Gender on an Anglo-Hispanic Frontier in the American Midwest, 1880–1940* (New York: Oxford University Press, 1987). Vicki L. Ruiz devotes *From Out of the Shadows* to the issue of Mexican women breaking past the economic, social, and educational barriers set before them to improve their lives and those of their loved ones.

20. For a good overview of the Chicano movement, see Manuel G. Gonzales, *Mexicanos: A History of Mexicans in the United States* (Bloomington: Indiana University Press, 1999), 199–222.

21. A detailed description of Arizona's English-Only Proposition, Proposition 106, is provided in "The Armando Ruiz Papers, 1987–1989, " Arizona State University, Department of Archives and Manuscripts, ACC # 89-129, Call #MSS-73.

22. Vicki Ruiz, *From Out of the Shadows,* 112.

23. Estela Ruiz, interview with author, South Phoenix, Arizona, September 22, 1993.

24. There are several excellent sources on children of alcoholics, all of which elucidate themes in Estela's narrative. See Barbara L. Wood, *Children of Alcoholism: The Struggle for Self and Intimacy in Adult Life* (New York: New York University Press, 1987); Theodore Jacob and Ruth Ann Seilhamer, "The Impact on Spouses and How They Cope, " in *Alcohol and the Family* (New York: St. Martin's Press, 1982), 114–126; Charles P. Barnard, M.D., *Families with an Alcoholic Member: The Invisible Patient* (New York: Human Sciences Press, 1990); Peter Steinglass, M.D., *The Alcoholic Family* (New York: Basic Books, 1987); and Rachel V., *Family Secrets: Life Stories of Adult Children of Alcoholics* (San Francisco: Harper and Row, 1987).

25. Clare Wilson, "The Impact on Children, " in *Alcohol and the Family,* ed. Jim Orford and Judith Harwin (New York: St. Martin's Press, 1982), 156–159.

26. Tom Petrisko, *For the Soul of the Family* (Santa Barbara, Calif.: Queenship Publishing, 1996), 46.

27. Estela Ruiz, interview with author, South Phoenix, Arizona, September 22, 1993.

28. Vicki L. Ruiz, *From Out of the Shadows,* 51–52; George Sánchez, *Becoming Mexican American,* 184–185.

29. Sánchez, *Becoming Mexican American,* 137. Ruth Horowitz, *Honor and the American Dream: Culture and Identity in a Chicano Community* (New Brunswick, N.J.: Rutgers University Press, 1983), 111; Vicki Ruiz, *From Out of the Shadows,* 65.

30. Estela Ruiz, interview with author, South Phoenix, Arizona, September 22, 1993.

31. There are several excellent scholarly works on women's roles in ethnic and immigrant families: Robert Orsi's *The Madonna of 115th Street* (New Haven, Conn.: Yale University Press, 1985), esp. 129–150; Donna Gabbacia, *From the Other Side: Women, Gender, and Immigrant Life in the U.S. 1820–1990* (Bloomington: In-

diana University Press, 1994), 45–60; and John Bodnar, *The Transplanted: A History of Immigrants in Urban America* (Bloomington: Indiana University Press, 1985), 71–84.

32. Robert Orsi writes about how women, daughters of immigrants in World War II America, were the focus of worries, prayers, and tears. Orsi, *Thank You Saint Jude: Women's Devotion to the Patron Saint of Hopeless Causes* (New Haven, Conn.: Yale University Press, 1996), 44–47.

33. Estela Ruiz, interview with author, South Phoenix, Arizona, September 22, 1993.

34. Wood, *Children of Alcoholism,* 39.

35. Estela Ruiz, interview with author, South Phoenix, Arizona, September 22, 1993.

36. Ibid.

37. Estela Ruiz, interview with author, South Phoenix, Arizona, December 6, 2000.

38. Ibid.

39. David Blackbourn, *Marpingen: Apparitions of the Virgin Mary in Bismarckian Germany* (Oxford: Clarendon Press, 1993), 23–24.

40. Estela Ruiz, interview with author, South Phoenix, Arizona, September 19, 1998.

41. Medjugorje, a small village in the former Yugoslavia, is the site of the most famous and popular Marian visions of the twentieth century. The Virgin Mary is said to have appeared to six children, beginning in June 1981 and ending in the fall of 1998. In the messages the Virgin gives to the children for the public, conversion to God is emphasized, in addition to praying the rosary and working on one's spiritual life. There are similarities between the messages these children received and those Estela has been given from the Virgin of the Americas—a call to evangelization, ecumenicism, and a priority for the poor. For a more detailed academic description of these messages, see Sandra Zimdars-Swartz, *Encountering Mary: Visions of Mary from La Salette to Medjugorje* (New York: Avon Books, 1991), esp. 20–21, 233–240, 242–245. For a devotee's/believer's perspective on the Medjugorje phenomenon, see Wayne Weibel, *Medjugorje: The Message* (Orleans, Mass.: Paraclete Press, 1997), and *Medjugorje: The Mission* (Orleans, Mass.: Paraclete Press, 1994).

42. Estela Ruiz, interview with author, South Phoenix, Arizona, September 19, 1998.

43. Ibid.

44. *Cursillos* are weekend retreats held for Catholics who want to deepen their relationship with God. *Cursillo* is Spanish for "short course in Christianity, " and the courses were popularized by Mexican Americans in the Southwest during the 1960s and 1970s. They were brought from Majorca, Spain, to the United States in the mid-1950s and have their beginnings in Latin American Pentecostalism.

45. Estela Ruiz, interview with author, South Phoenix, Arizona, September 22, 1993.

46. Estela, December 10, 1988; transcripts from the Ruiz family's private collection of taped conversations.

47. Estela Ruiz, Ruiz family tapes.

48. Virginia Lieson Brereton writes that this use of "before" and "after" language is also common in nineteenth- and twentieth-century Protestant women's conversion stories. Protestant women's conversion stories, like Estela's, also emphasize a "changed heart" and the desire to evangelize in the name of God. See *From Sin to Salvation: Stories of Women's Conversions, 1800 to the Present* (Bloomington: Indiana University Press, 1991), 4, 5.

49. Estela Ruiz, interview with author, South Phoenix, Arizona, April 14, 1993.

50. Ibid.

51. Estela Ruiz, interview with author, South Phoenix, Arizona, September 22, 1993.

52. Estela Ruiz, interview with author, South Phoenix, Arizona, April 14, 1993.

53. Nancy Chodorow, *The Reproduction of Mothering* (Berkeley: University of California Press, 1978), 73.

54. Estela Ruiz, interview with author, South Phoenix, Arizona, October 27, 1993.

55. Ibid.

56. Marina Warner, *Alone of All Her Sex* (New York: Alfred A. Knopf, 1976).

57. Martha Cotera, "Marianismo, " in *Dona Doormat no esta aqui!* ed. Irene Dominguez (Washington, D.C.: U.S. Department of Education, 1985), 147.

58. Gloria Ines-Loya, "The Hispanic Woman: *Pasionaria* and *Pastora* of the Hispanic Community, " in *Frontiers of Hispanic Theology in the United States,* ed. Allan Figueroa Deck (New York: Orbis Books, 1992), 125.

59. Judith Stacey, *Brave New Families: Stories of Domestic Upheaval in Late Twentieth Century America* (San Francisco: Basic Books, 1991).

60. Elizabeth Brusco, *The Reformation of Machismo: Evangelical Conversion and Gender in Colombia* (Austin: University of Texas Press, 1995), 6.

NOTES TO CHAPTER 2

1.William Christian Jr. writes about how visions become intertwined with others' stories and lives in *Visionaries: The Spanish Republic and the Reign of Christ* (Berkeley and Los Angeles: University of California Press, 1996).

2. Paolo Apolito, *Apparitions of the Madonna at Oliveto Citra* (University Park: Pennsylvania State University Press, 1998), 4.

3. Apolito, *Apparitions of the Madonna at Oliveto Citra,* 7. These kitchen-table talks and the tape recording of them took place December 10, 17, 20, 22, 24, 25, 27, and 30, 1988; and January 3, 4, 7, 10, 14, 15, and 20, 1989.

4. Estela Ruiz, December 10, 1988, transcripts from the Ruiz family's private collection of taped conversations.

5. Reyes Sr., December 12, 1988, transcripts from the Ruiz family's private collection.

6. Armando Ruiz, January 4, 1989, transcripts from the Ruiz family's private collection.

7. Ibid.

8. Armando Ruiz, interview with author, South Phoenix, Arizona, April 14, 1993.

9. Rosie Ruiz, December 30, 1988, transcripts from the Ruiz family's private collection.

10. Ibid., December 12, 1988.

11. Leticia Ruiz, December 10, 1988, transcripts from the Ruiz family's private collection.

12. Ibid.

13. Fernando Ruiz, December 10, 1988, transcripts from the Ruiz family's private collection.

14. Estela Ruiz, December 10, 1988, transcripts from the Ruiz family's private collection.

15. Becky Ruiz, December 10, 1988, transcripts from the Ruiz family's private collection.

16. Ibid., December 17, 1988. At the time, Father Doug Nohava was the parish priest of the family's home parish, St. Catherine of Siena, in South Phoenix. Father Doug, like Father Jack Spaulding of St. Maria Goretti in Scottsdale, was an early supporter of the Ruiz family and became the family's spiritual advisor when Bishop Thomas O'Brien told Father Jack that he could no longer function in that role because of the investigations that were under way concerning both Estela's visions and those of the St. Maria Goretti visionaries.

17. Estela Ruiz, December 24, 1988, transcripts from the Ruiz family's private collection.

18. Father Jack Spaulding, interview with author, St. Thomas the Apostle rectory, Phoenix, Arizona, November 4, 1998.

19. Father Jack Spaulding, interview with author, November 4, 1998.

20. Ibid.

21. There are several published sources from a believer's perspective on the St. Maria Goretti visionaries. These include: Robert Faricy, S.J. and Lucy Rooney, S.N.D. de N., *Our Lady Comes to Scottsdale: Is It Authentic?* (Santa Barbara, Calif.: Queenship Publishing Company, 1993); Faricy and Rooney, *Return to God: The Scottsdale Message* (Santa Barbara, Calif.: Queenship Publishing, 1993); and *I Am Your Jesus of Mercy,* volumes I–V (Milford, Ohio: Riehle Foundation, 1989, 1990, 1991, 1992, 1996). Father Faricy and Sister Rooney conducted their own investigations of the visionaries and of the visions' contents, and conclude that they are authentic.

22. Sandra Zimdars-Swartz, "The Marian Revival in American Catholicism: Focal Points and Features of the New Marian Enthusiasm, " in *Being Right: Conservative Catholics in America,* ed. Mary Jo Weaver and R. Scott Appleby (Bloomington: Indiana University Press, 1995), 230–234.

23. Ibid.

24. Ibid.

25. Estela Ruiz, January 3, 1989, transcripts from the Ruiz family's private collection.

26. Estela Ruiz, interview with author, South Phoenix, Arizona, September 19, 1998.

27. Apolito, *Apparitions of the Madonna at Oliveto Citra,* 10.

28. See Apolito, *Apparitions of the Madonna at Oliveto Citra;* William Christian Jr., *Apparitions in Late Medieval and Renaissance Spain* (Princeton, N.J.: Princeton University Press, 1981), and *Visionaries;* David Blackbourn, *Marpingen: Apparitions of the Virgin Mary in Bismarckian Germany* (Oxford: Clarendon Press, 1993); and Sandra Zimdars-Swartz, *Encountering Mary: Visions of the Virgin Mary From LaSalette to Medjugorje* (New York: Avon Books, 1991).

29. Apolito, in *Apparitions of the Madonna at Oliveto Citra,* uses this phrase to mean speech that is not hierarchically valued; every person's voice counts the same.

30. Christian, *Visionaries,* 5.

31. The messages of Medjugorje will be examined in greater detail in chapter 3.

32. Christian, *Visionaries,* 11.

NOTES TO CHAPTER 3

1. In virtually all of her public messages, which lasted from December 1989 to December 1998, the Virgin of the Americas relates her hope as well as her frustration and anguish that her "children" are not, as she tells Estela, "turning their hearts to God." The Virgin's messages from December 1989 to October 1994 are available in *Our Lady of the Americas: The Messages of the Blessed Virgin Mary as Received by Estela Ruiz of South Phoenix, Arizona* (McKees Rocks, Pa.: Pittsburgh Center for Peace, 1994). The rest of the public messages are available in a pamphlet, "Our Lady of the Americas' Messages from November '94–Present, " from Mary's Ministries, 30 East Cody Drive, Phoenix, Arizona 85040.

2. Academic studies of contemporary American Marian apparitions include: John McGreevy's "Bronx Miracle, " *American Quarterly* 52, no. 3 (September 2000): 405–443; Sandra Zimdars-Swartz, *Encountering Mary* (Princeton, N.J.: Princeton University Press, 1991); Daniel Wojcik, *The End of the World as We Know It* (New York: New York University Press, 1997).

3. Wojcik, *The End of the World as We Know It,* 12.

4. *Our Lady of the Americas: The Messages,* February 3, 1996.

5. The Virgin gave Estela this message December 5, 1998:
My Immaculate Heart will be victorious because through My great warriors we will win the war. It only takes a few good men and women to be willing and obedient servants. I have gained many, many willing and obedient soldiers in My coming to the world. There are many battles yet to be won as we forge ahead. Remember My beloved warriors that you must never put down your weapons.

6. Tom Petrisko, *For the Soul of the Family* (Santa Barbara, Calif.: Queenship Publishing, 1996), 249.

7. According to Estela, the Virgin gave her the following message on February 3, 1996:
I have been sent into the world for a very special purpose. As the destruction of the children of God continues because of hate and anger, heaven cries to see how lightly God's children have taken the gist of life that God creates. The purpose of My coming is that I may come to touch hearts, to call all souls to come back to God's ways. It is only if God's children return to the ways of God that you, My children of the world, can begin to stop the destruction of mankind on earth.

8. Petrisko, *For the Soul of the Family*, 8.

9. Estela Ruiz, interview with author, South Phoenix, Arizona, 19 September 1998.

10. *Our Lady of the Americas: The Messages*, October 1, 1994.

11. Ibid., February 4, 1995.

12. Ibid., September 6, 1997.

13. Fr. Rene Laurentin, *The Apparitions of the Blessed Virgin Mary Today* (Dublin: Veritas, 1990), 131.

14. Ibid.

15. *Dictionary of Mary* (New Jersey: Catholic Book Publishing, 1997), 477.

16. Ibid.

17. For academic approaches to these ultimately condemned visions, see: Thomas Kselman, "Our Lady of Necedah: Marian Piety and Cold War," CUSHWA Working Paper Series, University of Notre Dame, series 12, no. 2 (fall 1982):18; and Keven Lahart, "Miracle in Bayside," *The Critic* 1 (fall/winter 1974): 36. For "insider perspectives" on these apparitions, and for a detailed account of the messages, see: Henry Swan, *My Work with Necedah*, volumes I–IV (Necedah, Wis.: For My God and My Country, 1959); *Revelations and Messages as Given through Mary Ann Van Hoof, at Necedah, Wisconsin* (Necedah, Wis.: For My God and My Country, Inc., 1971); *Our Lady Help of Roses Mary Help of Mothers: An Introduction Booklet on the Apparitions of Bayside* (Lowell, Mass.: The Last Days, 1979); *Our Lady of the Roses Mary, Help of Mothers: A Booklet about the Heavenly Apparitions to Veronica Leuken of Bayside, New York* (Lowell, Mich.: These Last Days, 1979).

18. Fr. Rene Laurentin, *The Church and Apparitions: Their Status and Function, Criteria and Reception* (Milford, Ohio: Riehle Foundation, 1989), 9, 10; Fr. Edward O'Connor, *Marian Apparitions Today: Why So Many?* (Santa Barbara, Calif.: Queenship Publishing, 1996), 106, 107.

19. Laurentin, *The Church and Apparitions*, 9–11; *Dictionary of Mary*, 38–39. The investigating committee poses a series of questions based on the "Criteria to judge, at least with probability, the nature of presumed apparitions and revelations." As stated in the document, the committee looks at the following: whether the event is in harmony with or is contrary to revelation, or to faith and morals; if the seers are sincere persons or hypocrites, healthy or sick, saints or sinners; if there are signs such as healings that have been scientifically recognized; and whether "spiritual fruits" have been shown. This fourth criterion refers to Matthew 7:16–20, where Jesus says, "You can tell a tree by its fruits. . . . A sound tree cannot bear bad fruit any more than a decayed tree can bear good fruit."

20. Laurentin, *The Church and Apparitions*, 10–11.

21. Ibid., 13. In addition to the four "positive criteria, " another four questions are asked which establish "negative criteria": whether the apparitions manifest error as to the fact; if the apparitions show a doctrinal error, which would point to the visionary adding "human elements" to supernatural revelation; whether or not there is evidence of financial advantage in direct relation to the apparitions; and if there are "seriously immoral acts" that have been committed before or after the visions began, by the visionary and/or the "acolytes."

22. Ibid., 5.

23. Father Jack's and the visionaries' stories are provided in detail in the five-volume series *I Am Your Jesus of Mercy* (Santa Barbara, Calif.: Queenship Publishing, 1993–1996); and in Robert Faricy, S.J., and Lucy Rooney, S.N.D. de N., *Our Lady Comes to Scottsdale: Is It Authentic?* (Santa Barbara, Calif.: Queenship Publishing, 1993) and *Return to God: The Scottsdale Message* (Santa Barbara, Calif.: Queenship Publishing, 1993).

24. Bishop O'Brien's report included the following:

1.) The prayer meetings and public devotions at St. Maria Goretti Church may continue for the spiritual welfare of all concerned. There may not be, however, any unequivocal claim of miraculous intervention. This is due to the absence of any external evidence that the messages are directly from Our Lord Jesus Christ or the Blessed Virgin Mary. 2.) In order to maintain the unity of the prayer group at St. Maria Goretti Church with the whole Church, I am establishing a Community of Discernment. The Community . . . will: aid the prayer group in interpreting any future events; direct the development of devotion to Our Lady; monitor the circulation of any publications produced by the prayer group. *The Catholic Sun,* 18 January 1990, 14.

25. Ibid., 14.

26. Father Jack Spaulding, interview with author, St. Thomas parish, Scottsdale, Arizona, November 4, 1998.

27. *The Catholic Sun,* May 13, 1990, 12.

28. For the best historical overview of Marian apparitions. see Zimdars-Swartz, *Encountering Mary.* Several other sources provide detailed and valuable information on the history of apparitions, including William Christian Jr., *Visionaries: The Spanish Republic and the Reign of Christ* (Berkeley: University of California Press, 1997), and *Apparitions of Late Medieval and Renaissance Spain* (Princeton, N.J.: Princeton University Press, 1981); Paolo Apolito, *Apparitions of the Madonna at Oliveto Citra* (University Park: Pennsylvania State University Press, 1998); and Ruth Harris, *Lourdes: Body and Spirit in the Secular Age* (New York: Penguin Books, 1999).

29. Zimdars-Swartz calls attention to the interrelatedness of public and private revelations, most thoroughly in the Introduction to *Encountering Mary.* In "Religious Experience and Public Cult: The Case of Mary Ann Van Hoof, " *Journal of Religion and Health* 28, no. 1 (1989): 36–57, she explores the relationship between the public's demands and the private experiences in a case study of a mid-twentieth-century Marian visionary. Michael P. Carroll explores why children claim to be visionaries in "The Virgin Mary at LaSalette and Lourdes: Whom Did the Children See?" *Journal for the Scientific Study of Religion* 24, no. 1 (1985): 56–74.

30. Robert E. Wright, "If It's Official, It Can't Be Popular? Reflections on Popular and Folk Religion, " *Journal of Hispanic/Latino Theology* 1, no. 3 (1994): 53. Robert Orsi offers a devastating critique of "popular" and "official" in *The Madonna of 115th Street: Faith and Devotion in Italian Harlem,* 2d ed. (New Haven, Conn.: Yale University Press, 2002).

31. Mary's Ministries' popular Catholicism is deeply entwined with and informed by the Catholicism of the Church. The family and the organization have been actively supported by several Phoenix-area priests, in Glendale, Scottsdale, Mesa, and South Phoenix, who sponsored Mary's Ministries faith courses in their churches. The organization has also been supported on an international scale by the Catholic Church hierarchy, most notably by Father Tom Forrest of the Vatican's Evangelization 2000. The Ruizes and their organization have managed to retain their original enthusiasm and family-based piety as they have sought institutional support for what they see as their mission, the evangelization of the Americas. Their close associations with various priests and bishops in the United States and the Americas enable them to achieve more success through institutional validation and legitimation.

32. Fowler describes herself this way prior to her visions in an interview with Ann Marie Hitchcock in *Wake Up America! Take My Heart, Take My Hand* (Virginia: Hampton Roads Publishing Co., 1993), 20. Estela has described herself this way in numerous conversations and more formal interviews, spanning the years from 1992 to 2003.

33. Theologians and scholars alike note that Marian visionaries become stronger in their Catholic faith after the onset of the visions. Fr. Rene Laurentin, *Our Lord and Our Lady in Scottsdale: Fruitful Charisms in a Traditional American Parish* (Milford, Ohio: Faith Publishing Company, 1992); O'Connor, *Marian Apparitions Today;* Zimdars-Swartz, "The Marian Revival in American Catholicism," in *Being Right,* ed. Mary Jo Weaver and R. Scott Appleby (Bloomington: Indiana University Press, 1995), 213–239. Perhaps even more striking than theologians' or historians' verification are Marian visionaries' narratives, all of which describe how the visionary has experienced a conversion to God and renewed his/her faith in very specific ways, such as attending daily mass, taking the sacraments, praying the rosary, and fasting. Nancy Fowler, the Georgia visionary, sums up virtually every contemporary visionary's narrative when she points to her renewed Catholic faith: "Before the visions began, I did not have a serious prayer life. I was a bench-warmer Catholic. I could not tell you what the Gospel was about five minutes after I heard it. I did not believe in visions. . . . The turning point in my life came when I went to Reconciliation. I poured out my heart." Fowler, *Wake Up America!* 20.

34. Colleen McDannell, *Material Christianity* (New Haven, Conn.: Yale University Press, 1995).

35. Zimdars-Swartz, *Encountering Mary,* 50.

36. There has been a proliferation of U.S. Marian visions since Medjugorje, and the messages received by the visionaries are close to those given by the *Gospa.* See Mart Bax, *Medjugorje: Religion, Politics, and Violence in Rural Bosnia* (Amsterdam: VU University Press, 1995).

37. Daniel Wojcik writes that the third secret as given to Lucia has been the basis for contemporary Marian apocalypticism. Wojcik, *The End of the World as We Know It,* 66–67, 87–88.

38. Ibid., 12.

39. Robert Wuthnow, *The Restructuring of American Religion: Society and Faith since World War II* (Princeton, N.J.: Princeton University Press, 1988), 201.

40. Ibid., 199–299.

41. James Hitchcock, "Catholic Activist Conservatism in the United States," in *Fundamentalisms Observed,* ed. Martin E. Marty and R. Scott Appleby (Chicago: University of Chicago Press, 1991), 105.

42. Ibid., 107.

43. James Hitchcock writes: "Conservatives on both sides of the denominational line began to realize that as far as these issues were concerned, they had more in common with conservative counterparts on the other side of the line than with their liberal coreligionists. This in turn led to the discovery of a theological basis for such conservatism—a traditional view of truth and of religious authority. Both Catholic and Protestant conservatives believe that God's Word has been revealed to humanity and must be obeyed." Ibid., 108.

44. For a history of fundamentalisms and evangelicals, see George Marsden, *Understanding Fundamentalism and Evangelicalism* (Lansing, Mich.: William B. Eerdmans Publishing, 1991), and *Fundamentalism and American Culture: The Shaping of Twentieth-Century Evangelicalism, 1870–1925* (New York: Oxford University Press, 1980). See also Wuthnow, *The Restructuring of American Religion.*

45. Mark A. Noll, "The History of an Encounter: Roman Catholics and Protestant Evangelicals, " in *Evangelicals and Catholics Together: Toward a Common Mission,* ed. Charles Colson and Richard John Neuhaus (London: Word Publishing, 1995), 82–89.

46. Wojcik, *The End of the World as We Know It,* 34–35.

47. Mary's messages to the visionaries at Conyers, Georgia; Medjugorje, former Yugoslavia; Cold Spring, Kentucky; Hillside, Illinois; Belleville, Illinois; Batavia, Ohio; Cleveland, Ohio; Mesquite, Texas; Worcester, Massachusetts; San Bruno, California; Scottsdale, Arizona; and South Phoenix, Arizona, all have apocalyptic tones, interspersed with hope for the future. Of all these groups, the most technologically advanced is the Conyers group, "Our Loving Mother's Children": www.conyers.org/body.htm. This address is the most comprehensive of any apparition group in the United States: all of the messages to Nancy Fowler are available, in addition to pilgrims' testimonies. Mary's Ministries also has a web site: www.ourlovingmother.org. Other Marian groups have addresses to which prayers can be mailed and where copies of the messages can be obtained. A Call To Peace, in response to the reported messages to Cyndi Cane, has the messages published through Mir-A-Call Center, 1515 North Town East Boulevard, Suite 138, Mesquite, Texas 75150. Our Lady of the Holy Spirit Center has newsletters that tell of the messages given to the unnamed Batavia, Ohio visionary: 5540 Moeller Avenue, Norwood, Ohio 45212. And Holy Love Ministries in Cleveland, Ohio, makes available the messages to Ellen Drwal: P.O. Box 44185, Cleveland, Ohio 44144.

NOTES TO CHAPTER 4

1. So far Mary's Ministries has teamed up with Latin American dioceses and has sponsored faith courses in central Chile (Linares, San Bernardo); south, central, and northern Peru (Sulyana, Lima); eastern Ecuador (Cuenca); southern Colombia (Hirador); northern Brazil (Franca); Guatemala; and in Chihuahua, Coahuila, Durango, and Hermosillo, Mexico. The priests and bishops who work with Mary's Mnistries are of mixed orders. Bishop José Alemany of Peru is currently Mary's Ministries spiritual director. There are close to one hundred Mary's Ministries missionaries today, the majority of whom are Peruvian and Mexican women. There are about fifteen Mexican American missionaries from South Phoenix who have each given a year's commitment to missionize in Latin American communities supported by local dioceses. During their stay, they live in Mary Houses, paid for by Mary's Ministries.

2. Father Tom Forrest, CSs.R., personal letter to Father Doug Nohava, September 11, 1996.

3. Locally, the Ruiz family has worked closely with a handful of supportive priests. Father Doug Nohava, formerly of St. Catherine of Siena parish, the Ruizes' home parish, was their most avid supporter and ally and encouraged other parishes in the greater Phoenix area to have parish-based Mary's Ministries faith courses. Until his death in November 1998, Father Doug was the Ruiz family's spiritual advisor and was himself a devout Marianist and Charismatic Catholic who spoke in tongues. He was also a community activist, and he was well known for speaking out against gang violence in South Phoenix. His successor at St. Catherine parish, Father Charles Goraieb, is also openly supportive of Mary's Ministries and had a faith course offered in his former parish, St. Charles Borromeo in Glendale, Arizona, as well as at St. Catherine. Both priests have spoken at the annual December retreat in honor of the Virgin of the Americas' apparitions to Estela. Father Jack Spaulding of St. Thomas parish in Scottsdale, Arizona, discussed in chapter 2, is another supporter of the Ruiz family and Mary's Ministries.

4. The book Deacon George used is an example of a medieval predecessor of the currently used, post–Vatican II *Rituale*. The book Deacon George used, the *Manuale Curatorum*, "contains the blessing of salt and water, baptism, marriage, blessing of a house, visitation of the sick with viaticum and extreme unction, prayers for the dead, funeral services, funeral of infants, prayers for pilgrims, blessing of fire on Holy Saturday, and other blessings." www.newadvent.org, "Ritual."

5. For a good overview of American evangelicalism, see James Davidson Hunter, *Evangelicalism: The Coming Generation* (Chicago: University of Chicago Press, 1987). See also Hunter, *American Evangelicalism: Conservative Religion and the Quandary of Modernity* (New Brunswick, N.J.: Rutgers University Press, 1983); David Harrington Watt, *A Transforming Faith: Explorations of Twentieth-Century American Evangelicalism* (New Brunswick, N.J.: Rutgers University Press, 1991); Randall Balmer, *Mine Eyes Have Seen the Glory: A Journey into the Evangelical Subculture in America* (New York: Oxford University Press, 1993); and Robert Wuthnow, *The Struggle For America's Soul: Evangelicals, Liberals, and Secularism* (Grand Rapids, Mich.: William B. Eerdmans Publishing Company, 1989), for careful coverage of the main issues and concerns of evangelicals. For a comparative look at American evangelicalism, see *The Variety of American Evangelicalism,* ed. Donald W. Dayton and Robert K. Johnston (Knoxville: University of Tennessee Press, 1991).

6. There are several excellent sources that explore women and their ability to transcend everyday gender restrictions and to create a space for themselves. Lila Abu-Lughod, *Writing Women's Worlds: Bedouin Stories* (Berkeley and Los Angeles: University of California Press, 1993); Karen McCarthy Brown, *Mama Lola: A Vodou Priestess in Brooklyn* (Berkeley and Los Angeles: University of California Press, 1991); Carolyn Walker Bynum, *Holy Feast and Holy Fast: The Religious Signi-*

ficance of Food to Medieval Women (Berkeley and Los Angeles: University of California Press, 1987); R. Marie Griffith, *God's Daughters: Evangelical Women and the Power of Submission* (Berkeley: University of California Press, 1997); Laurel Kendall, *Shamans, Housewives, and Other Restless Spirits* (Honolulu: University of Hawaii Press, 1985); Elaine J. Lawless, *God's Peculiar People: Women's Voices and Folk Tradition in a Pentecostal Church* (Lexington: University Press of Kentucky, 1988), and *Women Preaching Revolution: Calling for Connection in a Disconnected Time* (Philadelphia: University of Pennsylvania Press, 1996).

7. Griffith, *God's Daughters*, 197.

8. Ibid. Women in evangelical Global Ministries, for example, are encouraged to "trade in" their abusive partners for "a more rewarding marriage to Jesus."

9. Luís León discusses Alcance Victoria, Victory Outreach, at length in "Born Again in East LA: The Congregation as Border Space," in *Gatherings in the Diaspora*, ed. R. Stephen Warner and Judith G. Wittner (Philadelphia: Temple University Press, 1998), 163–196.

10. R. Marie Griffith talks about this "openness" to Jesus in *God's Daughters*, 98.

11. María, a faith course graduate in October 1998, spoke openly about her many troubles. A single mother, she works all day as a housekeeper and takes care of her children. She says she is tired all of the time and doesn't feel very well. She is extremely grateful to the Ruizes and to her "*nuevos hermanas y hermanos*" (new brothers and sisters), the people she met in the course. María took the faith course with her sister, and both had to be driven there by friends, as neither has a car.

12. Matthew Barton, "A Stadium of Hope: A Rhetorical Analysis of the Promise Keepers" (unpublished Master's thesis, University of Nevada-Las Vegas, 1998), 1.

13. For more detailed information on the Promise Keepers' gender ideology, see Ken Abram, *Who Are the Promise Keepers? Understanding the Christian Men's Movement* (New York: Doubleday, 1997); Brian Brickner, *The Promise Keepers: Politics and Promise* (Lanham, Md.: Lexington Books, 1999); Edwin Louis Cole, *On Becoming a Real Man* (Nashville: Thomas Nelson Publishers, 1992); Greg Lewis, *The Power of a Promise Kept* (Colorado Springs: Focus on the Family Publishing, 1995); Bill McCartney, *From Ashes to Glory* (Nashville: Thomas Nelson Publishing Company, 1995), and *Sold Out: Becoming Man Enough to Make a Difference* (Nashville: Word Publishing, 1997); Bill McCartney, Greg Laurie, and Jack Hayford, *Seven Promises of a Promise Keeper* (Nashville: Word Publishers, 1999). Recent unpublished dissertations that explore PK rhetoric and gender ideology include Larry Dean Allen, "A Comparative Analysis of the Men and Religion Forward Movement and Promise Keepers," Boston University, 2000; Michael James Chrasta, "Jesus People and Promise Keepers: A Revival Sequence and Its Effect on Late Twentieth-Century Evangelical Ideas of Masculinity," University of Texas at Dallas, 1998; and John Richard Delbridge, "Partners or Patriarchs? Promise Keepers and the Rhetoric of Gender Reconciliation," Bowling Green State University, 1998.

14. Michael Messner, *Politics of Masculinities: Men in Movements* (Thousand Oaks, Calif.: Sage Publications, 1997), 34–35.

15. For a well-researched study on men's involvement in Promise Keepers and how it affects their relationships with their children, see Michael John Walcheski, "The Influence of Promise Keepers on Father's Involvement with Their Children" (Ph.D. dissertation, Western Michigan University, 1998).

16. Ibid., 24–25.

17. Sánchez, *Becoming Mexican American,* 32–33. What Sánchez is referring to here is the immense pressure Mexican and Mexican American men feel to be the providers for their family, and the frustration they feel, which leads to disillusionment and anger, when they fail to fulfill their duty.

18. Elizabeth Brusco, *The Reformation of Machismo: Evangelical Conversion and Gender in Colombia* (Austin: University of Texas Press, 1995), 136–137. Brusco's argument that evangelicalism can provide women with a powerful tool to reform their men goes a step further than the assertions Griffith makes in *God's Daughters;* the evangelical Aglow meetings Griffith describes, while they provide women with a much-needed outlet for spiritual healing, do not venture into "reforming" their men.

19. Luís León, "Metaphor and Place: The U.S.–Mexico Border as Center and Periphery in the Interpretation of Religion," *Journal of the American Academy of Religion* 67, no. 3 (September 1999): 553.

20. Ibid.

21. Robert Orsi explores the meanings behind the embrace of suffering by American Catholics in "'Mildred, Is It Fun to Be a Cripple?' The Culture of Suffering in Mid-Twentieth-Century American Catholicism," *South Atlantic Quarterly* 93, no. 3 (summer 1994): 547–590. Similar to the Catholic Church's encouragements and admonitions to American Catholics to embrace their suffering during this era, the Ruizes and Mary's Ministries encourage those who participate in the courses to accept their suffering. Reyes Sr. goes so far as to tell participants to "offer it up" for loved ones as well as souls in purgatory.

Notes to Chapter 5

1. Gastón Espinoza, "*El Azteca:* Francisco Olazábal and Latino Pentecostal Charisma, Power, and Faith Healing in the Borderlands," *Journal of the American Academy of Religion* 67, no. 3 (1999): 597.

2. Interview with author, South Phoenix, Arizona, March 31, 2002.

3. The essays in *Latin American Religion in Motion* explore the tensions and overlap between Catholicism and Protestantism (specifically Pentecostalism) throughout Latin America. The five essays on Catholicism show that Catholics are well aware of Protestants' successes and utilize and incorporate similar methods in

their new evangelization. Christian Smith and Joshua Prokopy, eds., *Latin American Religion in Motion* (New York: Routledge, 1999).

4. James Davidson Hunter, *Culture Wars: The Struggle to Define America* (New York: Basic Books, 1991), 89; Robert Wuthnow, *Sharing the Journey: Support Groups and America's New Quest for Community* (New York and London: Free Press, 1994).

5. Jeffrey M. Burns, "The Mexican Catholic Community in California," in *Mexican Americans and the Catholic Church, 1900–1965,* ed. Jay P. Dolan and Gilberto M. Hinojosa (Notre Dame, Ind.: University of Notre Dame Press, 1994), 222.

6. Ibid., 223.

7. Gilberto M. Hinojosa, "Mexican-American Faith Communities in Texas and the Southwest," in *Mexican Americans and the Catholic Church, 1900–1965,* ed. Jay P. Dolan and Gilberto M. Hinojosa (Notre Dame, Ind.: University of Notre Dame Press, 1994), 117.

8. Greater Phoenix's Mount Claret Center embodies the contemplative philosophy of *Cursillo* retreats in its physical geography. Nestled in the Camelback Mountain chain in North Phoenix, the Center, formerly La Fonda Fiesta Guest Ranch, borders wealthy Scottsdale and is far away from the noisy highways.

9. George Joseph Kramer, "The Intensive Group Process and the Cursillo Experience: Implications for Spiritual Formations of Participants" (Ph.D. dissertation, The Catholic University of America, 1985), 2.

10. Mount Claret Cursillo Movement, *Voice* 6, no. 6 (October 1998): 2.*Palanca* is translated in the *Cursillo Movement's Leader's Manual,* seventh edition, as the self-denial that is necessary for "securing God's grace" (Dallas: Office of the National Secretariat of the Cursillo Movement in the United States, 1998), 136. Mexican families make "offerings," or *palanca,* when the Guadalupe statue visits their homes.

11. The quotation continues: "especially among couples who would be concerned with the immediate ramifications of the Weekend on their own relationship if they lived it together. . . . Since it is possible for persons to come to a Weekend absorbed in their own personal concerns and to be satisfied only with a personal solution to them, it is even more likely for couples to come to a Weekend solely intent on their own concerns as spouses and a family and thereby resist integration into the community." *The Cursillo Movement's Leader's Manual,* 7th ed., 86–88.

12. Thomas Csordas, *The Sacred Self: A Cultural Phenomenology of Charismatic Healing* (Berkeley and Los Angeles: University of California Press, 1994), 16. Several sources discuss the religious pluralism of the charismatic movement. Michael Harper, in his *Three Sisters* (Bloomington, Ill.: Tyndale House, 1979), discusses evangelicals, charismatics, and Catholic charismatics and their relationship to one another; *The Religious Reawakening in America,* ed. Joseph Newman (Washington, D.C.: Books by U.S. News & World Report, 1972), contains a chapter on "Catholic Pentecostals," another terminology and take on Catholic charismatics. Robert H.

Culpepper provides a good overview of the charismatic movement in *Evaluating the Charismatic Movement* (Valley Forge, Pa.: Judson Press, 1977). In *Pentecostal Movements as an Ecumenical Challenge,* ed. Jürgen Moltmann and Karl-Josef Kuschel (Maryknoll, N.Y.: Orbis Books, 1996), prominent Catholic theologians discuss the Pentecostal roots of Catholic charismatic movements, citing direct communication with the Holy Spirit and healing as key aspects of charismatic influence and popularity.

13. Thomas J. Csordas, *Language, Charisma, and Creativity: The Ritual Life of a Religious Movement* (Berkeley and Los Angeles: University of California Press, 1997), 4.

14. Csordas, *The Sacred Self,* 18.

15. Mary Jo Neitz, *Charisma and Community: A Study of Religious Commitment within the Charismatic Renewal* (New Brunswick, N.J.: Transaction Books, 1987), 24.

16. Csordas, *Language, Charisma, and Creativity,* 29.

17. Ibid., 166–167.

18. Neitz, *Charisma and Community,* xix.

19. Meredith McGuire, *Pentecostal Catholics: Power, Charisma and Order in a Religious Movement* (Philadelphia: Temple University Press, 1982), 64. See also Neitz, *Charisma and Community.*

NOTES TO CHAPTER 6

1. The organization's urban renewal and reform is directed toward what is geographically designated by the city as "Target Area B," the roughly triangular South Phoenix neighborhood bounded by south Central Avenue, Roeser Avenue, and Broadway Avenue. "Project America: Leadership, Ecology, & Educational Center; Item I: Development Concept," August 9, 1994, 1.

2. Vivi Stenberg, "'Super' Gift Helps Build Dream; NFL-Funded Center to Open in January," *The Arizona Republic* (hereafter *TAR*), December 17, 1997 A-6.

3. "Project America: Leadership, Ecology, & Educational Center; Item I. Development Concept," August 9, 1994, 2.

4. Ibid., 2.

5. The official Articles of Incorporation, filed by the Arizona Corporation Commission January 18, 1994, state that the purpose of the organization is "combatting [sic] deterioration in the South Phoenix community." ESPIRITU was established as a nonmember corporation that is run by the board of directors, who retain all the rights and powers vested in them by the articles of incorporation. "Articles of Incorporation of ESPIRITU Community Development Corporation," January 18, 1994, 1.

6. Ruiz's political career is detailed in "The Armando Ruiz Papers, 1987–1989," Arizona State University, Department of Archives and Manuscripts, ACC # 89-129,

Call #MSS-73. See also Chris Fiscus, "New 'Y' Unites Community; Neighborhood Called Worthy of Best, " *The Phoenix Gazette* (hereafter *TPG*), March 3, 1995, B1; John Davis, "KJ Drives for Goal; Suns Star Courts Donations for YMCA Gym, " *TPG*, November 18, 1994, A1; Alfredo Azula, "YMCA Expanding Child-Care Options, " *TAR*, September 8, 1993, 1, Downtown/South Community; Editorial, Armando Ruiz, "Even Some of South Phoenix's Weaknesses Underscore Its Strengths, " *TAR*, December 12, 1994, B4; Mike Padgett, "Grant Will Allow Minority Preschool to Purchase School, " *TAR*, January 4, 1995, 4.

7. Ed Foster, "Symington Visits Community Center, Helps Mark Neighborhoods' Rebirth, " *TAR*, December 17, 1993, A6; "Ex-Senator Named to Consumer Office, " *TAR*, December 4, 1993, B2; William H. Carille, "Symington Will Visit South Phoenix, " *TAR*, September 13, 1991, B3.

8. Armando Ruiz, interview with author, South Phoenix, Arizona, October 20, 1998.

9. Ibid.

10. In 1981, at twenty-four years of age, Ruiz was the youngest ever Mexican American elected in the state of Arizona. "Ruiz Leaves Legislature, " *TPG*, April 20, 1992, A8.

11. Susan Curtis, *A Consuming Faith: The Social Gospel and Modern American Culture* (Baltimore and London: Johns Hopkins University Press, 1991), 10.

12. NCLR Newsrelease, January 24, 1996.

13. Ruiz is responding to critics like Tempe Councilman Ben Arredondo ("NFL Gives S. Phoenix $1 Million, " *TAR*, January 25, 1996, A1) who said that politics played a part in the NFL's decision to award $1 million to ESPIRITU. Ruiz says that it is imperative to have political connections in the competitive world of grants and financial gifts. Ruiz, interview with author, South Phoenix, Arizona, November 10, 1998.

14. Diane Winston, *Red Hot and Righteous: The Urban Religion of the Salvation Army* (Cambridge: Harvard University Press, 1999), 4.

15. Robert Orsi, *Gods of the City: Religion and the American Urban Landscape* (Bloomington: Indiana University Press, 1999), 43. Orsi's book is the most comprehensive source on urban religion and urban religious theory, and there are few other sources on urban religion. See also Winston, *Red Hot and Righteous;* and *Public Religion and Urban Transformation: Faith in the City,* ed. Lowell W. Livezey (New York: New York University Press, 2000) for recent academic inquiries on urban religions.

16. These descriptions are based in part on my fieldwork from 1992 to 1994 and in the fall of 1998. Conversations and interviews with local residents confirm that South Phoenix is known as a place where gang activity and shootings, drug activity, and juvenile delinquency are higher than in surrounding areas. Phoenix's established gang presence is reflected in South Phoenix, where the South Side Posse, subsets of Wet Back Power (WBP), and Los Angeles–based Crips and Bloods are

active and visible. Subsets tend to reflect what part of Mexico the majority of the gang members' families are from and to have regional and Mexican national emphases. More detailed elaboration of Phoenix's gang phenomena and how gang culture has affected the city's residents is provided in "Ground Zero, " *Phoenix New Times* (hereafter *PNT*), October 21, 1999; "The Strong Arm of the Law, " *PNT*, October 14, 1999; Patti Epler, "Gang Influence Runs Deep in Phoenix's Roots, " *PNT*, September 16, 1999; Amy Silverman, "Out of God's Hands, " *PNT*, September 16, 1999; Michael Kiefer, "Gang, Bang, You're Dead, " *PNT*, September 9, 1999; Terry Greene Sterling, "Loco Motive, " *PNT*, August 26, 1999; Graciela Smith and Jesus Lopez Jr., "Crime Magnet Is Razed; Rainbow Market Comes Down in Bid to Rebuild Area, " *TAR*, August 12, 1999, B1; Tony Ortega, "Mentor's Lament, " *PNT*, July 8, 1999; Chris Farnsworth, "Crackdown, " *PNT*, June 24, 1999; "Anti-Gang Force to Begin 10th Year, " *TAR*, April 28, 1999, B3; Kelly Ettenborough, "Lives Resurrected; Every Day Is Like Easter at South Phoenix Church, " *TAR*, April 4, 1999, B1; Brent Whiting, "Police Resume Anti-Gang Operation; Phoenix Squads Hit the Streets, " *TAR*, June 10, 1998, 5; Stephen Tuttle, "Anti-Gang Plan Treads on Bill of Rights, " *TAR*, June 7, 1998, H3; Editorial, "A War on Gangs; Taking a Controversial Step, " *TAR*, June 1, 1998, B4; Editorial, "Cooling Off the City's Streets, " *TPG*, August 7, 1995, B4; Mary Jo Pitzl and Judi Villa, "100 Lawmen Target Area of Attack on Cops; Mayor Pledges 'To Break Backs' of Gangs' Zone, " *TAR*, March 24, 1995, A1; Russ Hemphill, "Cost of War on Gangs Keeps Rising; Police Want $2.2 Million to Expand Special Unit, " *TPG*, December 7, 1994, B1; Don Harris, "Basketball Credited in Crime Cut; Gang Members Play in Tourney, " *TAR*, September 2, 1991, A14; Lisa Davis, "Neighborhood Terrorized by 91 Fires in 4 Months; 80% Blamed on Arson, " *TPG*, September 11, 1991, B4.

For a greater understanding of the gang members' perspectives and reasons for joining gangs, see Susan M. Raymond, "Symbolic Relationships of Graffiti by Phoenix Metropolitan Area Gangs" (Master's thesis, Arizona State University, 1991), 52–100; Chris Paul Faulkner, "Understanding Homeboys: A Cultural Perspective, " unpublished paper, Arizona State University, fall 1987; Scott W. Renshaw, "Thrasher Revisited: Thrill-Seeking within Mexican-American Gangs in Phoenix, Arizona, " Master's thesis, Arizona State University, 1997.

17. For more information on school dropout rates and Phoenix-based outreach programs for Mexican Americans and Hispanic youth, see Donna Olvera, "Education Reform and Census Information Center Project, " unpublished report submitted to the Hispanic Research Center Community Based Documentation Program, Arizona State University, June 4, 1991; Gene T. Chavez and Kurt Organista, "Barriers to Chicano Participation in Higher Education: Admissions Selection Criteria, " unpublished paper, adopted as the official position paper of the RAZA Graduate Student Caucus, Arizona State University, fall 1979, 1–8; Careers for Youth, Inc., "High School Graduation Rates in Downtown and South Phoenix: A Preliminary Study, " unpublished report, 1961.

18. Mike Davis, *Magical Urbanism: Hispanics Reinvent the City* (London and New York: Verso, 2000), 112.

19. Pete Dimas, "Perspectives on Progress and a Mexican American Community's Struggle for Existence" (Ph.D. dissertation, Arizona State University, 1991), 53–54.

20. Mike Davis, *City of Quartz: Excavating the Future in Los Angeles* (New York: Vintage Books, 1990), 270. Robert Orsi also discusses the culture of fear that arises in relation to the city and to ethnic and racial "otherness." See *Gods of the City,* Introduction and chapter 6, "The Religious Boundaries of an In-Between People, " 257–288.

21. Linda Greenhouse and Ken Herman, "English-Only Case Headed to High Court, " *Austin-American Statesman* (hereafter *AAS*), March 26, 1996, A1.

22. See Paul Davenport, "Arizona Supreme Court Rules State English-Only Law Unconstitutional, " *San Diego Tribune,* April 29, 1998, A3; Randy Kull, "Official-English Amendment Challenged, " *TPG*, November 7, 1992, B1; Anne Rackham, "Ruiz: Legislators to Withhold Budget Votes to Push Proposal, " *The Mesa Tribune* (hereafter *TMT*), March 26, 1988, B5; Rackham, "English Bill Gains Panel OK; Legislator Helps Alternative Cause, " *TMT,* March 10, 1988, B8; Linda Greenhouse and Ken Herman, "English-Only Case Headed to High Court; Arizona Law Governing Workers' On-the-Job Language Is at Issue, " *AAS,* March 26, 1996, A1; Victoria Harker, "'English' Backer to Talk at ASU, " *TAR,* September 12, 1991; Jonathan Sidener, "Legionnaires Back 'Official English' Idea, " *TAR,* September 1, 1991, B1; Anne Rackham, "'Official English' Foes Vow to Continue Fight, " *TMT,* July 2, 1988, B1; Editorial, "Linguistic Jingoism, " *TMT,* April 1, 1988, A12. Arizona's 1988 referendum is part of a larger movement in the Southwest to declare English the official language. Mark Shaffer, "Arizona Next for Prop. 187? California Leader at the Forefront, " *TAR,* March 2, 1996, A1. Bilingual education programs in schools continue to be a hotly contested topic. Arthur H. Rotstein, "Deep Rifts Divide Those Favoring, Opposed to Bilingual Education, " *Associated Press State and Local Wire,* January 2, 1999; Cathryn Creno, "Bilingual Ed Fight Erupts in Arizona, " *TAR,* December 10, 1998, A1.

23. See Deborah Laake, "Who Killed King? The Valley's Hottest Political Strategists Teamed Up to Push MLK Day. No Wonder It Failed, " *PNT,* December 5, 1995; Steve Yozwiak, "King Issue Still Alive, " *TAR,* November 3, 1991, B1; Bob Cohn and Norm Frauenheim, "Fear of Backlash Mostly Unfounded, " *TAR,* November 3, 1991, D1; Betty Beard, "King Aftermath: 90 Groups Cancel, " *TAR,* November 3, 1991, F1; James E. Cook, "Climate in Arizona Still Nurturing Intolerance, " *TAR,* September 1, 1991, E2.

24. Daniel Gonzalez, phone conversation with author, June 3, 2003.

25. Ibid.

26. Armando Ruiz, interview with author, South Phoenix, Arizona, September 10, 1998.

27. Pat Kossan, "Arizona Center Braces for New Crowd, " *TAR,* March 2, 1998, A1; Lisa Davis, "S. Phoenix Waiting for the Movies, " *TAR,* September 4, 1991, C1; Alan Thurber, "'We Love' Arizona Center, " *TAR,* November 8, 1991, F1, 5.

28. Kossan, "Arizona Center Braces for New Crowd, " A1.

29. Peter C. Baldwin, *Domesticating the Street: The Reform of Public Space in Hartford, 1850–1930* (Columbus: Ohio State University Press, 1999), 8.

30. According to Alan J. Rankin, President of the Canadian company Icynene, the company that produces the foam insulation, the foam is sprayed as a liquid and has the capability of expanding one hundred times its volume within seconds, permanently adhering to the surfaces of the surrounding building materials and filling and sealing all joints, crevices, and gaps. The result is also said to be superior to traditional insulation methods, as it provides an effective air and moisture barrier. It is also supposed to reduce energy costs by as much as 30 to 50 percent, according to Rankin. Icynene is water-based and is reported to emit no harmful gases, formaldehyde, CFCs, or HCFCs. According to Rankin, it is the only insulation material certified by the Envirodesic! Certification Program for maximum indoor air quality. See http://www.icynene.com/news/japan.html for more information on the new insulation material.

31. The NFL has a grant competition each year in the city in which the Super Bowl is hosted. When the event was held in Phoenix in 1996, ECDC was able to apply for the $1 million in grant money offered that year. The NFL normally disperses the money to several groups, but that particular year it awarded the money exclusively to ECDC, whose proposal for its expanded charter school demonstrated how it would form links throughout the community with South Mountain YMCA, local community colleges, and neighborhood groups. Pat Kossan, "Charter School Is Legacy of Valley's Super Bowl, " *TAR,* January 14, 1998, B1; Vivi Stenberg, "'Super' Gift Helps Build Dream; NFL-Funded Center to Open in January, " *TAR,* December 17, 1997, Scottsdale/Foothills Community, 6; Stenberg, "NFL-Funded Center Kicks Off in January; $1 Million Super Bowl Gift Helps Realize Dream, " *TAR,* December 12, 1997, Central Phoenix Community, 1; Stenberg, "NFL-Funded Community Center to Kick Off Programs in January, " *TAR,* December 10, 1997, Chandler Community, EV7; Pat Flannery, "NFL Gives S. Phoenix $1 Million, " January 25, 1996, A1; Hal Mattern, "Phoenix Site Will Give Rise to One of State's 1st Charter Schools, " *TAR,* October 4, 1994, A1; Mary Rourke, "Field of Dreams, " *Los Angeles Times* (hereafter *LAT*), September 15, 1995, E1, E5.

32. Hal Mattern, "4 Alternative Schools Win 1st Charters Given by State, " *TAR,* March 3, 1995, B1, B2; Hal Mattern, "Charter Schools Map Uncharted Territory, " *TAR,* May 12, 1995, A1, 18, 20. More detailed general information on Arizona's charter schools can be found in State Board for Charter Schools, "Introduction to Arizona's Charter Schools, " June 15, 1998, 1; State Board For Charter Schools, "Arizona Charter Schools, " March 4, 1998, 1–3; State Board for Charter Schools, "Charter School Fact Sheet, " n.d., 1–4; Mary Gifford, "Charter Schools: Double

the Accountability" (Phoenix: Goldwater Institute, April 28, 1998), 1–4. See "State and Federal Regulations Applicable to Charter Schools, " revised July 1997, 1–18; Arizona Department of Education, "The Charter Schools Handbook: A Resource Book for Charter School Applicants, " revised November 26, 1997; State Board for Charter Schools, "1999–2000 Application Information & Requirements, " 1–12; and "Charter Contract between Arizona State Board for Charter Schools and Esperanza Montessori Academy, " May 8, 1995, 1–11, for the most recent, detailed information.

33. Monica Rohr, "School Maze, " *Latina* (January 1999): 84.

34. April Gresham, Frederick Hess, et al., "Desert Bloom: Arizona's Free Market in Education, " *Kappan* 81, no. 10 (June 2000): 753.

35. Joe Nathan, *Charter Schools: Creating Hope and Opportunity for American Education* (San Francisco: Jossey-Bass, 1996), 176–177.

36. Thomas L. Good and Jennifer S. Braden, "Charter Schools: Another Reform Failure or a Worthwhile Investment?" *Kappan* 81, no. 10 (June 2000): 746–748. Good and Braden provide an even more comprehensive account of charter schools, the successes and areas needing improvement, in *The Great School Debate: Choice, Vouchers, and Charters* (Mahwah, N.J.: Lawrence Erlbaum Associates, 2000).

37. Good and Braden acknowledge the heterogeneity of charter schools and note that some states have better defined rules and regulations than others, which results in fewer loopholes. Arizona, which has the most charter schools of any state, possesses "all five attributes" of strong charter school laws, according to a 1999 Brookings Institution–supported study. The five issues addressed by the Brookings Institution are: (1) entity other than local board as able to authorize a charter school; (2) wide range of people and organizations able to start a charter school; (3) charter schools able to be legally and fiscally independent of the local school board; (4) charter schools receiving automatic exemption from a broad range of state and local policies; and (5) a law that enables many charter schools to open. The Arizona charter school laws are viewed as strong in all five areas. Bryan C. Hassel, *The Charter School Challenge: Avoiding the Pitfalls, Fulfilling the Promise* (Washington, D.C.: Brookings Institution Press, 1999), Table 2-1, 20.

38. Manno et al., "Beyond the Schoolhouse Door, " 738–739.

39. Rourke, "Field of Dreams, " E5.

40. As one teacher and critic of charter schools was quoted as saying, "The charter system lets people do things the way they want to. But you have to understand, everything in the education code is there because somebody made a mistake." Rourke, "Field of Dreams, " E5.

Lisa Graham Keegan, Arizona School Board Superintendent, asserts that Arizona's charter school laws aggressively track those schools that are not meeting educational standards put forth by the state; as of December 1998, six charter schools were effectively closed.

41. Reyes Ruiz Jr., interview with author, South Phoenix, Arizona, November 10, 1998.

42. Ibid., November 10, 1998.

43. Armando Ruiz as quoted in Rourke, "Field of Dreams, " E5.

44. Winston, *Red Hot and Righteous,* 252–253.

45. The Mark Ten building is named after a passage in the Gospel according to Mark (Mark 10:41-45) in which Jesus calls his ten disciples and tells them that they must be servants to all: "For the Son of Man came not to be served but to serve, and to give his life a ransom for many." See *The Harper Collins Study Bible: New Revised Standard Version* (London: HarperCollins Publishers, 1989), 1938–1939.

46. Susan Curtis, *A Consuming Faith,* 8.

47. Mary Hartley, "A Voice from the State Legislature: Don't Do What We Did!" in *School Choice in the Real World: Lessons from Arizona Charter Schools,* ed. Roberto Maranto et al. (Boulder, Colo.: Westview Press, 1999), 202.

48. There are numerous sources on Maria Montessori and her teaching philosophy and methods. See Maria Montessori's *The Discovery of the Child* (Notre Dame, Ind.: Fides Publishers, 1967); *Maria Montessori's Own Handbook* (New York: Schocken Books, 1965); *Education and Peace* (Chicago: Henry Regnery Company, 1972); *The Montessori Method* (New York: Schocken, 1989); *The Secret of Childhood* (New York: APT Books, 1984); *The Absorbent Mind* (New York: Dell, 1984). The following provide background information on Montessori, her training in medicine and child psychology, and her pedagogy: Elizabeth G. Hainstock, *The Essential Montessori: An Introduction to the Woman, the Writings, the Method, and the Movement* (New York: Plume, 1997); E. M. Standing, *Maria Montessori: Her Life and Work* (New York: Mentor-Omega Books, 1957); Phyllis Applebaum, "The Growth of the Montessori Movement in the United States" (Ph.D. dissertation, New York University, 1971); Rita Kraemer, *Maria Montessori: A Biography* (New York: G. P. Putnam's Sons, 1976); R. C. Orem, *Montessori Today* (New York: G. P. Putnam's Sons, 1971); *Montessori: Her Method and the Movement* (New York: G. P. Putnam's Sons, 1974).

49. Estela Ruiz, interview with author, South Phoenix, Arizona, September 19, 1998.

50. An outing in October 1998 to see the movie *Smoke Signals,* for instance, and the follow-up essay assignment, asked students to think about larger issues such as how tradition is shaped by culture, how traditions change over time, and how young people within a particular ethnic group can strengthen and contribute to the group's identity—the very issues and questions the dozen or so students deal with on a regular basis. The students enjoyed the outing, for reasons other than that it allowed them to miss some of their classes that day. The general consensus was that the movie was "cool" for showing how young people like them deal with the challenges such as poverty, racism, and abuse, in their lives. I was invited to accompany the group as an adult chaperone and was able to talk with the students

and listen in on the discussion session Fernando held after the movie was over, on September 24, 1998.

51. I spoke with and interviewed approximately twenty female students and five male students, most of whom were eager to talk about their experiences at the school. I have used pseudonyms for all of the students to protect their identities. While this is admittedly not a social scientific survey, it does provide a sense of the average student's perspective. All of the students emphasized that they feel safe and cared for at the school and that they appreciate the individualized attention, which they say sets the school apart from other high schools.

52. While most portrayals of Mexican American families before the 1980s depicted them as unidimensional (see Alfredo Mirandé and Evangelina Enríquez, *La Chicana: The Mexican American Woman* [Chicago: University of Chicago Press, 1979]), more recent, post–Chicano era, revisionist histories portray the Mexican American family as a stabilizing unit that provides economic, social, and kinship networks while showing a remarkable adaptability to change. Richard Griswold Del Castillo, in *La Familia: Chicano Families in the Urban Southwest, 1848 to the Present* (Notre Dame, Ind.: University of Notre Dame Press, 1984), writes that the Mexican American family has undergone changes in response to the "dynamic pressures" of industrial and postindustrial United States and that the Mexican American family contends with a continuous tension between its expectations and ideals and "the actual conditions of day-to-day reality" (9). According to Del Castillo, Mexican American families adapted to their surroundings in the United States, and familistic kinship networks were oftentimes strengthened in response to a frequently hostile Anglo environment. George J. Sánchez, in *Becoming Mexican American,* also points to the adaptive abilities of Mexican American families of different classes who contended with discrimination and drew on family resources in varying ways (130–132). Sánchez also notes that gender roles were fluid, as Mexican women and men did whatever they could to ensure the survival and continuation of their families (132). Manuel G. Gonzales, *Mexicanos: A History of Mexicans in the United States* (Bloomington: Indiana University Press, 1999), 165–167, points to the "special significance" of families in rural, pre-industrial Mexico, from which "customs are maintained" in the Southwestern United States. The Mexican family was the basic economic and social unit for immigrants, and this carried over to contemporary Mexican American culture. Despite the importance of family in Mexican culture, Gonzales writes, Chicano nationalists have painted a highly idealized picture of the Mexican family that overlooks domestic violence, alcoholism, abandonment, and divorce (165). Norma Williams, *The Mexican American Family: Tradition and Change* (New York: General Hall, 1990), looks at the changing power relationships within Mexican American families.

53. The historic Golden Gate barrio community was demolished in the 1970s and 1980s to make room for an expansion of Phoenix's Sky Harbor airport and is a

prime example of how urban renewal is, for minorities, urban removal. Armando J.'s grandfather, Abraham Arvizu, was one of the former residents who fought to have Sacred Heart parish designated a historic site—it was this parish that became a symbol of resistance to wealthy, greedy city developers. For more in-depth information on the Golden Gate barrio and struggles, see Pete Dimas, *Progress and a Mexican American Community's Struggle for Existence: Phoenix's Golden Gate Barrio* (New York: Peter Lang, 1990); David Rossmiller, "Tradition Imperiled; Deterioration of Church May Prevent Christmas Mass, Reunion, " *TPG,* December 23, 1991, B1, B2; David Schwartz, "Closed Church to Reopen Christmas, Ex-Parishioners, Phoenix Agree, " *TAR,* December 25, 1991, B1; David Rossmiller, "Neighborhood Was Like a Family; Mass Rekindles Life in Barrio, " *TPG,* December 26, 1991, A1, A18. Bradford Luckingham, in *Minorities in Phoenix,* also mentions the forced removal of Golden Gate residents in the 1970s and 1980s, 68–69.

54. Laura Trujillo, "Youths Find Author 'Like Me'; Words from the Barrio, " *TAR,* May 8, 1999, A1.

55. The sense of being in between cultures is something immigrants and children of immigrants experience in the United States as they attempt to map out a new identity for themselves and to negotiate their ethnicity and American culture. As cultural and social historians and anthropologists argue, ethnic persons and immigrants occupy a position that is in between that of their parents and that of Anglo American culture. This situatedness can be the site for fruitful encounters and endeavors, as well as frustrating, painful, and even dangerous situations. Puerto Rican Piri Thomas writes about the danger of being in between cultures, of not "fitting" into any category, and the occasional physical consequences, in *Down These Mean Streets* (New York: Vintage, 1974), 26. Robert Orsi addresses in-betweenness most directly in "The Religious Boundaries of an In-Between People: Street *Feste* and the Problem of the Dark-Skinned Other in Italian Harlem, " in *Gods of the City,* 257–288. He uses the term racially, in reference to Italian Americans' skin color, which was somewhere in between that of blacks and whites, and which was therefore a constant source of confusion for non-Italians and for Italians themselves. Like Piri Thomas, Italians experienced the perils of being in-between, Orsi argues. Richard Rodriguez, in *Hunger of Memory: The Education of Richard Rodriguez* (New York: Bantam Books, 1982), addresses the notion of in-betweenness in a direct and oftentimes heartwrenching way as he grapples with his growing distance from his immigrant, Spanish-speaking parents and faces the painful emotions he associates with his childhood and with living in a bicultural world. For Rodriguez, being Mexican American is fraught with conflicting emotions and desires, is necessarily painful, and is predicated on losing one's native language in order to succeed.

56. Deborah Laake, "Seeing the Light: Now Appearing in South Phoenix: The Virgin Mary, " *PNT,* July 15, 1992, 4.

57. Mary Hartley, "A Voice from the State legislature, " 201–203.

58. Ibid., 210.

59. Complaints against NFL-YET are on file at the State of Arizona Department of Education. The following allege that NFL-YET failed to maintain state standards concerning education special education children: complaint filed by the Arizona Center for Disability Law and staff attorney, August 1, 1996; complaint filed by L. P., June 20, 1996 and September 18, 1996. The following allege mismanagement and misallocation of funds on the part of the school's administration: The Concerned Parent Group of NFL-YET Academy, June 17, 1997; R. M., complaint filed September 10, 1996. The following letters filed are in support of the school: M. T., open letter, undated. The following complaints are in regards to the firing of three teachers by NFL-YET: R. S., n.d.; Concerned Parent Group of NFL-YET Academy, April 21, 1997; Concerned Parents Minutes, May 1, 1997; L. T., April 22, 1997; B. M., D. T., April 22, 1997; L. U., E. U., April 22, 1997; P. G., C. G., April 23, 1997; R. V., April 22, 1997; L. T., R. T., April 21, 1997; I. L., E. L., n.d. The following are responses from NFL-YET Academy to the Concerned Parents Group in open letters: F. R., April 10, 1997; A. R., n.d.; A. R., April 25, 1997.

60. A. R., April 25, 1997.

61. José, interview with author, South Phoenix, Arizona, October 22, 1998.

62. José has since resigned and is currently employed by a Phoenix public school. Since his experience at NFL-YET he has "sworn off" teaching at charter schools.

63. Fernando Ruiz, letter to parents, students, and staff, April 10, 1997.

64. ESPIRITU Community Development Corporation, "School Improvement Plans 1998–1999" (school improvement manual distributed to teachers and parents), 1–60.

65. Hudson Institute, "Project on 'Charter Schools in Action, '" June 1997 survey, NFL-YET Youth Education Town Academy (Washington, D.C.: Hudson Institute).

66. Up to the present publication of this book, the only formal accusation against ECDC's expenditures on file is the one previously listed. No other charges have been filed against the Ruizes. While I do not want to downplay the seriousness of these accusations, it should also be noted that they were made by a disgruntled individual who is no longer an ECDC employee and that the majority of employees have told me in interviews and conversations that they are committed to the mission of ECDC. Moreover, the state board which oversees the school and its expenditures thus far has not found any evidence of improper use of funds.

NOTES TO CHAPTER 7

1. Deidre Sklar, in *Dancing with the Virgin: Body and Faith in the Fiesta of Tortugas, New Mexico* (Berkeley: University of California Press, 2001), provides the

most thorough description and analysis of the Matachina dancers (*danzantes*), their sacred dance, and the community in which they live.

2. Kay Turner, "Mexican-American Women's Home Altars: The Art of Relationship" (Ph.D. dissertation, University of Texas at Austin, 1990), 5.

3. Turner, "Mexican American Women's Home Altars, " 5.

4. Jill Dubisch, *In a Different Place: Pilgrimage, Gender, and Politics at a Greek Island Shrine* (Princeton, N.J.: Princeton University Press, 1995), 36, 37. Dubisch writes that pilgrimage sites are places removed from ordinary time and space, and are experienced as sacred by all pilgrims. Alan Morinis also writes that the distance of the journey is irrelevant and that what makes a journey a pilgrimage is the "quest for the ideal." See Morinis, ed., *Sacred Journeys: The Anthropology of Pilgrimage* (Westport, Conn.: Greenwood Press, 1992), 7.

5. James Preston, "Spiritual Magnetism: An Organizing Principle for the Study of Pilgrimage, " in *Sacred Journeys: The Anthropology of Pilgrimage,* ed. Alan Morinis (Westport, Conn.: Greenwood Press, 1992), 35.

6. William Christian Jr., *Person and God in a Spanish Valley* (Princeton, N.J.: Princeton University Press, 1989), 182; Dubisch, *In a Different Place,* 37.

7. Eric Wolf, "The Virgin of Guadalupe: A Mexican National Symbol, " in *Reader in Comparative Religion: An Anthropological Approach,* 3d edition, ed. William A. Lessa and Evon Z. Vogt (New York: Harper & Row, 1972), 149–153.

8. Bernadette, interview with author, South Phoenix, Arizona, September 5, 1993.

9. Jeffrey M. Burns, "The Mexican Catholic Community in California, " in *Mexican Americans and the Catholic Church, 1900–1965,* ed. Jay P. Dolan and Gilberto Hinojosa (Notre Dame, Ind.: University of Notre Dame Press, 1994), 181–182. Jo Anne Schneider writes about how ethnicity is presented in parades in her article "Defining Boundaries, Creating Contacts: Puerto Rican and Polish Presentation of Group Identity through Ethnic Parades, " *Journal of Ethnic Studies* 18 (spring 1990): 33–57.

10. Karen Mary Davalos, "The Real Way of Praying: The Via Crucis, *Mexicano* Sacred Space, and the Architecture of Domination, " in *Horizons of the Sacred: Mexican Traditions in U.S. Catholicism,* ed. Timothy Matovina and Gary Riebe-Estrella, SVD (Ithaca, N.Y.: Cornell University Press, 2002), 43.

11. Eileen Oktavec discusses Mexican Americans' devotion to saints and the relationships they form with them in *Answered Prayers: Miracles and Milagros along the Border* (Tucson: University of Arizona Press, 1995), esp. 3–42.

12. Kay Turner, "Mexican American Home Altars: Towards Their Interpretation, " *Aztlan* 13, no. 1 (1982): 310. Turner explores the sense connectedness women form with saints and deities in *Beautiful Necessity: The Art and Meaning of Women's Altars* (New York: Thames and Hudson, 1999).

13. Oktavec, *Answered Prayers,* 18. This merging of saints by devotees is also seen in a South Phoenix chapel dedicated to a hybrid version of Saint Francis Xavier

who combines histories and physical resemblances of Saint Francis Xavier, Saint Francis of Assisi, and southwestern Jesuit missionary Padre Eusebio Kino. See Anna Dooling, "Miracle on 24 Street, " *PNT,* December 29–4 January 1995, 20–28.

14. Robert Orsi, *Thank You, Saint Jude* (New Haven, Conn.: Yale University Press, 1996), xi. Orsi writes about Italian Americans' devotion to the Virgin in *The Madonna of 115th Street: Faith and Community in Italian Harlem, 1880–1950* (New Haven, Conn.: Yale University Press, 1985), 163–178.

Victor Turner writes that devotion to saints is common in a Catholic concept of communion with the saints in *Image and Pilgrimage in Christian Culture* (New York: Columbia University Press, 1978), 146. Kay Turner's work focuses on the relationships women form with saints. See Kay Turner, *Beautiful Necessity* (New York: Thames and Hudson, 1999); Kay Turner and Suzanne Seriff, "'Giving an Altar': The Ideology of Reproduction in a St. Joseph's Day Feast, " *Journal of American Folklore* 100 (1987): 446–459; Turner, "Mexican American Home Altars, " 309–326; and Turner, "Mexican American Women's Home Altars: The Art of Relationship." Richard M. Dorson describes Peruvians' adoration for the Virgin of the Doors in "Material Components Celebration, " in *Celebration: Studies in Festivity and Ritual,* ed. Victor Turner (Washington, D.C.: Smithsonian Institution Press, 1982), 34–35.

15. Robert A. Orsi, "The Cult of the Saints and the Reimagination of the Space and Time of Sickness in Twentieth-Century American Catholicism, " *Literature and Medicine* 8 (1989): 70–71.

16. Deidre, interview with author, South Phoenix, Arizona, October 22, 1998.

17. Reyes Ruiz Sr., interview with author, South Phoenix, Arizona, September 27, 1998.

18. Ibid.

19. Robert Orsi discusses this taking control of spaces in "Cult of the Saints and the Reimagination of the Space and Time of Sickness, " 73.

20. Dubisch, *In a Different Place,* 33. Colin Turnbull also writes about the anthropologist's journey and the necessity of joining in the pilgrimage as an academic in "Postscript: Anthropology as Pilgrimage, Anthropologist as Pilgrim, " in *Sacred Journeys,* ed. Morinis, 257–274.

21. Colleen McDannell provides an insightful account of how the Lourdes waters became famous for their healing properties and how they became part of Catholic material culture in *Material Christianity: Religion and Popular Culture in America* (New Haven, Conn.: Yale University Press, 1995), 132–162. Pilgrims' beliefs in the healing waters of Lourdes is explored in Andrea Dahlberg, "The Body as a Principle of Holism: Three Pilgrimages to Lourdes, " 30–50, and John Eade, "Order and Power at Lourdes: Lay Helpers and the Organization of a Pilgrimage Shrine, " 51–76, both in *Contesting the Sacred: The Anthropology of Christian Pilgrimage,* ed. John Eade and Michael J. Sallnow (London and New York: Routledge, 1991).

22. McDannell, *Material Christianity,* 135.

23. Sabine MacCormack, "Loca Sancta: The Organization of Sacred Topography in Late Antiquity, " in *The Blessings of Pilgrimage,* ed. Robert Ousterhout (Urbana and Chicago: University of Illinois Press, 1990), 21. In the same edited volume, Maggie Duncan-Flowers also writes about the healing powers, or "mana, " that are associated with the shrine grounds in "A Pilgrim's Ampulla from the Shrine of St. John the Baptist at Epheseus, " 130.

24. David Haberman discusses how bodily discomfort is an intricate part of the pilgrimage experience in northern India in his book *Journey through the Twelve Forests* (Oxford and New York: Oxford University Press, 1994). Though the pilgrimage I am writing about is in a contained urban area rather than spread out over miles as is the Ban-Yantra pilgrimage Haberman writes about, pilgrims at this South Phoenix shrine are encouraged to make themselves uncomfortable, and do so, by kneeling, and they have to sit outside in the nighttime cold and the daytime heat.

25. Haberman, *Journey through the Twelve Forests,* 7, 130. For other discussions of pilgrimage as gendered performance see Dubsich, *In a Different Place,* 218–229.

26. David Morgan, *Visual Piety: A History and Theory of Popular Religious Images* (Berkeley: University of California Press, 1998), 3. A growing body of scholarship focuses on the interrelatedness of religion and material culture. The art historian David Freedberg also discusses relationships people form with objects in *The Power of Images: Studies in the History and Theory of Response* (Chicago: University of Chicago Press, 1989). Colleen McDannell writes about the religious significance of material culture and how people assign meaning to these objects in *Material Christianity,* Introduction. Robert Orsi notes the importance of St. Jude's appearance to the women who pray to him; as one woman told him, "a lot of times I'll look at his face [on a statue], and I'll see if he's smiling, everything will be OK." See *Thank You, St. Jude,* 97.

27. See Barbara Myerhoff and Jay Ruby, eds., *A Crack in the Mirror: Reflexive Perspectives in Anthropology* (Philadelphia: University of Pennsylvania Press, 1982), 1, Introduction.

28. Dominic, interview with author, Tempe, Arizona, October 27, 1998.

29. Robert Orsi, "The Cult of the Saints, " 69.

30. Ibid., 75.

31. Mike, interview with author, South Phoenix, Arizona, December 4, 1998. According to Sandra Zimdars-Swartz, a historian of religion in the United States, the 1988 Lubbock, Texas, phenomenon was primarily attended by charismatic Catholics who claimed to see sun miracles as well as visions of Mary and Jesus in the clouds. The gathering corresponded with the early stages of the Medjugorje apparitions and marked the culmination of Pope John Paul II's declared Marian Year. See Zimdars-Swartz, *Encountering Mary,* 17–18, 162.

32. *The Catholic Sun,* May 13, 1990, 12. In his official report, the former Bishop O'Brien commended the Ruiz family for their devotion and for "adding greatly to

the devotion of the people of God to their Church" and added that the prayer services could continue for the "spiritual welfare of the Ruiz family and the people who attend the devotional services."

33. Robert Orsi, *Thank You Saint Jude,* 169.

34. At the December 2002 retreat, Bishop Alemany of Peru, wearing his stole and alb, presided and read from the Pope's Apostolic Letter *Rosarium Virginis Mariae* on "The Most Holy Rosary," which he distributed in Spanish and English and read aloud over the course of three days.

NOTES TO CONCLUSION

1. David Gutiérrez, "Migration, Emergent Ethnicity, and the 'Third Space': The Shifting Politics of Nationalism in Greater Mexico," *Journal of American History* (September 1999): 18–19. Gina Maria Pitti also explores the concept of third space in "The Sociedades Guadalupanas in the San Francisco Archdiocese, 1942–1962," *U.S. Catholic Historian* (winter 2003): 91–92.

2. Lara Medina and Gilbert R. Cadena, "Días de los Muertos: Public Ritual, Community Renewal, and Popular Religion in Los Angeles," in *Horizons of the Sacred: Mexican Traditions in U.S. Catholicism,* ed. Timothy Matovina and Gary Riebe-Estrella, SVD (Ithaca, N.Y.: Cornell University Press, 88.

3. Fenggang Yang, *Chinese Christians in America: Conversion, Assimilation, and Adhesive Identities* (University Park: The Pennsylvania State University Press, 1999), 17.

4. There has been much recent scholarly work on religion and the "empowerment" of women. See R. Marie Griffith, *God's Daughters: Evangelical Women and the Power of Submission* (Berkeley and Los Angeles: University of California Press, 1997); Brenda Brasher, *Godly Women: Fundamentalism and Female Power* (New Brunswick, N.J.: Rutgers University Press, 1998); Ruth Behar, *Translated Woman* (Boston: Beacon Press, 1993); Laurel Kendall, *Shamans, Housewives, and Other Restless Spirits* (Honolulu: University of Hawaii Press, 1993); Karen McCarthy Brown, *Mama Lola: A Vodou Priestess in Brooklyn* (Berkeley and Los Angeles: University of California Press, 1991) for well-written, thoughtful studies of how women are empowered through their faith.

5. Timothy Matovina, "U.S. Catholicism in One América," *American Catholic Studies Newsletter* 29, no. 2 (fall 2002): 9.

Bibliography

BOOKS AND ARTICLES

Abram, Ken. *Who Are the Promise Keepers? Understanding the Christian Men's Movement.* New York: Doubleday Books, 1997.

Abu-Lughod, Lila. "Writing against Culture. " In *Recapturing Anthropology: Working in the Present,* ed. Richard Fox. Santa Fe, N. M. : School of American Research, 1991.

———. *Writing Women's Worlds: Bedouin Stories.* Berkeley and Los Angeles: University of California Press, 1993.

Allen, Larry Dean. "A Comparative Analysis of the Men and Religion Forward Movement and Promise Keepers. " Ph. D. dissertation, Boston University, 2000.

Aloy, Marc. "Barrio: A Living Community. " Arizona State University, Chicano Reading Room Collection, 1973.

Apodaca, Maria Linda. "They Kept the Home Fires Burning: Mexican-American Women and Social Change. " Ph. D. dissertation, University of California, Irvine, 1994.

Apolito, Paolo. *Apparitions of the Madonna at Oliveto Citra: Local Visions and Cosmic Drama.* University Park: Pennsylvania State University Press, 1998.

Appadurai, Arjun. "Theme Issue: Place and Voice in Anthropological Theory. " *Cultural Anthropology* 3, no. 1 (February 1988): 16–20.

Applebaum, Phyllis. "The Growth of the Montessori Movement in the United States. " Ph. D. dissertation, New York University, 1971.

Acquistapace, Fred. *Miracles that Never Were: Natural Explanations of the Bible's Supernatural Stories.* Santa Rosa, Calif. : Eye-Opener Books, 1991.

Arvey, Michael. *Miracles: Opposing Viewpoints.* San Diego, Calif. : Greenhaven Press, 1990.

Arroyo, Antonio M. Stephens. *Prophets Denied Honor: An Anthology of the Hispano Church of the United States.* Maryknoll, N. Y. : Orbis Books, 1980.

Ashton, Joan. *Mother of All Nations: Visions of Mary.* San Francisco: HarperCollins, 1989.

———. *The People's Madonna.* San Francisco: HarperCollins, 1991.

Baca Zinn, Maxine. "Political Familism: Toward Sex Role Equality in Chicano

Families. " *Aztlán: Chicano Journal of the Social Sciences and the Arts* 6, no. 1 (spring 1975): 13–26.

Baldwin, Peter C. *Domesticating the Street: The Reform of Public Space in Hartford, 1850–1930.* Columbus: The Ohio State University Press, 1999.

Balmer, Randall. "Apocalypticism in America: The Argot of Premillennialism in Popular Culture. " *Prospects: An Annual of American Cultural Studies* 13 (1988): 417–433.

———. *Mine Eyes Have Seen the Glory: A Journey into the Evangelical Subculture in America.* New York: Oxford University Press, 1993.

Barnard, Charles P., M. D. *Families with an Alcoholic Member: The Invisible Patient.* New York: Human Sciences Press, 1990.

Barton, Matthew. "A Stadium of Hope: A Rhetorical Analysis of the Promise Keepers. " Master's thesis, University of Nevada–Las Vegas, 1998

Bax, Mart. "Marian Apparitions in Medjugorje: Rivalling Religious Regimes and State-Formation in Yugoslavia. " In *Religious Regimes and State-Formation,* ed. Eric R. Wolf. New York: State University of New York Press, 1991.

———. *Medjugorje: Religion, Politics, and Violence in Rural Bosnia.* Amsterdam: Paul & Co. Publishing Consortium, 1995.

Behar, Ruth. *Translated Woman.* Boston: Beacon Press, 1993.

———. *The Vulnerable Observer: Anthropology that Breaks Your Heart.* Boston: Beacon Press, 1996.

Berger, Peter. *The Sacred Canopy: Elements of a Sociological Theory of Religion.* New York: Anchor Books, 1969.

Betancur, John J., et al. "Economic Restructuring and the Process of Incorporation of Latinos into the Chicago Economy. " In *Latinos in a Changing U. S. Economy,* ed. Rebecca Morales and Frank Bonilla. Newbury Park, Calif. : Sage Publications, 1993.

Blackbourn, David. *Marpingen: Apparitions of the Virgin Mary in Bismarckian Germany.* Oxford: Clarendon Press, 1993.

Blea, Irene. *La Chicana and the Intersection of Race, Class, and Gender.* New York: Praeger Publishers, 1992.

Bodnar, John. *The Transplanted: A History of Immigrants in Urban America.* Bloomington: Indiana University Press, 1985.

Bonilla-Santiago, Gloria, ed. *Breaking Ground and Barriers: Hispanic Women Developing Effective Leadership.* San Diego, Calif. : Marin Publications, 1992.

Bourguignon, Erika. *Altered States of Consciousness and Social Change.* Columbus: The Ohio State University Press, 1973.

Brasher, Brenda. *Godly Women: Fundamentalism and Female Power.* New Brunswick, N. J. : Rutgers University Press, 1998.

Bravman, Bill. *Making Ethnic Ways: Communities and Their Transformations in Taita, Kenya, 1800–1950.* Woburn, Mass. : Heinemann, 1998.

Brereton, Virginia Lieson. *From Sin to Salvation: Stories of Women's Conversions, 1800 to the Present.* Bloomington: Indiana University Press, 1991.

Brettel, Caroline B., ed. *When They Read What We Write: The Politics of Ethnography.* Westport, Conn., and London: Bergin & Garvey, 1993.

Brickner, Brian. *The Promise Keepers: Politics and Promise.* Lanham, Md. : Lexington Books, 1992.

Bright, Brenda Jo. "'Heart Like a Car': Hispano/Chicano Culture in Northern New Mexico. " *American Ethnologist* 25, no. 4 (November 1998): 583–609.

————. "Mexican American Low Riders: An Anthropological Approach to Popular Culture. " Ph. D. dissertation, Rice University, 1994.

————. "Nightmares in the New Metropolis: The Cinematic Poetics of Lowriders. " *Studies in Latin American Popular Culture* 16 (1997): 13–30.

————. "Remappings: Los Angeles Low Riders. " In *Looking High and Low: Art and Cultural Identity,* ed. Brenda Jo Bright and Liza Blakewell. Tucson: University of Arizona Press, 1995.

Brown, Karen McCarthy. *Mama Lola: A Vodou Priestess in Brooklyn.* Berkeley and Los Angeles: University of California Press, 1991.

Brown, Michael. *The Final Hour.* Milford, Ohio: Faith Publishing Company, 1992.

Brusco, Elizabeth. "The Peace that Passes All Understanding: Violence, the Family, and Fundamentalist Knowledge in Colombia. " In *Mixed Blessings: Gender and Religious Fundamentalism Cross-Culturally,* ed. Judy Brink and Joan Mencher. London and New York: Routledge, 1997.

————. *The Reformation of Machismo: Evangelical Conversion and Gender in Colombia.* Austin: University of Texas Press, 1995.

Burns, Jeffrey M. "The Mexican Catholic Community in California. " In *Mexican Americans and the Catholic Church, 1900–1965,* ed. Jay P. Dolan and Gilberto N. Hinojosa. Notre Dame, Ind. : University of Notre Dame Press, 1994.

Careers for Youth, Inc. "High School Graduation Rates in Downtown and South Phoenix: A Preliminary Study. " Unpublished report, 1961.

Carroll, Michael P. *Catholic Cults and Devotions: A Psychological Enquiry.* Montreal: McGill-Queen's University Press, 1989.

————. *The Cult of the Virgin Mary: Psychological Origins.* Princeton, N. J. : Princeton University Press, 1986.

————. *Madonnas that Maim: Popular Catholicism in Italy since the Fifteenth Century.* Baltimore, Md. : Johns Hopkins University Press, 1992.

————. *Veiled Threats: The Logic of Popular Catholicism in Italy.* Baltimore, Md. : Johns Hopkins University Press, 1996.

————. "The Virgin Mary at LaSalette and Lourdes: Whom Did the Children See?" *Journal for the Scientific Study of Religion* 24, no. 1 (1985): 56–74.

————. "Visions of the Virgin Mary: The Effect of Family Structures on Marian Apparitions. " *Journal for the Scientific Study of Religion* 22, no. 3 (1983): 205–221.

Chavez, Gene T., and Kurt Organista. "Barriers to Chicano Participation in Higher Education: Admissions Selection Criteria. " Arizona State University, RAZA Graduate Student Caucus, fall 1979.

Chrasta, Michael James. "Jesus People and the Promise Keepers: A Revival Sequence and Its Effect on Late Twentieth-Century Evangelical Ideas of Masculinity. " Ph. D. dissertation, University of Texas at Dallas, 1998.

Christian, William A. Jr. *Apparitions in Late Medieval and Renaissance Spain.* Princeton, N. J. : Princeton University Press, 1981.

———. *Person and God in a Spanish Valley.* Princeton, N. J. : Princeton University Press, 1989.

———. *Visionaries: The Spanish Republic and the Reign of Christ.* Berkeley and Los Angeles: University of California Press, 1996.

City of Phoenix Planning Department. "Draft: General Plan Element, Housing. " Unpublished draft, May 1985.

———. "South Mountain Village: A Plan for Our Future. " Unpublished draft, February 1985.

Clifford, James. *The Predicament of Culture: Twentieth-Century Ethnography, Literature, and Art.* Cambridge: Harvard University Press, 1988.

———. "Spatial Practices: Fieldwork, Travel, and the Disciplining of Anthropology. " In *Anthropological Locations: Boundaries and Grounds of a Field Science,* ed. Akhil Gupta and James Ferguson, 185–222. Berkeley: University of California Press, 1997.

Clifford, James, and George E. Marcus, eds. *Writing Culture: The Poetics and Politics of Ethnography.* Berkeley and Los Angeles: University of California Press, 1986.

Cohen, Ronald D. *Children of the Mill: Schooling and Society in Gary, Indiana, 1906–1960.* Bloomington: Indiana University Press, 1990.

Cole, Edwin Louis. *On Becoming a Real Man.* Nashville, Tenn. : Thomas Nelson Publishers, 1992.

Comaroff, John, and Jean Comaroff. *Ethnography and the Historical Imagination.* Boulder, Colo. : Westview Press, 1992.

Connell, Janice. *Meetings with Mary: Visions of the Blessed Mother.* New York: Ballantine Books, 1995.

———. *The Visions of the Children: The Apparitions of the Blessed Mother at Medjugorje, 1981–1983.* New York: St. Martin's Press, 1992.

Corley, Julie. "Conflict and Community: St. Mary's Parish, Phoenix, Arizona. " Master's thesis, Arizona State University, 1992.

Cornell, Stephen, and Douglas Hartmann, eds. *Ethnicity and Race: Making Identities in a Changing World.* Thousand Oaks, Calif. : Pine Forge Press, 1998.

Cotera, Martha. "Marianismo. " In *Dona Doormat no esta aqui!* ed. Irene Dominguez, 147. Washington, D. C. : U. S. Department of Education, 1985.

Coteran, Martha, and Larry Hufford, eds. *Bridging Two Cultures.* Austin, Tex. : National Educational Laboratory Publishers, 1980.

Cousins, John W., C. P. "Signpost: Your Questions Answered. " *Sign* (December 1965): 46–47.

Crowley, Michael. "Spiritual Winds over a Cultural Sea: Grass-Roots Patterns in Latin America. " *Religion* 28, no. 3 (1998): 257–270.

Csordas, Thomas. *Language, Charisma, and Creativity: The Ritual Life of a Religious Movement.* Berkeley and Los Angeles: University of California Press, 1997.

———. *The Sacred Self: A Cultural Phenomenology of Charismatic Healing.* Berkeley and Los Angeles: University of California Press, 1994.

Culpepper, Robert H. *Evaluating the Charismatic Movement.* Valley Forge, Pa. : Judson Press, 1977.

Curtis, Susan. *A Consuming Faith: The Social Gospel and Modern American Culture.* Baltimore and London: Johns Hopkins University Press, 1991.

Dahlberg, Andrea. "The Body as a Principle of Holism: Three Pilgrimages to Lourdes. " In *Contesting the Sacred: The Anthropology of Christian Pilgrimage,* ed. John Eade and Michael J. Sallnow. London and New York: Routledge, 1991.

Davalos, Karen Mary. "The Real Way of Praying: The Via Crucis,*Mexicano* Sacred Space, and the Architecture of Domination. " In *Horizons of the Sacred: Mexican Traditions in U. S. Catholicism,* ed. Timothy Matovina and Gary Riebe-Estrella, S. V. D., 41–68. Ithaca, N. Y. : Cornell University Press, 2002.

Davis, Mike. *City of Quartz: Excavating the Future in Los Angeles.* New York: Vintage Books, 1990.

———. *Magical Urbanism: Latinos Reinvent the City.* London and New York: Verso, 2000.

Dayton, Donald W., and Robert K. Johnston. *The Variety of American Evangelicalism.* Knoxville: University of Tennessee Press, 1991.

De Anda, Roberto M. *Chicanas and Chicanos in Contemporary Society.* Boston: Allyn and Bacon, 1996.

Deck, Allan Figueroa, S. J. *The Second Wave: Hispanic Ministry and the Evangelization of Cultures.* New York: Paulist Press, 1989.

Delbridge, John Richard. "Partners or Patriarchs? Promise Keepers and the Rhetoric of Gender Reconciliation. " Ph. D. dissertation, Bowling Green State University, 1998.

Del Castillo, Richard Griswold. *La Familia: Chicano Families in the Urban Southwest, 1848 to the Present.* Notre Dame, Ind. : University of Notre Dame Press, 1984.

Delgado, Richard, and Jean Stefancic, eds. *The Latino/a Condition: A Critical Reader.* London and New York: New York University Press, 1998.

Deutsch, Sarah. *No Separate Refuge: Culture, Class, and Gender on an Anglo-Hispanic Frontier in the American Midwest, 1800–1940.* New York: Oxford University Press, 1987.

Díaz-Stevens, Ana Maria. "From Puerto Rican to Hispanic: The Politics of the Fiestas Patronales in New York. " *Latino Studies Journal* 1, no. 1 (January 1990): 28–47.

Dictionary of Mary. New Jersey: Catholic Book Publishing Company, 1997.

Dimas, Pete. "Perspectives on Progress and a Mexican American Community's Struggle for Existence. " Ph. D. dissertation, Arizona State University, 1991.

———. *Progress and a Mexican American Community's Struggle for Existence: Phoenix's Golden Gate Barrio.* New York: Peter Lang, 1990.

Dinges, William. "Roman Catholic Traditionalism and Activist Conservatism in the United States. " In *Evangelicals and Catholics Together,* ed. Charles Colson and Richard John Neuhaus. London: Word Publishing, 1995.

Dorson, Richard M. "Material Components of Celebration. " In *Celebration: Studies in Festivity and Ritual,* ed. Victor Turner. Washington, D. C. : Smithsonian Institution Press, 1982.

Dubisch, Jill. *In a Different Place: Pilgrimage, Gender, and Politics at a Greek Island Shrine.* Princeton, N. J. : Princeton University Press, 1995.

Durkheim, Emile. *The Elementary Forms of the Religious Life.* New York: Free Press, 1915.

Eade, John. "Order and Power at Lourdes: Lay Helpers and the Organization of a Pilgrimage Shrine. " In *Contesting the Sacred: The Anthropology of Christian Pilgrimage,* ed. John Eade and Michael J. Sallnow. London and New York: Routledge, 1991.

Eade, John, and Michael J. Sallnow, eds. *Contesting the Sacred.* London and New York: Routledge, 1991.

Elizondo, Virgilio. *The Future Is Mestizo: Life Where Cultures Meet.* Bloomington, Ill. : Meyer-Stone Books, 1988.

———. *Galilean Journey: The Mexican American Promise.* Maryknoll, N. Y. : Orbis Books, 1983.

———. "Popular Religion and Support of Identity: A Pastoral-Psychological Case-Study Based on the Mexican American Experience in the USA. " In *Popular Religion,* ed. Norbert Greinacher and Norbert Mette. Edinburgh: T. & T. Clark, Ltd., 1986.

Engle, Michael. *The Struggle for Control of Public Education: Market Ideology vs. Democratic Values.* Philadelphia: Temple University Press, 2000.

Espinosa, Gastón. "*El Azteca*: Francisco Olazábal and Latino Pentecostal Charisma, Power, and Faith Healing in the Borderlands. " *Journal of the American Academy of Religion* 67, no. 3 (1999): 597–616.

ESPIRITU Community Development Corporation. "School Improvement Plans 1998–1999. " Unpublished article, 1999.

Faricy, Robert, S. J., and Lucy Roony, S. N. D. de N. *Medjugorje Up Close: Mary Speaks to the World.* Chicago: Franciscan Herald Books, 1986.

———. *Our Lady Comes to Scottsdale: Is It Authentic?* Santa Barbara, Calif. : Queenship Publishing Company, 1993.

———. *Return to God: The Scottsdale Message.* Santa Barbara, Calif. : Queenship Publishing Company, 1993.

Faulkner, Chris Paul. "Understanding Homeboys: A Cultural Perspective. " Chicano Reading Room, Arizona State University, 1987.

Feeney, Robert. *Mother of the Americas.* Washington, D. C. : Aquinas Press, 1989.

Filas, Francis L., S. J. "What of Lucy's Claims?" *America* 101 (July 1959): 490–491.

Finn, Chester, et al. *Charter Schools in Action: Renewing Public Education.* Princeton, N. J. : Princeton University Press, 2000.

Freedberg, David. *The Power of Images: Studies in the History and Theory of Response.* Chicago and London: University of Chicago Press, 1989.

Gabbacia, Donna. *From the Other Side: Women, Gender and Immigrant Life in the U. S. 1820–1990.* Bloomington: Indiana University Press, 1994.

Galarza, Ernesto, et al. *Mexican-Americans in the Southwest.* Santa Barbara, Calif. : McNally & Loftin, Publishers, 1970.

Gallagher, Charles A., ed. *Rethinking the Color Line.* London: Mayfield Publishers, 1999.

García, Ignacio. "Backwards from Aztlán: Politics in the Age of Hispanics. " In *Chicanas and Chicanos in Contemporary Society,* ed. Roberto M. De Anda. Boston: Allyn and Bacon, 1996.

Garvey, Mark. *Searching for Mary: An Exploration of Marian Apparitions across the U. S.* New York: Penguin Books, 1998.

Geertz, Clifford. *The Interpretation of Cultures.* New York: Basic Books, 1973.

Glazier, Stephen D. "Pilgrimages of the Caribbean: A Comparison of Cases from Haiti and Trinidad. " In *Sacred Journeys,* ed. Alan Morinis. Westport, Conn. : Greenwood Press, 1992.

Gonzales, Manuel G. *Mexicanos: A History of Mexicans in the United States.* Bloomington: Indiana University Press, 1999.

Good, Thomas L., and Jennifer S. Braden. "Charter Schools: Another Reform Failure or a Worthwhile Investment?" *Kappan* 81, no. 10 (June 2000): 745–750.

———. *The Great School Debate: Choice, Vouchers, and Charters.* Mahwah, N. J. : Lawrence Erlbaum Associates, 2000.

Goodman, Felicitas D. *Trance, Healing, and Hallucination: Three Field Studies in Religious Experience.* New York: Wiley, 1974.

Gracia, Jorge J. *Hispanic/Latino Identity: A Philosophical Perspective.* Boston: Blackwell Publishers, 2000.

Graham Keegan, Lisa. "The Empowerment of Market-Based School Reform. " In *School Choice in the Real World,* ed. Robert Maranto et al. Boulder, Colo. : Westview Press, 1999.

Greenhouse, Carol J. *Praying for Justice: Faith, Order, and Community in an American Town.* Ithaca, N. Y. : Cornell University Press, 1986.

Gresham, April, Fredrick Hess, et al. "Desert Bloom: Arizona's Free Market in Education. " *Kappan* 81, no. 10 (June 2000): 751–757.

Griffith, R. Marie. *God's Daughters: Evangelical Women and the Power of Submission.* Berkeley and Los Angeles: University of California Press, 1997.

Gutiérrez, David. "Migration, Emergent Ethnicity, and the 'Third Space': The Shifting Politics of Nationalism in Greater Mexico. " *Journal of American History* (September 1999): 18–19.

Gutiérrez, Lorraine, and Zulema Suarez. "Empowerment with Latinas. " In *Empowering Women of Color,* ed. Lorraine M. Gutiérrez and Edith A. Lewis. New York: Columbia University Press, 1999.

Haberman, David. *Journey through the Twelve Forests.* Oxford and New York: Oxford University Press, 1994.

Hainstock, Elizabeth G. *The Essential Montessori: An Introduction to the Woman, the Writings, the Method, and the Movement.* New York: Plume, 1997.

Hancock, Ann Marie. *Wake Up America! Take My Heart, Take My Hand.* Norfolk, Va. : Hampton Roads Publishing Company, 1993.

Haney López, Ian. "Chance, Context, and Choice in the Social Construction of Race. " In *The Latino/a Condition: A Critical Reader,* ed. Richard Delgado and Jean Stefancic. London and New York: New York University Press, 1998.

Hardy-Fanta, Carol. *Latina Politics, Latino Politics: Gender, Culture, and Political Participation in Boston.* Philadelphia: Temple University Press, 1993.

Harper, Michael. *Three Sisters.* Bloomington, Ill. : Tyndale House, 1979.

Harris, Ruth. *Lourdes: Body and Spirit in the Secular Age.* New York: Penguin, 1999.

Hart, John Mason. "The Evolution of the Mexican and Mexican-American Working Classes. " In *Border Crossings: Mexican and Mexican-American Workers,* ed. John Mason Hart. Wilmington, Del. : S. R. Books, 1998.

Hartley, Mary. "A Voice from the State Legislature: Don't Do What We Did!" In *School Choice in the Real World: Lessons from Arizona Charter Schools,* ed. Roberto Maranto et al. Boulder, Colo. : Westview Press, 1999.

Hassel, Bryan C. *The Charter School Challenge: Avoiding the Pitfalls, Fulfilling the Promise.* Washington, D. C. : Brookings Institution Press, 1999.

Heinz, Donald. "The Struggle to Define America. " In *The New Christian Right: Mobilization and Legitimation,* ed. Robert C. Liebman and Robert Wuthnow. New York: Aldine Publishing Company, 1983.

Hinojosa, Gilberto M. "The Mexican-American Church, 1930–1965. " In *Mexican Americans and the Catholic Church, 1900–1965,* ed. Jay P. Dolan and Gilberto M. Hinojosa. Notre Dame, Ind. : University of Notre Dame Press, 1994.

———. "Mexican-American Faith Communities in Texas and the Southwest. " In *Mexican Americans and the Catholic Church, 1900–1965,* ed. Jay P. Dolan and Gilberto M. Hinojosa. Notre Dame, Ind. : University of Notre Dame Press, 1994.

Hitchcock, James. "Catholic Activist Conservatism in the United States. " In *Fundamentalisms Observed,* ed. Martin A. Marty and R. Scott Appleby. Chicago and London: University of Chicago Press, 1991.

Holler, Stephen. "Exploring the Popular Religion of U. S. Hispanic/Latino Ethnic Groups. " *Latino Studies Journal* 6, no. 3 (September 1995): 3–29.

Horowitz, Ruth. *Honor and the American Dream: Culture and Identity in a Chicano Community.* New Brunswick, N. J. : Rutgers University Press, 1983.

Hunter, James Davidson. *American Evangelicalism: Conservative Religion and the Quandary of Modernity.* New Brunswick, N. J. : Rutgers University Press, 1983.

———. *Culture Wars: The Struggle to Define America.* New York: Basic Books, 1991.

———. *Evangelicalism: The Coming Generation.* Chicago: University of Chicago Press, 1987.

Ines-Loya, Gloria. "The Hispanic Woman: *Pasionaria* and *Pastora* of the Hispanic Community. " In *Frontiers of Hispanic Theology in the United States,* ed. Allan Figueroa Deck, 125. New York: Orbis Books, 1992.

Isasi-Diaz, Ada María, and Yolanda Tarango. *Hispanic Women: Prophetic Voice in the Church.* San Francisco: Harper & Row, 1988.

Jackson, Michael. *Minima Ethnographica: Intersubjectivity and Anthropological Art.* Chicago: University of Chicago Press, 1998.

———. *Things as They Are: New Directions in Phenomenological Anthropology.* Bloomington: Indiana University Press, 1996.

Jacob, Theodore, and Ruth Ann Seilhamer. "The Impact on Spouses and How They Cope. " In *Alcohol and the Family,* ed. Jim Orford and Judith Harwin. New York: St. Martin's Press, 1982.

Jenkins, Richard. *Rethinking Ethnicity: Arguments and Explorations.* Thousand Oaks, Calif. : Sage Publications, 1997.

Jensen, Lone. *Gifts of Grace: A Gathering of Personal Encounters with the Virgin Mary.* San Francisco: HarperCollins, 1995.

Kendall, Laurel. *The Life and Hard Times of a Korean Shaman.* Honolulu: University of Hawaii Press, 1988.

———. *Shamans, Housewives, and Other Restless Spirits.* Honolulu: University of Hawaii Press, 1985.

Kinsley, David. *Health, Healing, and Religion: A Cross-Cultural Perspective.* Upper Saddle River, N. J. : Prentice Hall, 1996.

Kraemer, Rita. *Maria Montessori: A Biography.* New York: G. P. Putnam's Sons, 1976.

Kraljevik, Svetozar, O. F. M. *The Apparitions of Our Lady at Medjugorje, 1981–1983.* Chicago: Franciscan Herald Press, 1984.

Kramer, George Joseph. "The Intensive Group Process and Cursillo Experience: Implications for Spiritual Formations of Participants. " Ph. D. dissertation, Catholic University of America, 1985.

Kselman, Thomas. "Our Lady of Necedah: Marian Piety and the Cold War. " CUSHWA Working Paper Series, University of Notre Dame, series 12, no. 2 (fall 1982): 1–38.

Lahart, Kevin. "Miracle in Bayside. " *The Critic* 33, no. 1 (fall/winter 1974): 36–44.

Lambeck, Michael. *Human Spirits: A Cultural Account of Trance in Mayotte.* New York: Cambridge University Press, 1981.

Laurentin, René. *The Apparitions of the Virgin Mary Today.* Dublin, Ireland: Veritas, 1990.

———. *The Church and Apparitions—Their Status and Function: Criteria and Reception.* Milford, Ohio: The Riehle Foundation, 1989.

———. *Medjugorje: Thirteen Years Later.* Milford, Ohio: The Riehle Foundation, 1994.

———. *Our Lord and Our Lady in Scottsdale: Fruitful Charisms in a Traditional American Parish.* Milford, Ohio: Faith Publishing Company, 1992.

———. *Ten Years of Apparitions: New Growth and Recognition of the Pilgrims.* Milford, Ohio: Faith Publishing Company, 1991.

———. *The Way of the Cross in Santa Maria, California.* Santa Barbara, Calif. : Queenship Publishing Company, 1993.

Lawless, Elaine J. *God's Peculiar People: Women's Voices and Folk Tradition in a Pentecostal Church.* Lexington: University Press of Kentucky, 1988.

———. Review of *God's Daughters: Evangelical Women and the Power of Submission,* by R. Marie Griffith, and *Godly Women: Fundamentalism and Female Power,* by Brenda E. Brasher. *Journal of the American Academy of Religion* 67, no. 4 (December 1999): 892–897.

———. *Women Preaching Revolution: Calling for a Connection in a Disconnected Time.* Philadelphia: University of Pennsylvania Press, 1996.

Léon, Luís. "Born Again in East L. A. : The Congregation as Border Space. " In *Gatherings in the Diaspora,* ed. R. Stephen Warner and Judith G. Wittner. Philadelphia: Temple University Press, 1998.

———. "Metaphor and Place: The U. S. –Mexico Border as Center and Periphery in the Interpretation of Religion. " *Journal of the American Academy of Religion* 67, no. 3 (September 1999): 541–572.

Lewis, Greg. *The Power of a Promise Kept.* Colorado Springs, Colo. : Focus on the Family Publishing, 1995.

Liebman, Robert C., and Robert Wuthnow. *The New Christian Right: Mobilization and Legitimation.* New York: Aldine Publishing Company, 1983.

Lippy, Charles H. "Millennialism and Adventism. " In *Encyclopedia of American Religious Experience: Studies of Traditions and Movements,* ed. Charles H. Lippy and Peter W. Williams. New York: Charles Scribner's Sons, 1988.

Livezey, Lowell W., ed. *Public Religion and Urban Transformation: Faith in the City.* New York: New York University Press, 2000.

Luckingham, Bradford. *Minorities in Phoenix: A Profile of Mexican American, Chinese American, and African American Communities, 1860–1992.* Tucson: University of Arizona Press, 1994.

———. *Phoenix: The History of a Southwestern Metropolis.* Tucson: University of Arizona Press, 1989.

Luckmann, Thomas. *The Invisible Religion: The Problem of Religion in Modern Society.* New York: Macmillan, 1967.

MacCormack, Sabine. "Loca Santa: The Organization of Sacred Topography in Late Antiquity. " In *The Blessings of Pilgrimage,* ed. Robert Ousterhout. Urbana and Chicago: University of Illinois Press, 1990.

Mac an Ghaill, Máirtín. *Contemporary Racisms and Ethnicities: Social and Cultural Transformations.* Buckingham and Philadelphia: Open University Press, 1999.

A Man Named Father Jozo. Milford, Ohio: The Riehle Foundation, 1989.

Manno, Bruno V., Chester Finn Jr., and Gregg Vanourek. "Beyond the Schoolhouse Door: How Charter Schools Are Transforming U. S. Public Education. " *Kappan* 81, no. 10 (June 2000): 736–744.

Marcus, George E., and Michael Fischer, eds. *Anthropology as Cultural Critique.* Chicago and London: University of Chicago Press, 1986.

Marsden, George. *Fundamentalism and American Culture: The Shaping of Twentieth-Century Evangelicalism, 1870–1925.* New York: Oxford University Press, 1980.

———. *Understanding Fundamentalism and Evangelicalism.* Grand Rapids, Mich. , : William B. Eerdmans Publishing Company, 1991.

Martínez, Elizabeth. "In Pursuit of Latina Liberation. " *Signs* 20, no. 4 (summer 1995): 1019–1028.

Mary's Ministries. "Our Lady of the Americas' Messages from November '94–Present. " Mary's Ministries, 30 E. Cody Drive, Phoenix, Arizona 85040.

Matovina, Timothy, and Gary Riebe-Estrella, S. V. D. *Horizons of the Sacred: Mexican Traditions in U. S. Catholicism.* Ithaca, N. Y. : Cornell University Press, 2002.

McBride, James D. "Liga Protectora Latina: A Mexican American Benevolent Society in Arizona. " Arizona State University, Chicano Reading Room Collection, 1975.

McCartney, Bill. *From Ashes to Glory.* Nashville, Tenn. : Thomas Nelson Publishing Company, 1995.

———. *Sold Out: Becoming Man Enough to Make a Difference.* Nashville, Tenn. : Word Publishing, 1997.

McCartney, Bill, Greg Laurie, and Jack Hayford. *Seven Promises of a Promise Keeper.* Nashville, Tenn. : Word Publishing, 1999.

McDannell, Colleen. *Material Christianity: Religion and Popular Culture in America.* New Haven, Conn. : Yale University Press, 1995.

McGreevy, John. "Bronx Miracle. " *American Quarterly* 52, no. 3 (September 2000): 405–443.

McGuire, Meredith. *Pentecostal Catholics: Power, Charisma, and Order in a Religious Movement.* Philadelphia: Temple University Press, 1982.

McLoughlin, Emmett. *People's Padre: An Autobiography.* Boston: Beacon Press, 1954.

Meier, Matt S., and Feliciano Ribera. *Mexican Americans/American Mexicans: From Conquistadores to Chicanos.* New York: Hill and Wang, 1993.

Mesa-Bains, Amalia. "Land and Spirituality in the Descansos. " In *Saber es poder/Interventions,* ed. Richard M. Carp. Los Angeles: Adobe L. A., 1994.

Messner, Michael. *Politics of Masculinities: Men in Movements.* Thousand Oaks, Calif. : Sage Publications, 1997.

Mirande, Alfredo, and Evangelina Enriquez. *La Chicana.* Chicago and London: University of Chicago Press, 1979.

Moltmann, Jürgen, and Karl-Josef Kuschel. *Pentecostal Movements as an Ecumenical Challenge.* Maryknoll, N. Y. : Orbis Books, 1996.

Montessori, Maria. *The Absorbent Mind.* New York: Dell Publishing Company, 1984.

———. *The Discovery of the Child.* Notre Dame, Ind. : Fides Publishers, 1967.

———. *Education and Peace.* Chicago: Henry Regnery Company, 1972.

———. *Maria Montessori's Own Handbook.* New York: Schocken Books, 1965.

———. *The Montessori Method.* New York: Schocken Books, 1989.

———. *The Secret of Childhood.* New York: APT Books, 1984.

Morgan, David. *Visual Piety: A History and Theory of Popular Religious Images.* Berkeley and Los Angeles: University of California Press, 1998.

Morinis, Alan, ed. *Sacred Journeys: The Anthropology of Pilgrimage.* Westport, Conn. : Greenwood Press, 1992.

Nathan, Joe. *Charter Schools: Creating Hope and Opportunity for American Education.* San Francisco: Jossey-Bass Publishers, 1996.

National Secretariat of the Cursillo Movement in the United States. *The Cursillo Movement's Leaders' Manual.* Dallas, Tex. : National Secretariat of the Cursillo Movement in the United States, 1981.

———. *Desarollo: The Evolution of the Cursillo Literature.* Dallas, Tex. : National Ultreya Publication, 1971.

———. *Encuentros del Movimiento De Cursillos.* Dallas, Tex. : Centro Nacional de Cursillos, 1971.

———. *The Fundamental Ideas of the Cursillo Movement.* Dallas, Tex. : National Ultreya Publications, 1992.

———. *Our Fourth Day.* Dallas, Tex. : National Ultreya Publications, 1985.

———. *¿Y después del Cursillo?* Dallas, Tex. : Centro Nacional de Cursillos, 1970.

Neitz, Mary Jo. *Charisma and Community: A Study of Religious Commitment within the Charismatic Renewal.* New Brunswick, N. J. : Transaction Books, 1987.

Newman, Joseph. *The Religious Reawakening in America.* Washington, D. C. : Books by U. S. News & World Report, 1972.

Nickell, Joe. *Looking for a Miracle: Weeping Icons, Relics, Stigmata, Visions and Healing Cures.* Buffalo, N. Y. : Prometheus Books, 1993.

———. *Secrets of the Supernatural.* Buffalo, N. Y. : Prometheus Books, 1988.

Noble, Thomas F. X., ed. *Soldiers of Christ: Saints and Saint's Lives from Late Antiquity and the Early Middle Ages.* University Park: Pennsylvania State University Press, 1995.

Nolan, Denis. *Medjugorje: A Time for Truth and a Time for Action.* Santa Barbara, Calif. : Queenship Publishing Company, 1993.

Noll, Mark A. "The History of an Encounter: Roman Catholics and Protestant Evangelicals. " In *Evangelicals and Catholics Together: Toward a Common Mission,* ed. Charles Colson and Richard John Neuhaus. London: Word Publishing, 1995.

Obeyesekere, Gananath. *Medusa's Hair: An Essay on Personal Symbols and Religious Experience.* Chicago and London: University of Chicago Press, 1981.

Oboler, Suzanne. *Ethnic Labels, Ethnic Lives: Identity and the Politics of Representation in the United States.* Minneapolis: University of Minnesota Press, 1995.

Ochoa, Gilda Laura. "Everyday Ways of Resistance and Cooperation: Mexican American Women Building *Puentes* with Immigrants. " *Frontiers* 20, no. 1 (1999): 1–20.

O'Connor, Edward, C. S. C. *Marian Apparitions Today: Why So Many?* Santa Barbara, Calif. : Queenship Publishing Company, 1996.

Oktavec, Eileen. *Answered Prayers: Miracles and Milagros along the Border.* Tucson: University of Arizona Press, 1995.

Olvera, Donna. "Education Reform and Census Information Center Project. " Arizona State University, Hispanic Research Center Community Based Documentation Program, June 4, 1991.

Omi, Michael, and Howard Winant, eds. *Racial Formation in the United States.* London and New York: Routledge, 1994.

Orem, R. C. *Montessori: Her Method and the Movement.* New York: G. P. Putnam's Sons, 1974.

———. *Montessori Today.* New York: G. P. Putnam's Sons, 1971.

Orsi, Robert A. "The Cult of the Saints and the Reimagination of the Space and Time of Sickness in Twentieth-Century American Catholicism. " *Literature and Medicine* 8 (1989): 63–77.

———. *Gods of the City: Religion and the American Urban Landscape.* Bloomington: Indiana University Press, 1999.

———. *The Madonna of 115th Street.* Second edition. New Haven, Conn. : Yale University Press, 2002.

———. "'Mildred, Is It Fun to Be a Cripple?': The Culture of Suffering in Mid-Twentieth-Century American Catholicism. " *South Atlantic Quarterly* 93, no. 3 (summer 1994): 547–591.

———. *Thank You, Saint Jude: Women's Devotion to the Patron Saint of Hopeless Causes.* New Haven, Conn. : Yale University Press, 1996.

Ortner, Sherry B. "Theory in Anthropology since the Sixties. " *Comparative Studies in Society and History* 26, no. 1 (January 1984): 126–166.

Our Lady Help of Mothers: A Book about the Heavenly Apparitions to Veronica Leuken of Bayside, New York. Lowell, Mich. : These Last Days, n. d.

Our Lady of the Americas: The Messages of the Blessed Virgin Mary as Received by

Estela Ruiz of South Phoenix, Arizona. McKees Rocks, Pa. : Pittsburgh Center for Peace, 1994.

"Our Lady of the Americas' Messages from November '94–Present. " Booklet photocopied by Mary's Ministries, 30 E. Cody Drive, Phoenix, Arizona 85040.

Our Lady of the Roses Mary Help of Mothers: An Introduction Booklet on the Apparitions of Bayside. Lowell, Mich. : These Last Days, n. d.

Padilla, Felix M. *Latino Ethnic Consciousness: The Case of Mexican Americans and Puerto Ricans in Chicago.* Notre Dame, Ind. : University of Notre Dame Press, 1985.

Pardo, Mary. "Creating Community: Mexican American Women in Eastside Los Angeles. " In *Community Activism and Feminist Politics: Organizing across Race, Class, and Gender,* ed. Nancy A. Naples. London and New York: Routledge, 1998.

———. *Mexican American Women Activists: Identity and Resistance in Two Los Angeles Communities.* Philadelphia: Temple University Press, 1998.

———. "Mexican American Women Grassroots Community Activists: 'Mothers of East Los Angeles. '" *Frontiers* 20, no. 1 (1990): 1–7.

Parsons, Heather. *Marja and the Mother of God.* Dublin: Robert Andrew Press, 1993.

Personal Knowledge and Beyond: Reshaping the Ethnography of Religion. Edited by James V. Spickard, J. Shawn Landres, and Meredith B. McGuire. New York: New York University Press, 2002.

Petrisko, Tom. *Call of the Ages.* Santa Barbara, Calif. : Queenship Publishing Company, 1995.

———. *For the Soul of the Family.* Santa Barbara, Calif. : Queenship Publishing Company, 1996.

———. *Mother of the Secret.* Santa Barbara, Calif. : Queenship Publishing Company, 1997.

———. *Our Lady of the Americas: The Messages of the Virgin Mary as Received by Estela Ruiz of South Phoenix, Arizona.* McKees Rocks, Pa. : Pittsburgh Center for Peace, 1994.

Pitti, Gina Maria. "The Sociedades Guadalupanas in the San Francisco Archdiocese, 1942–1962. " *U. S. Catholic Historian* (winter 2003): 91–92.

Preston, James. "Spiritual Magnetism: An Organizing Principle for the Study of Pilgrimage. " In *Sacred Journeys: The Anthropology of Pilgrimage,* ed. Alan Morinis. Westport, Conn. : Greenwood Press, 1992.

Randi, James. *The Faith Healers.* Buffalo, N. Y. : Prometheus Books, 1987.

Ratcliffe, Peter. *"Race" Ethnicity and Nation: International Perspectives on Social Conflict.* Lynn, U. K. : UCL Press, 1994.

Raymond, Susan. "Symbolic Relationships of Graffiti by Phoenix Metropolitan Area Gangs. " Master's thesis, Arizona State University, 1991.

Renshaw, Scott W. "Thrasher Revisited: Thrill-Seeking within Mexican-American Gangs in Phoenix, Arizona. " Master's thesis, Arizona State University, 1997.

Revelations and Messages as Given through Mary Ann Van Hoof at Necedah, Wisonsin. Necedah, Wis. : For My God and My Country, Inc., 1971.

Rodriguez, Jeanette. *Our Lady of Guadalupe: Faith and Empowerment among Mexican-American Women.* Austin: University of Texas Press, 1994.

———. "Toward an Understanding of Spirituality in U. S. Latina Leadership. " *Frontiers* 20, no. 1 (1999): 137–147.

Rodriguez, Richard. *Brown: The Last Discovery of America.* New York: Penguin, 2002.

———. *Hunger of Memory: The Education of Richard Rodriguez.* New York: Bantam Books, 1982.

Romero, Gilbert C. *Hispanic Devotional Piety: Tracing the Biblical Roots.* Maryknoll, N. Y. : Orbis Books, 1991.

Rosaldo, Renato. *When Natives Talk Back: Chicano Anthropology since the Late Sixties.* Renato Rosaldo Lecture Series Monograph, vol. 2. Tucson: University of Arizona Mexican American Studies and Research Center, 1986.

Ruby, Jay, and Barbara Meyerhoff, eds. *A Crack in the Mirror: Reflexive Perspective in Anthropology.* Philadelphia: University of Pennsylvania Press, 1982.

Ruiz, Vicki L. *From Out of the Shadows: Mexican Women in Twentieth-Century America.* New York: Oxford University Press, 1998.

Sánchez, George J. *Becoming Mexican American: Ethnicity, Culture, and Identity in Chicano Los Angeles.* Berkeley and Los Angeles: University of California Press, 1993.

Sandoval, Moises. *On the Move: A History of the Hispanic Church in the United States.* Maryknoll, N. Y. : Orbis Books, 1990.

———. "The Organization of a Hispanic Church. " In *Hispanic Catholic Culture in the U. S. : Issues and Concerns,* ed. Jay P. Dolan and Allan Figueroa Deck, 141–146. Notre Dame, Ind. : University of Notre Dame Press, 1994.

Sarason, Seymour B. *Charter Schools: Another Flawed Educational Reform?* New York and London: Teacher's College, Columbia University, 1998.

Schell, Patience A. "An Honorable Avocation for Ladies: The Work of Mexico City Unión de Damas Católicas Mexicanas, 1912–1926. " *Journal of Women's History* 10, no. 4 (winter 1999): 78–103.

Schneider, Jo Anne. "Defining Boundaries, Creating Contacts: Puerto Rican and Polish Presentation of Group Identity through Ethnic Parades. " *Journal of Ethnic Studies* 18, no. 1 (spring 1990): 33–58.

Sedillo López, Antoinette, ed. *Latinos in the United States: Historical Themes and Identity.* New York and London: Garland Publishers, 1995.

Sklar, Deidre. *Dancing with the Virgin: Body and Faith in the Fiesta of Tortugas, New Mexico.* Berkeley: University of California Press, 2001.

Smith, Bradford, Sylvia Shue, et al., eds. *Philanthropies in Communities of Color.* Bloomington: Indiana University Press, 1999.

Smith, Christian, and Joshua Prokopy. *Latin American Religion in Motion*. New York: Routledge, 1999.

Sollors, Werner. *Neither Black nor White yet Both*. Cambridge: Harvard University Press, 1997.

Stacey, Judith. *Brave New Families: Stories of Domestic Upheaval in Late Twentieth Century America*. San Francisco: Basic Books, 1990.

Standing, E. M. *Maria Montessori: Her Life and Work*. New York: Mentor-Omega Books, 1957.

Steinglass, Peter, M. D. *The Alcoholic Family*. New York: Basic Books, 1987.

Strathern, Marilyn. *Partial Connections*. Savage, Md. : Rowman & Littlefield Publishers, 1991.

Swan, Henry. *My Work with Necedah, vol. I. Mary Ann Van Hoof's Own Story of the Apparitions of the Blessed Virgin Mary*. Necedah, Wis. : For My God and My Country, 1959.

———. *My Work with Necedah*, vol. II. *The Narrative of the Passion from the Sufferings on the Fridays of Advent and Lent*. Necedah, Wis. : For My God and My Country, 1959.

———. *My Work with Necedah*, vol. III. Necedah, Wis. : For My God and My Country, 1959.

———. *My Work with Necedah*, vol. IV. Necedah, Wis. : For My God and My Country, 1959.

Swanson, Tod. "Through Family Eyes: Towards a More Adequate Perspective for Viewing Native American Religious Life. " *American Indian Quarterly* 21, no. 1 (winter 1997): 57–71.

Thomas, Piri. *Down These Mean Streets*. New York: Vintage, 1974.

Turnbull, Colin. "Postscript: Anthropology as Pilgrimage, Anthropologist as Pilgrim. " In *Sacred Journeys*, ed. Alan Morinis. Westport, Conn. : Greenwood Press, 1992.

Turner, Kay, and Suzanne Seriff. "Giving an Altar: The Ideology of Reproduction in a St. Joseph's Day Feast. " *Journal of American Folklore* 100, no. 398 (October-December 1987): 446–460.

Turner, Kay. *Beautiful Necessity: The Art and Meaning of Women's Home Altars*. New York: Thames and Hudson, 1999.

———. "Mexican American Home Altars: Towards Their Interpretation. " *Aztlán* 13, no. 1 (spring 1982): 309–326.

———. "Mexican-American Women's Home Altars: The Art of Relationship. " Ph. D. dissertation, University of Texas at Austin, 1990.

Turner, Victor. *Image and Pilgrimage in Christian Culture*. New York: Columbia University Press, 1978.

———. *The Ritual Process: Structure and Anti-Structure*. New York: Cornell University Press, 1969.

Tweed, Thomas A. *Our Lady of the Exile: Diasporic Religion at a Cuban Shrine in Miami.* New York and Oxford: Oxford University Press, 1997.

Tyler, Stephen A. "Post-Modern Ethnography: From Document of the Occult to Occult Document. " In *Writing Culture: The Poetics and Politics of Ethnography,* ed. James Clifford and George E. Marcus. Berkeley and Los Angeles: University of California Press, 1986.

V., Rachel. *Family Secrets: Life Stories of Adult Children of Alcoholics.* San Francisco: Harper & Row, 1987.

Vidal, Jaime. "Popular Religion among Hispanics in the General Area of the Archdiocese of Newark. " In *Presencia Nueva: Knowledge for Service and Hope. A Study of Hispanics in the Archdiocese of Newark.* Newark, N. J. : Office of Research and Planning, Archdiocese of Newark, 1988.

Villa, Raúl Homero. "'Aquí estamos y no nos vamos': Place Struggles in Latino Los Angeles. " In *La Vida Latina en L. A. : Urban Latino Cultures,* ed. Gustavo LeClerc, Raúl Villa, and Michael J. Dear. Thousand Oaks, Calif. : Sage Publications, 1999.

———. *Barrio-Logos: Space and Place in Urban Chicano Literature and Culture.* Austin: University of Texas Press, 2000.

Walcheski, Michael John. "The Influence of Promise Keepers on Fathers' Involvement with Their Children. " Ph. D. dissertation, Western Michigan University, 1998.

Walker Bynum, Carolyn. *Holy Feast and Holy Fast: The Religious Significance of Food to Medieval Women.* Berkeley and Los Angeles: University of California Press, 1987.

Wardle, Francis. "Multicultural Education. " In *The Multiracial Experience: Racial Borders as the New Frontier,* ed. Maria P. Root. Thousand Oaks, Calif. : Sage Publications, 1996.

Warner, Marina. *Alone of All Her Sex: Myth and Cult of the Virgin Mary.* San Francisco: Random House, 1983.

Watt, David Harrington. *A Transforming Faith: Explorations of Twentieth-Century American Evangelicalism.* New Brunswick, N. J. : Rutgers University Press, 1991.

Weibel, Wayne. *Medjugorje: The Message.* Orleans, Mass. : Paraclete Press, 1997.

———. *Medjugorje: The Mission.* Orleans, Mass. : Paraclete Press, 1994.

Wilcox, Clyde. *God's Warriors: The Christian Right in Twentieth-Century America.* Baltimore, Md. : Johns Hopkins University Press, 1992.

Williams, Norma. *The Mexican American Family: Tradition and Change.* New York: General Hall, 1990.

Wilson, Bryan. "Millennialism in Comparative Perspective. " *Comparative Studies in Society and History* 6 (1963): 93–116.

Wilson, Claire. "The Impact on Children. " In *Alcohol and the Family,* ed. Jim Orford and Judith Harwin. New York: St. Martin's Press, 1982.

Winston, Diane. *Red Hot and Righteous: The Urban Religion of the Salvation Army.* Cambridge: Harvard University Press, 1999.

Wojcik, Daniel. *The End of the World As We Know It: Faith, Fatalism, and Apocalypse in America.* New York: New York University Press, 1997.

———. "Polaroids from Heaven. " *Journal of American Folklore* 109, no. 432 (spring 1996): 129–177.

Wolf, Eric R. "The Virgin of Guadalupe: A Mexican National Symbol. " In *Reader in Comparative Religion,* ed. William Lessa and Evon Z. Vogt. New York: Harper & Row, 1972.

Wong, Paul, ed. *Race, Ethnicity and Nationality in the United States: Toward the Twenty-First Century.* Boulder, Colo. : Westview Press, 1999.

Wood, Barbara L. *Children of Alcoholism: The Struggle for Self and Intimacy in Adult Life.* New York: New York University Press, 1987.

Wood, Peter. "Pilgrimage and Heresy: The Transformation of Faith at a Shrine in Wisconsin. " In *Sacred Journeys,* ed. Alan Morinis. Westport, Conn. : Greenwood Press, 1992.

Wright, Robert E. "If It's Official, It Can't Be Popular? Reflections on Popular and Folk Religion. " *Journal of Hispanic/Latino Theology* 1, no. 3 (May 1994): 47–67.

Wuthnow, Robert. *The Restructuring of American Religion: Society and Faith since World War II.* Princeton, N. J. : Princeton University Press, 1988.

———. *Sharing the Journey: Support Groups and America's New Quest For Community.* New York and London: Free Press, 1994.

———. *The Struggle for America's Soul: Evangelicals, Liberals, and Secularism.* Grand Rapids, Mich. : William B. Eerdmans Publishing Company, 1989.

Yang, Fenggang. *Chinese Christians in America: Conversion, Assimilation, and Adhesive Identities.* University Park: Pennsylvania State University Press, 1999.

Zambrana, Ruth E., ed. *Understanding Latino Families.* Thousand Oaks, Calif. : Sage Publications, 1995.

Zamora, Emilio. "Labor Formation, Community, and Politics: The Mexican Working Class in Texas, 1900–1945. " In *Border Crossings: Mexican and Mexican-American Workers,* ed. John Mason Hart. Wilmington, Del. : S. R. Books, 1998.

Zimdars-Swartz, Sandra L. *Encountering Mary: Visions of the Virgin Mary from LaSalette to Medjugorje.* New York: Avon Books, 1991.

———. "The Marian Revival in American Catholicism: Focal Points and Features of the New Marian Enthusiasm. " In *Being Right: Conservative Catholics in America,* ed. Mary Jo Weaver and R. Scott Appleby. Bloomington: Indiana University Press, 1995.

———. "Religious Experience and Public Cult: The Case of Mary Ann Van Hoof. " *Journal of Religion and Health* 28, no. 1 (spring 1989): 36–57.

Zinn, Maxine Baca. "Political Familism: Toward Sex Role Equality in Chicano Families. " *Aztlán: Chicano Journal of the Social Sciences and the Arts* 6 (spring 1975): 13–26.

NEWSPAPERS AND PERIODICALS

The Arizona Daily Star (TADS)
The Arizona Republic (TAR)
Austin-American Statesman (AAS)
The Catholic Sun (TCS)
Los Angeles Times (LAT)
The Mesa Tribune (TMT)
The Phoenix Gazette (TPG)
Phoenix New Times (PNT)

Index

Page numbers in italics refer to illustrations on the page.

ABOUT THE AUTHOR

Kristy Nabhan-Warren is Assistant Professor of American Religions at Augustana College, in Rock Island, Illinois. Her research has focused on American Catholicism and Mexican American lived religion. In her work, she pays special attention to the interplay of ethnicity, gender, and faith. Her next project, on Mexican Americans and Cursillos in the southwestern United States, will explore gendered dynamics of this religious phenomenon.

BERNICE ORTIZ, COVER ART

I was very proud to be asked to design the book cover for Kristy Nabhan-Warren. I met Kristy at one of the Faith Courses, by Mary's Ministries in Phoenix, Arizona. Through this week-long course I underwent a conversion; a change took place in my heart. Hence the title of my painting is *Conversion*.

I have been working in graphic and fine art for over twenty-five years and have always felt a need to express myself, in symbols and messages. There happens to be symbols throughout *Conversion*, such as a rosary, which has played a huge part in my conversion.

The cross in the center depicts the cross we all take up. The virgins in the corners of the paintings depict the differences in our Blessed Mother and what she looks like.

Currently, I am living in Gilbert, Arizona. I live with my son, Dominic, and our five Shih Zzus. I teach high school art at Queen Creek High in Queen Creek, Arizona.